women

icons by oscar

women

icons by oscar

TERRA

The Women Oscar Saw

There was something unmistakably honest about the way Oscar Abolafia pointed his lens. He didn't just capture celebrities — he caught them mid-laugh, off guard, leaning into their fame or stepping quietly away from it. His work, deeply rooted in the cultural swirl of 1960s and '70s America, was both intimate and iconic. But among the thousands of images he created, there was a recurring presence, a kind of magnetic elegance: the women.

This book is a tribute to that gaze — not one that objectifies, but one that observes. It's a curated selection of portraits in which Abolafia captured women with a striking mix of tenderness and strength. These women — actresses, models, singers — are not simply muses here. They are collaborators in the frame, meeting Oscar halfway, allowing themselves to be seen, but never diminished.

Born in New York City in 1935 to a Spanish immigrant family, Oscar came of age in a world obsessed with stardom. He worked for *People*, *Vanity Fair*, and *Harper's Bazaar*, and found himself embedded in moments that would later define pop culture: photographing Raquel Welch together with Dolly Parton, catching Grace Jones in her prime, snapping candid shots of Liza Minnelli or Farah Fawcet without a single hair out of place. He wasn't interested in the myth of perfection — he was drawn to the real texture of fame, the humanity behind the glamour.

And yet, Oscar's work never felt intrusive. That was his quiet genius. His camera didn't steal moments; it preserved them. He was welcomed backstage, invited into green rooms, trusted in ways that few photographers ever are. That trust radiates from every image. In a world that often reduces women to stillness or spectacle, Oscar's portraits feel alive. His subjects are thinking, reacting, becoming. They are icons — yes — but also women, full of nuance and contradiction.

To peruse these pages is to move through decades of cultural transformation — when standards of beauty shifted, when the role of women in public life expanded, when fashion, art and rebellion collided in the spotlight. But more than that, it's to revisit the quiet power of the still image. To remember what it means to truly see someone.

This book doesn't claim to show every woman Oscar photographed — the archive is far too vast. Instead, it offers a personal selection: portraits that linger, that hint at the rapport between photographer and subject, that remind us of a time when photography was still film, still instinct, still moment rather than manipulation.

Oscar Abolafia passed away in 2020, but his photographs endure — not just as evidence, but as presence. They are reminders of a visual era defined not by filters or edits, but by trust, access, and an eye that knew when not to look away.

This is Oscar's America — glamorous, flawed, intimate. And these are the women who shaped it, and were shaped by it, one frame at a time.

"I never told them how to pose. I just waited for who they really were to show up."

Oscar Abolafia

Whoopi Goldberg
New York City, 1985

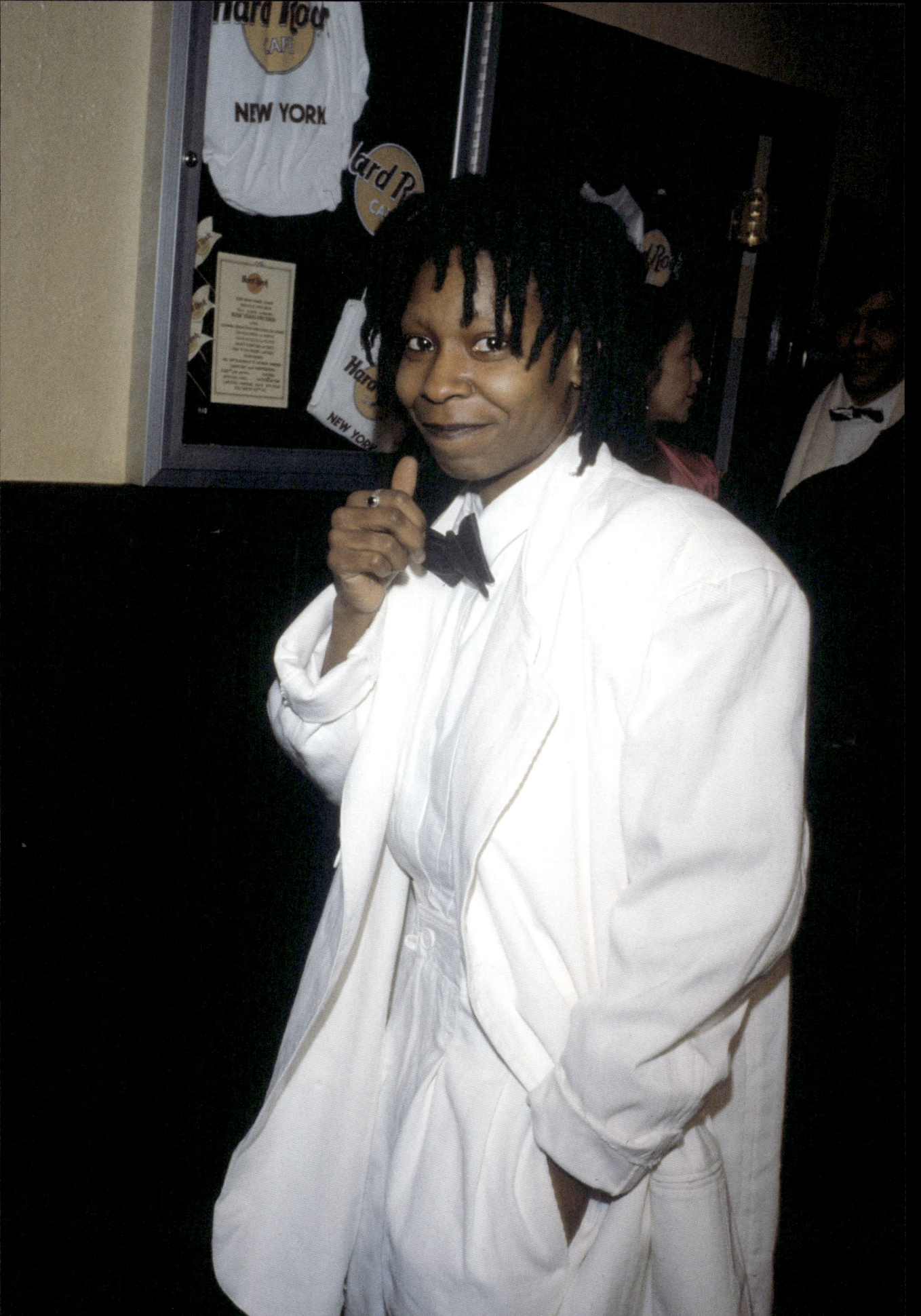

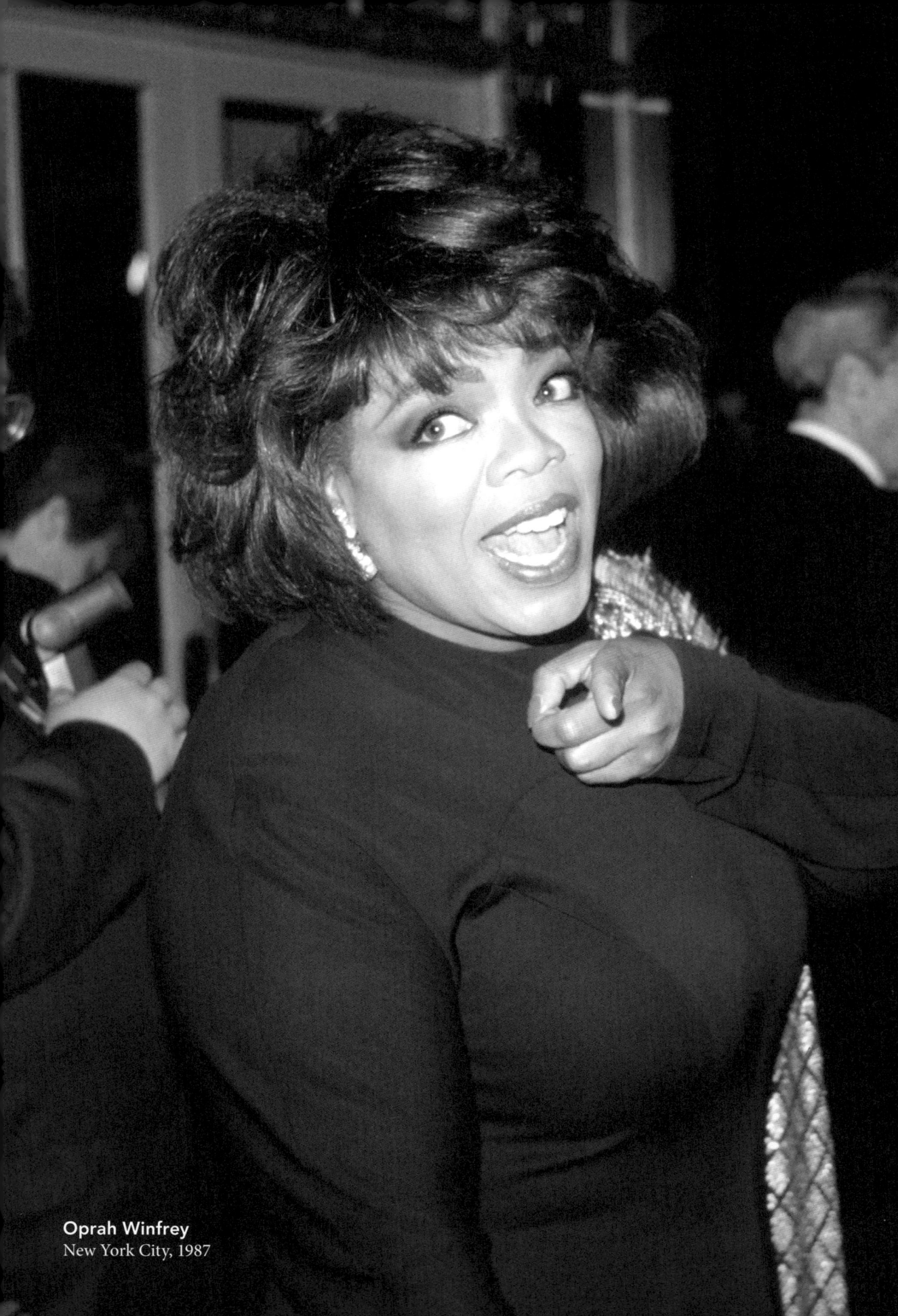

Oprah Winfrey
New York City, 1987

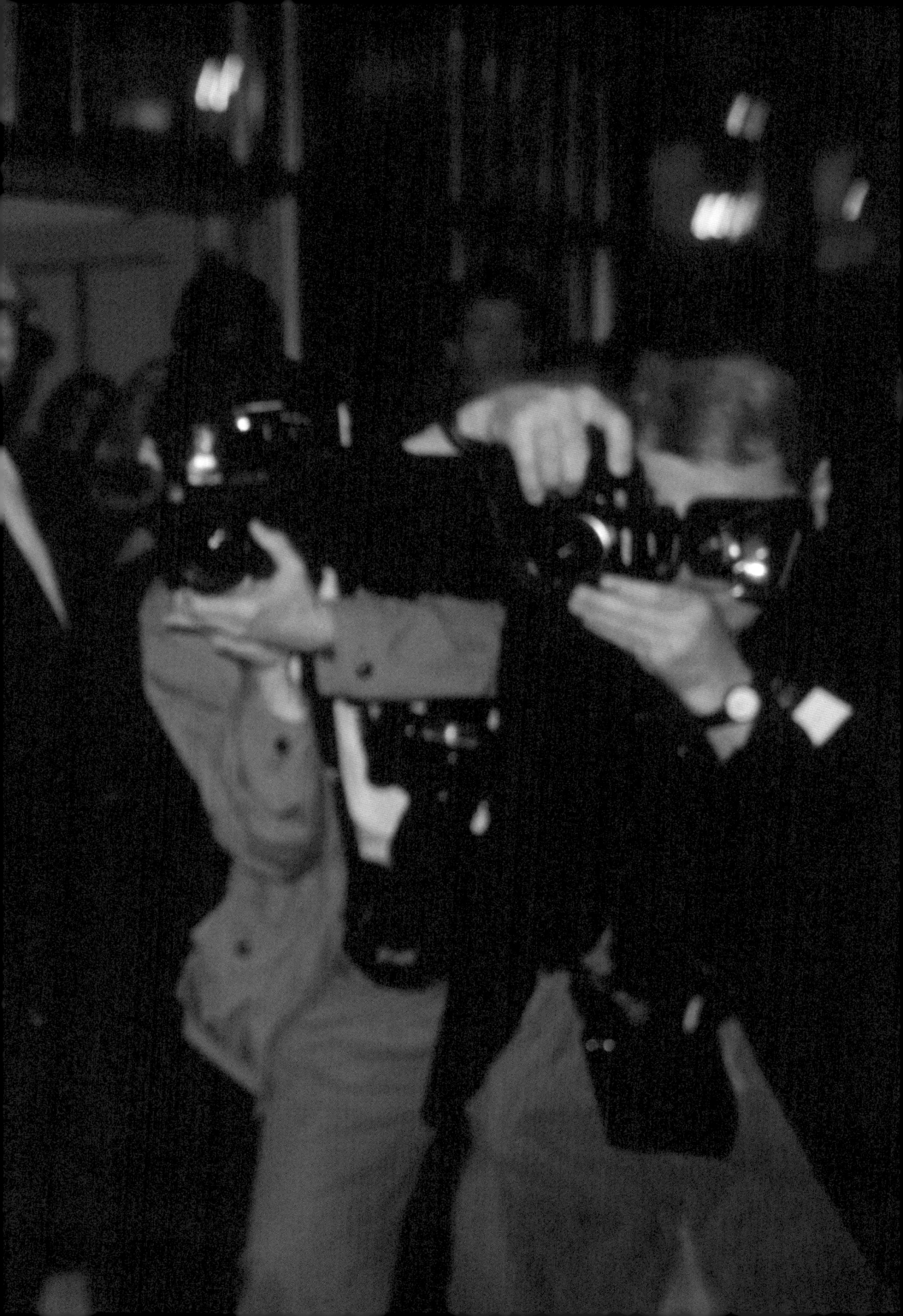

Priscilla Presley
Dallas, 1984

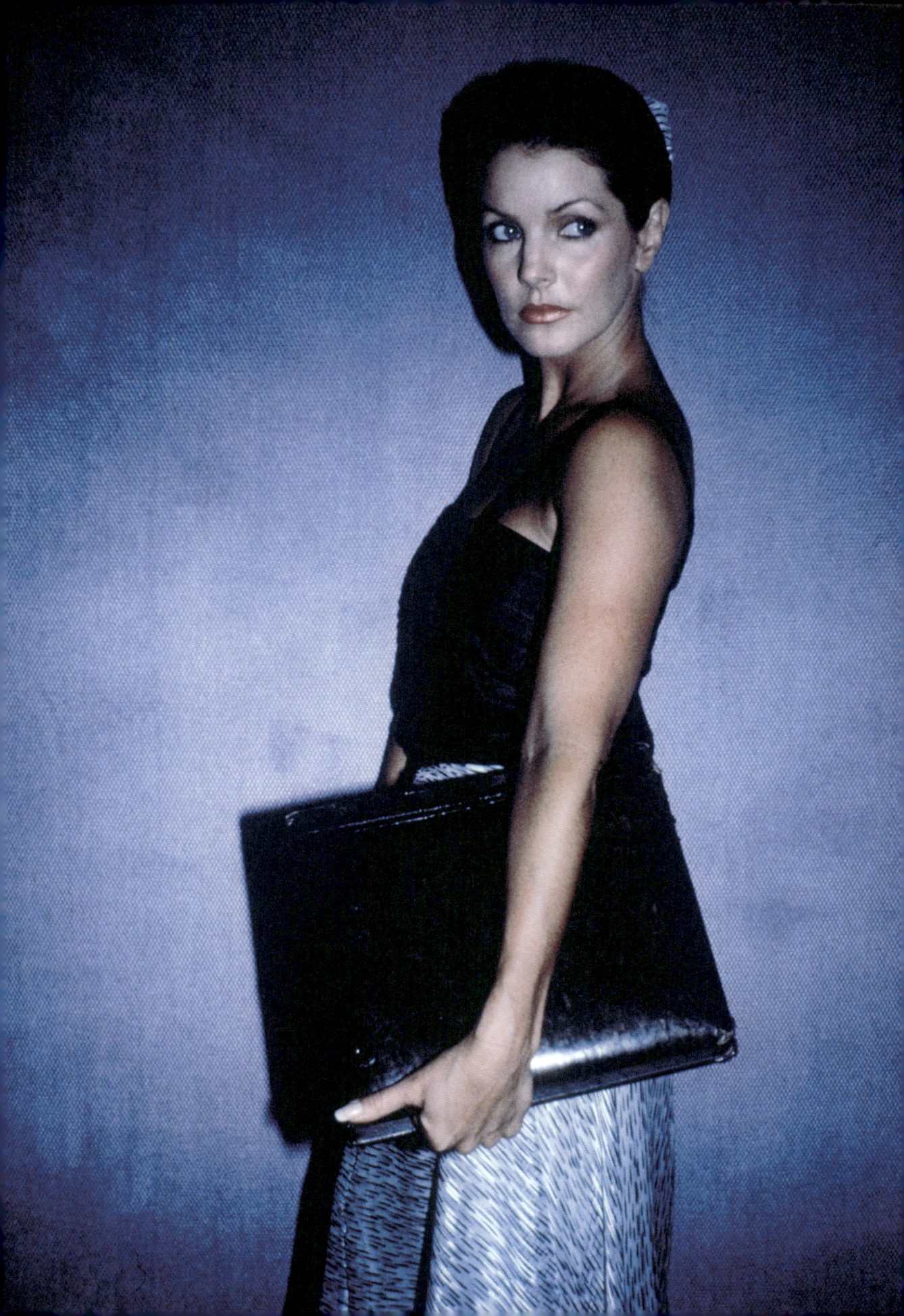

Big hair, bigger heart — and a mind sharper than you'd guess.

Everyone saw the sparkle first — the wigs, the waist, the rhinestones. That was the plan. Dolly Parton built her own myth out of glitter.

But what Oscar loved most was her clarity. She didn't pretend to be anything she wasn't. She was country wisdom in couture, kindness wrapped in camp. And behind the performance, a business mind more vivid than any spotlight.

He caught her smiling — not for him, but for herself.

Dolly Parton
Nashville, 1980

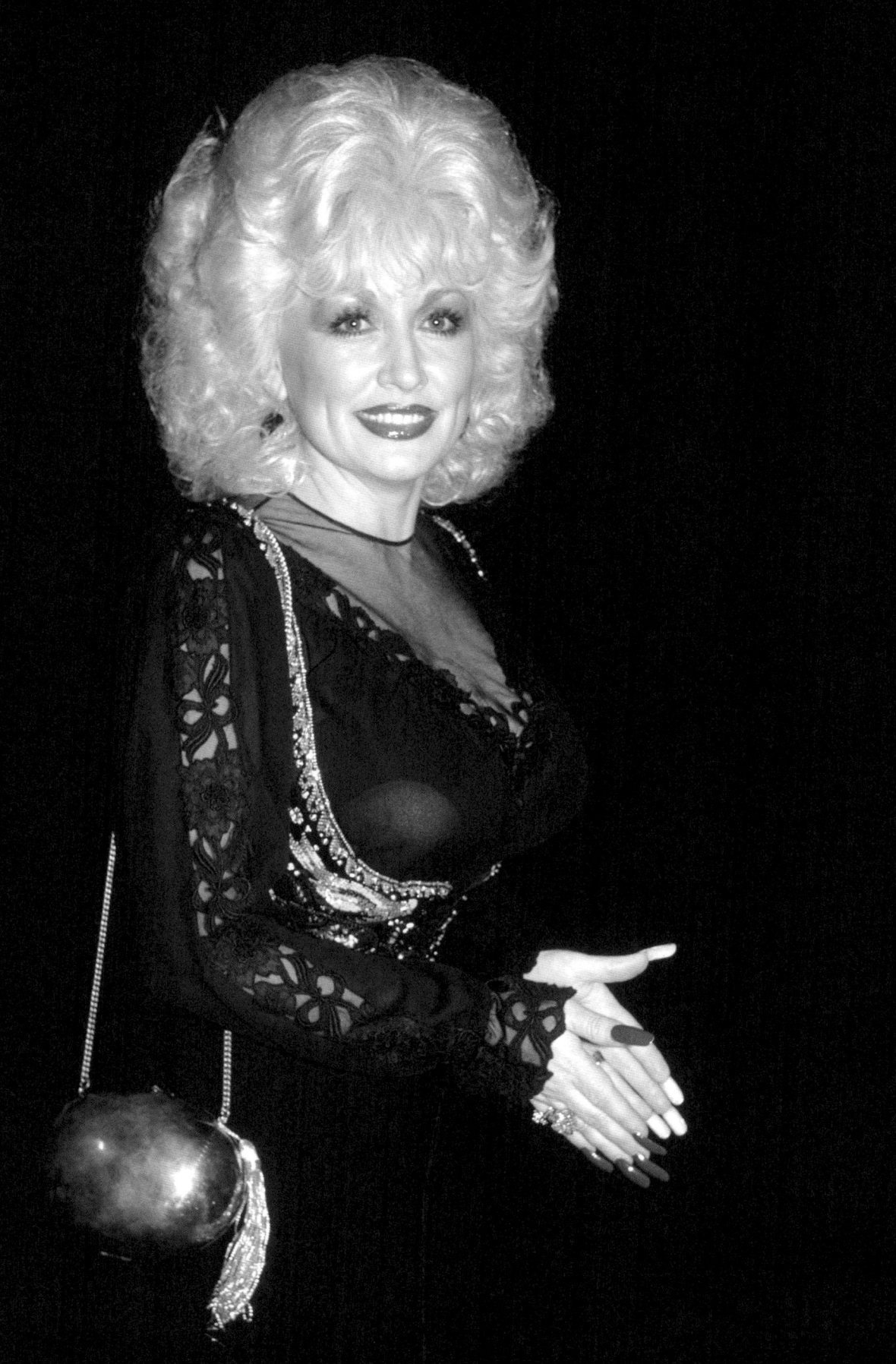

Agnetha Fältskog
Stockholm, ca. 1977

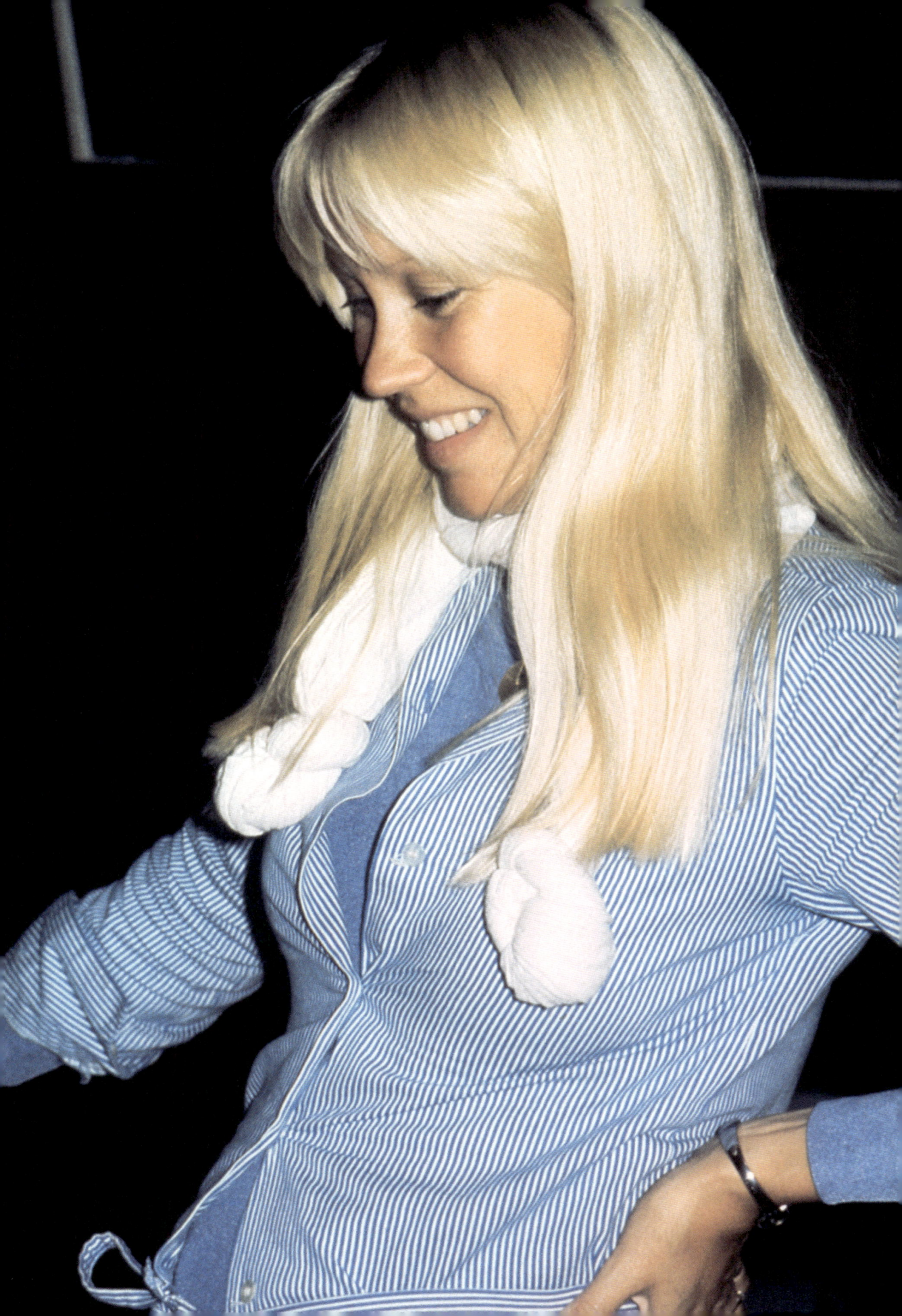

Anni-Frid Lyngstad
Stockholm, 1981

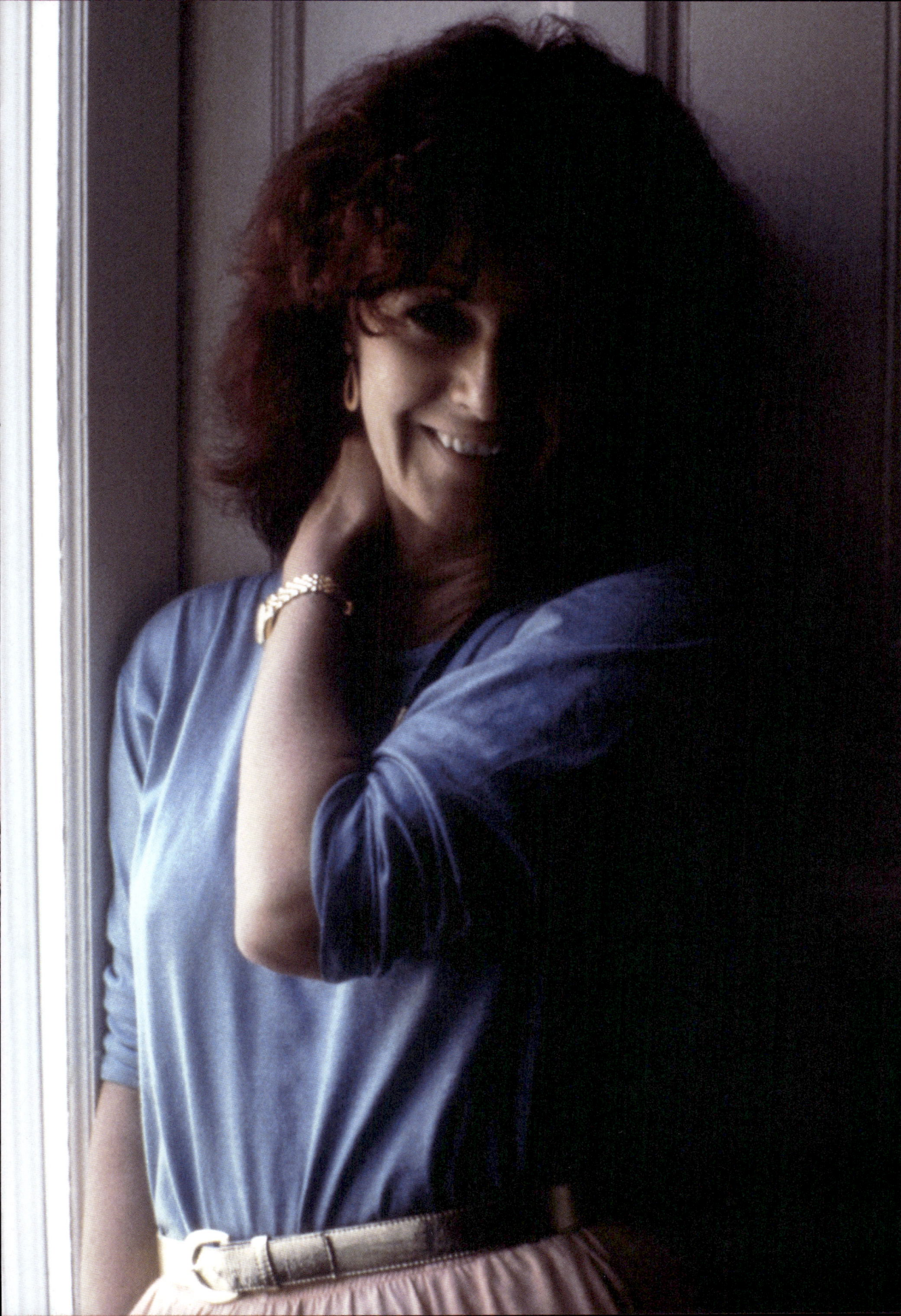

Grace Kelly
New York City, 1977

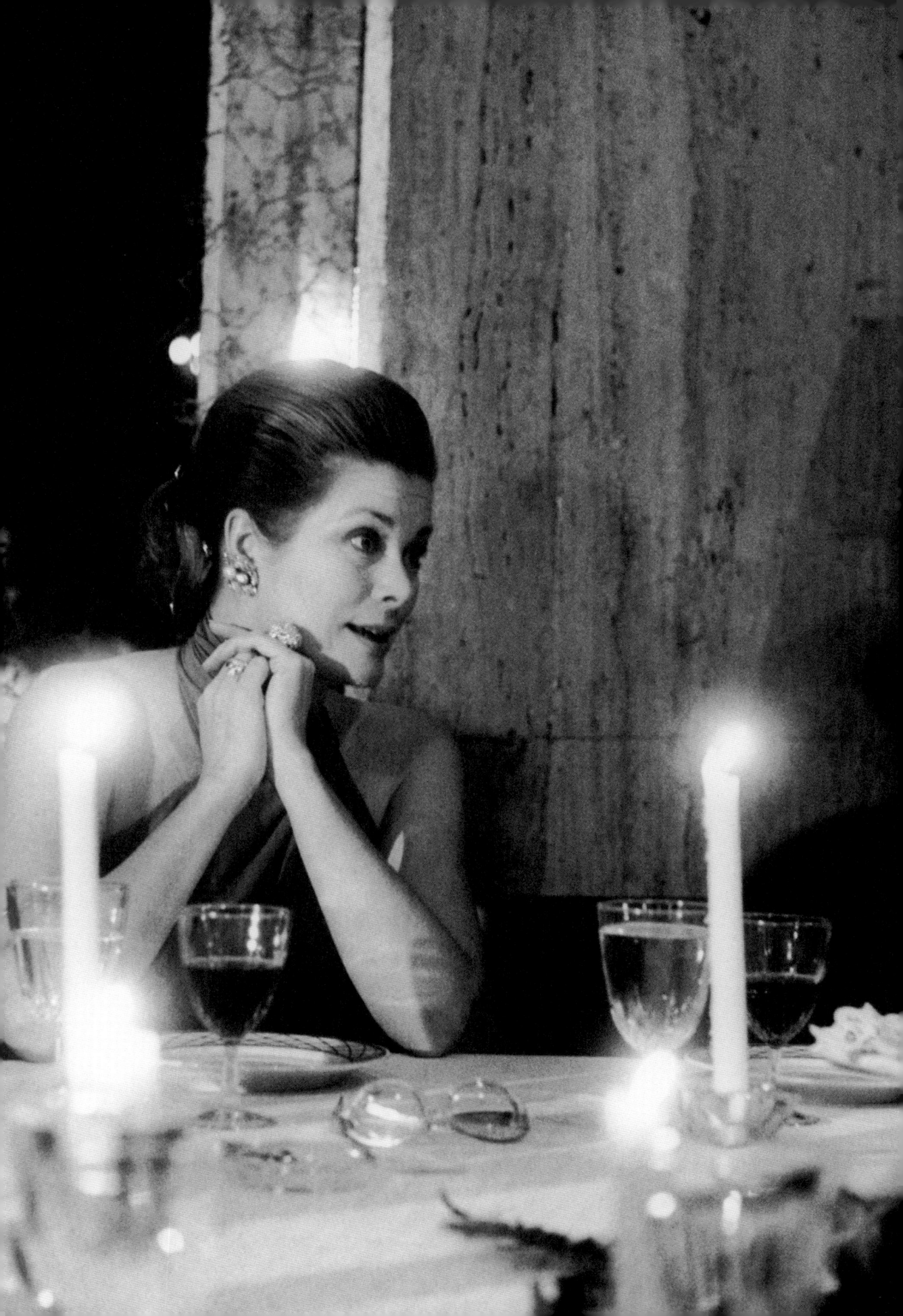

Christie Brinkley
New York City, 1987

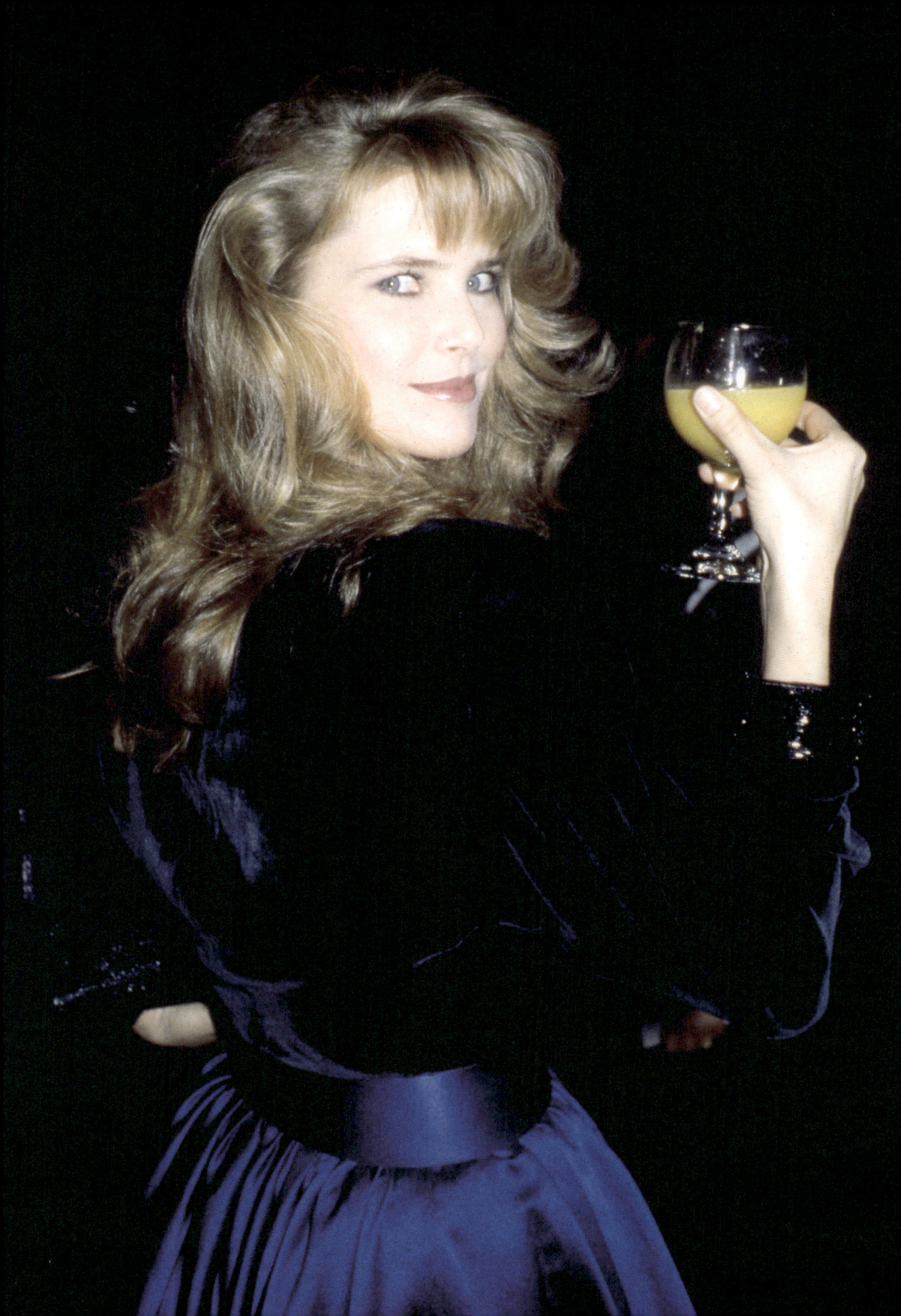

The edge of punk with the glamour of a movie star.

She didn't want to be a star. She simply didn't care if she became one.

That was Debbie Harry's power — magnetic, effortless, and just a little dangerous. Blondie had already blown open the doors of what punk-pop could be. But Oscar's portrait of her found the moment after: the eyeliner slightly smudged, the mood unexpectedly soft.

She didn't give him performance: she gave him permission. To capture not the icon, but the woman who never needed to prove what she was.

Debbie Harry
New York City, 1977

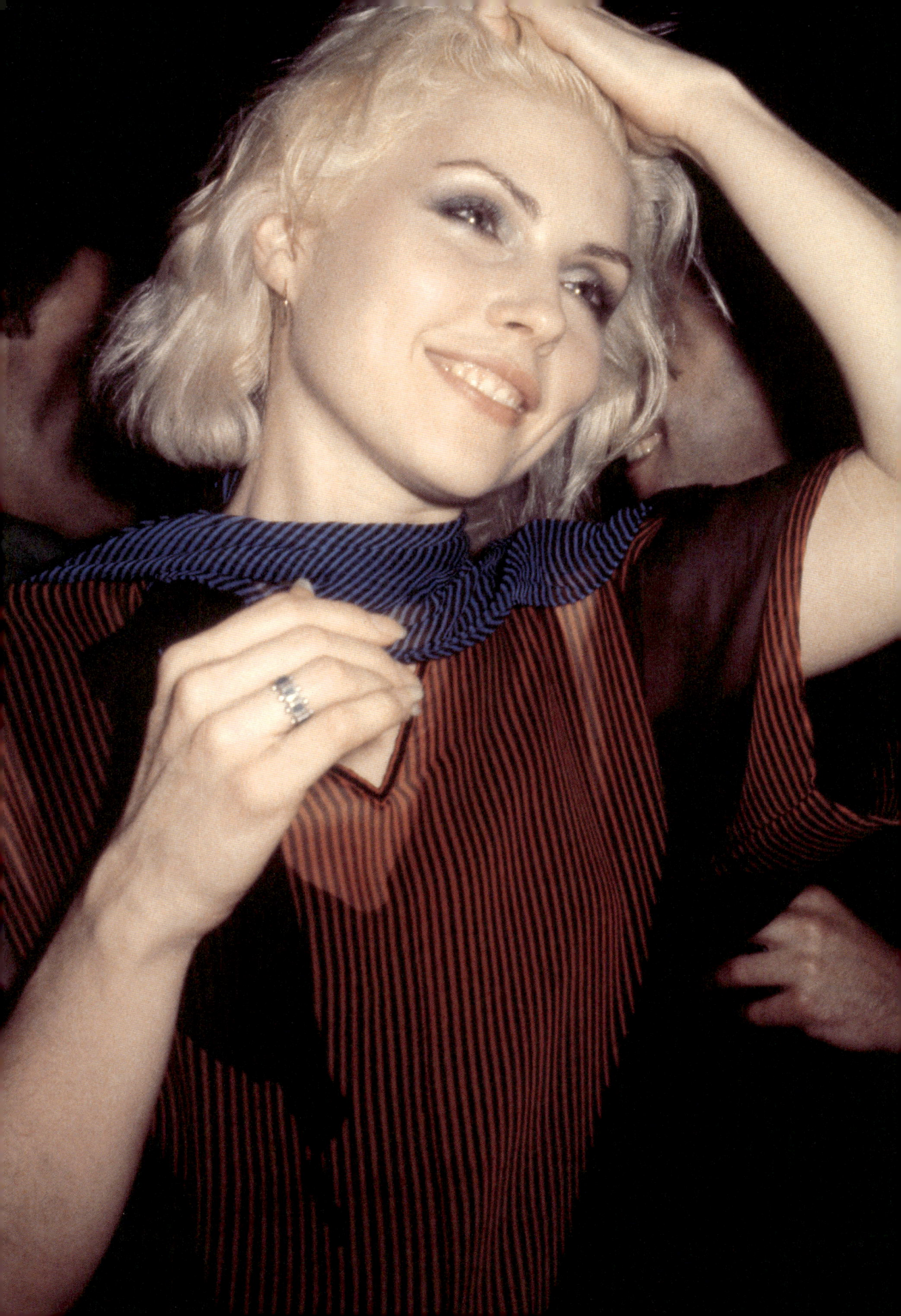

Aileen Quinn
New York City, 1982

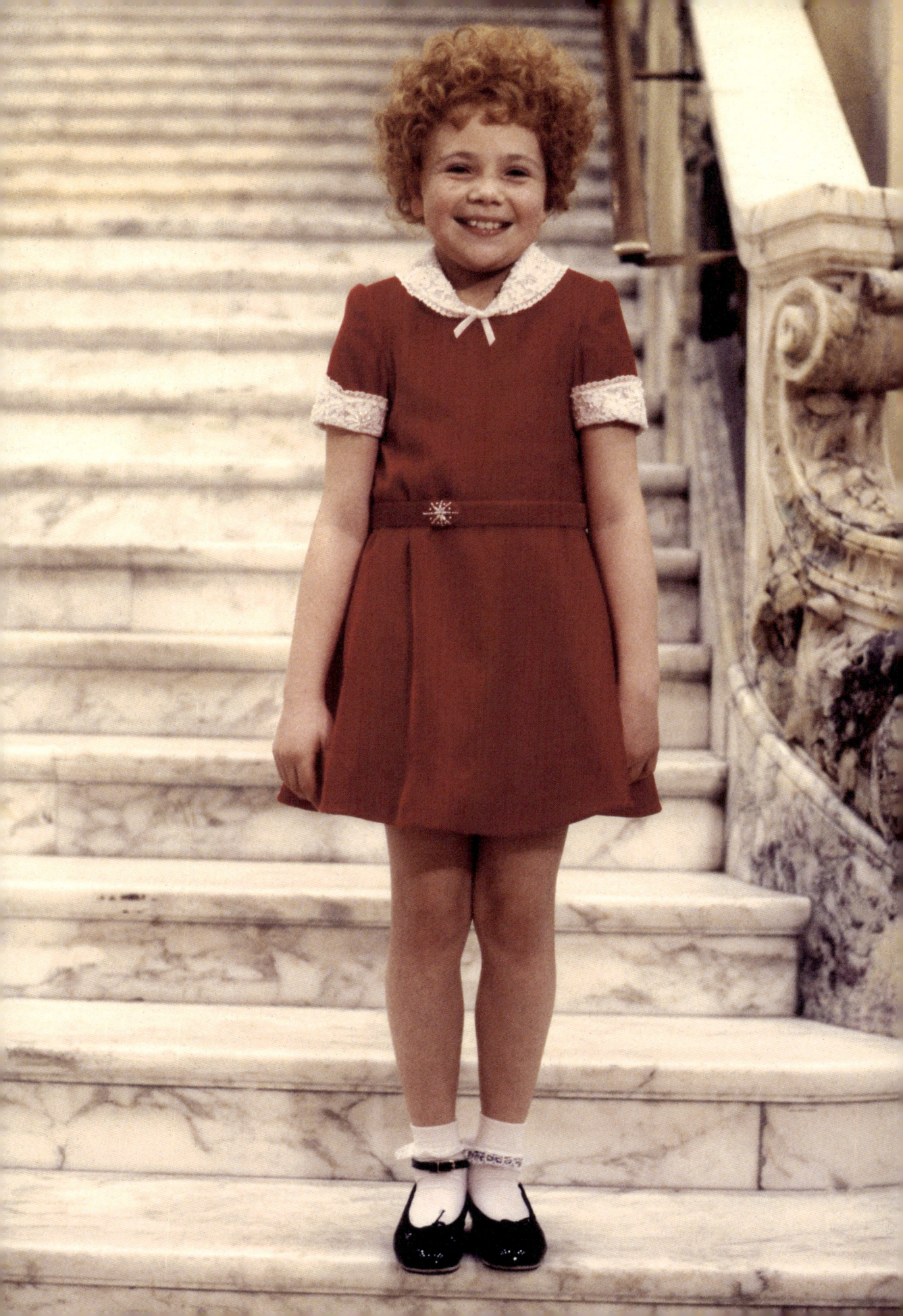

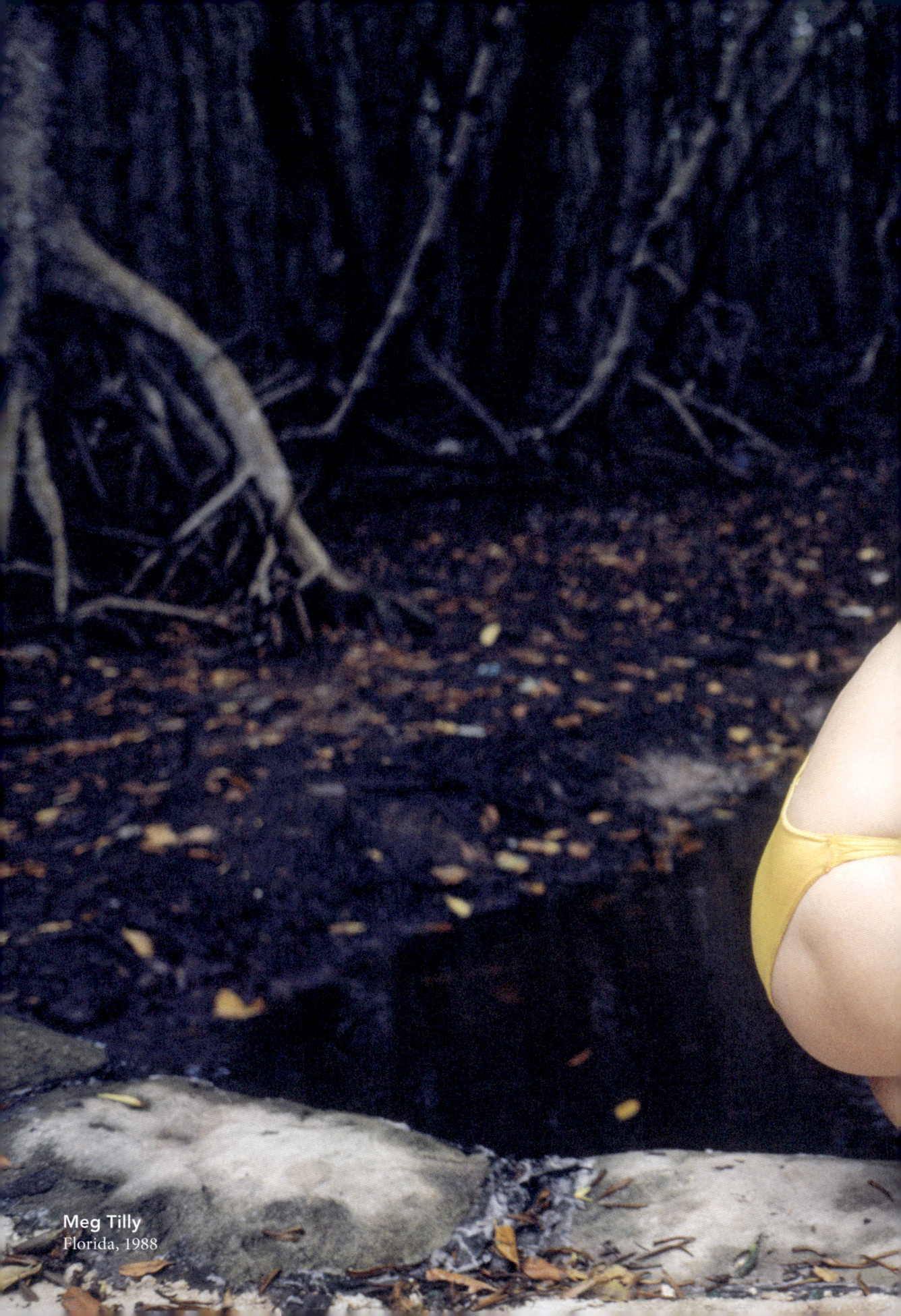

Meg Tilly
Florida, 1988

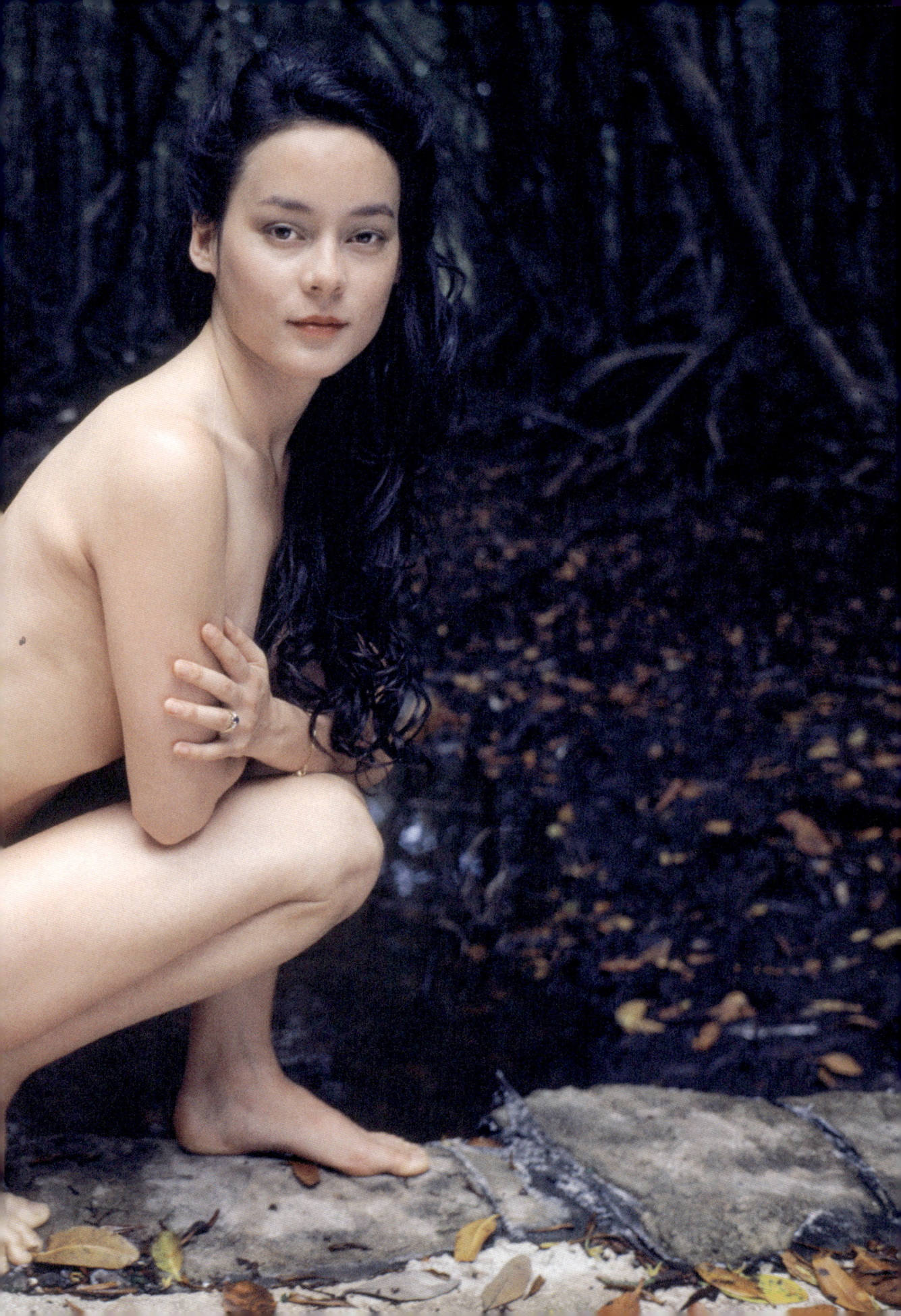

Jackie Kennedy Onassis
New York City, 1974

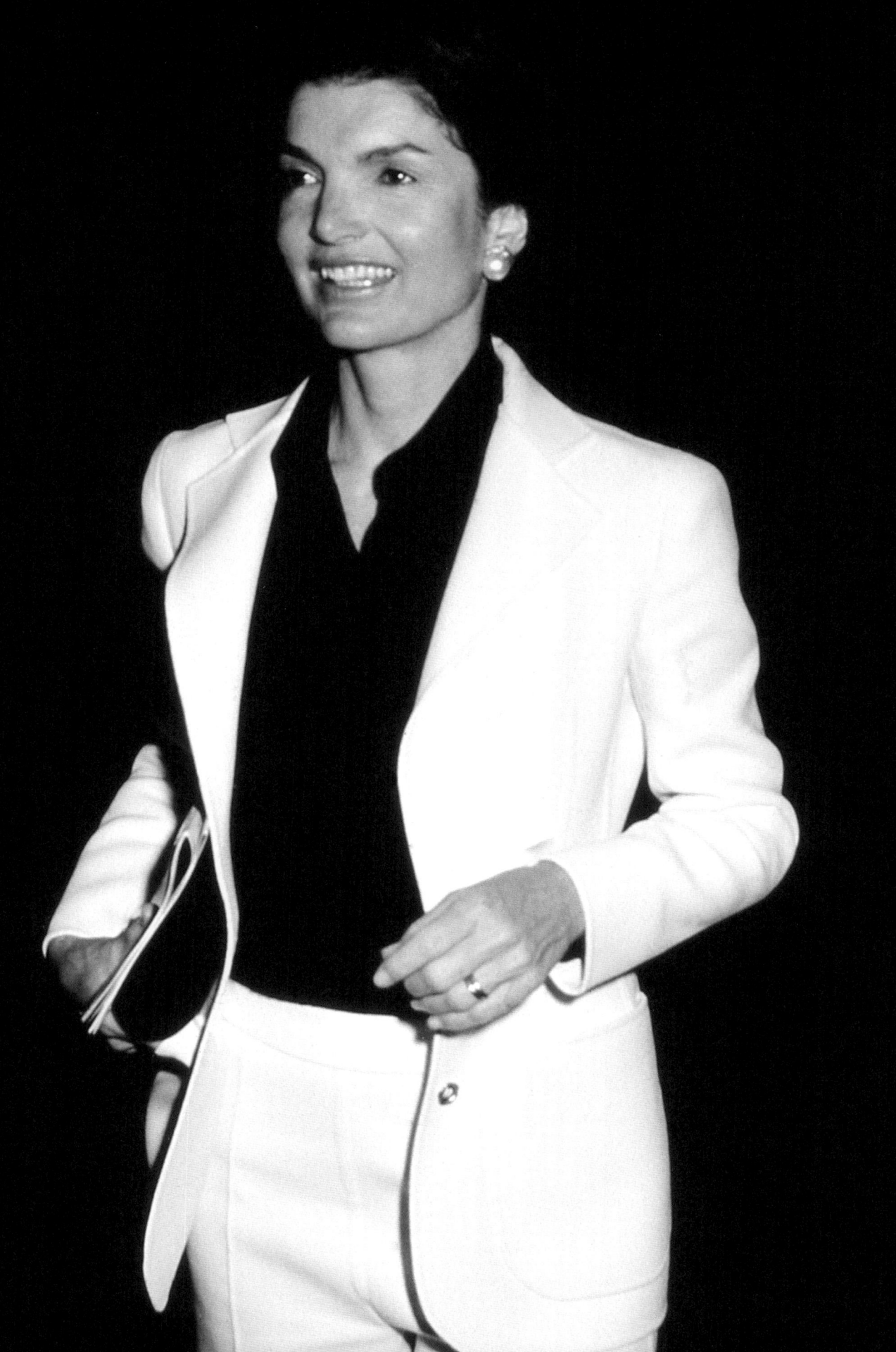

Drew Barrymore
New York City, 1985

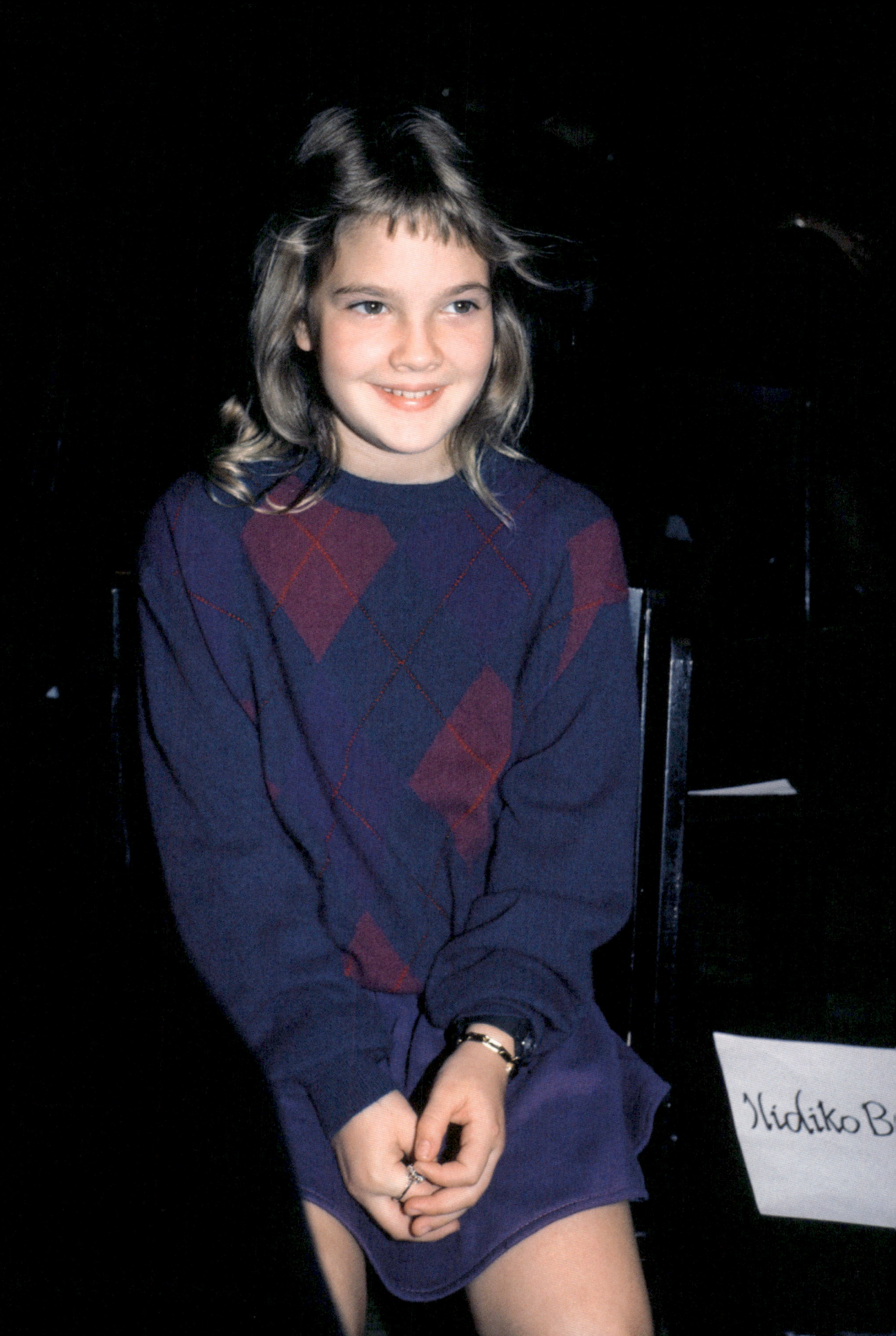

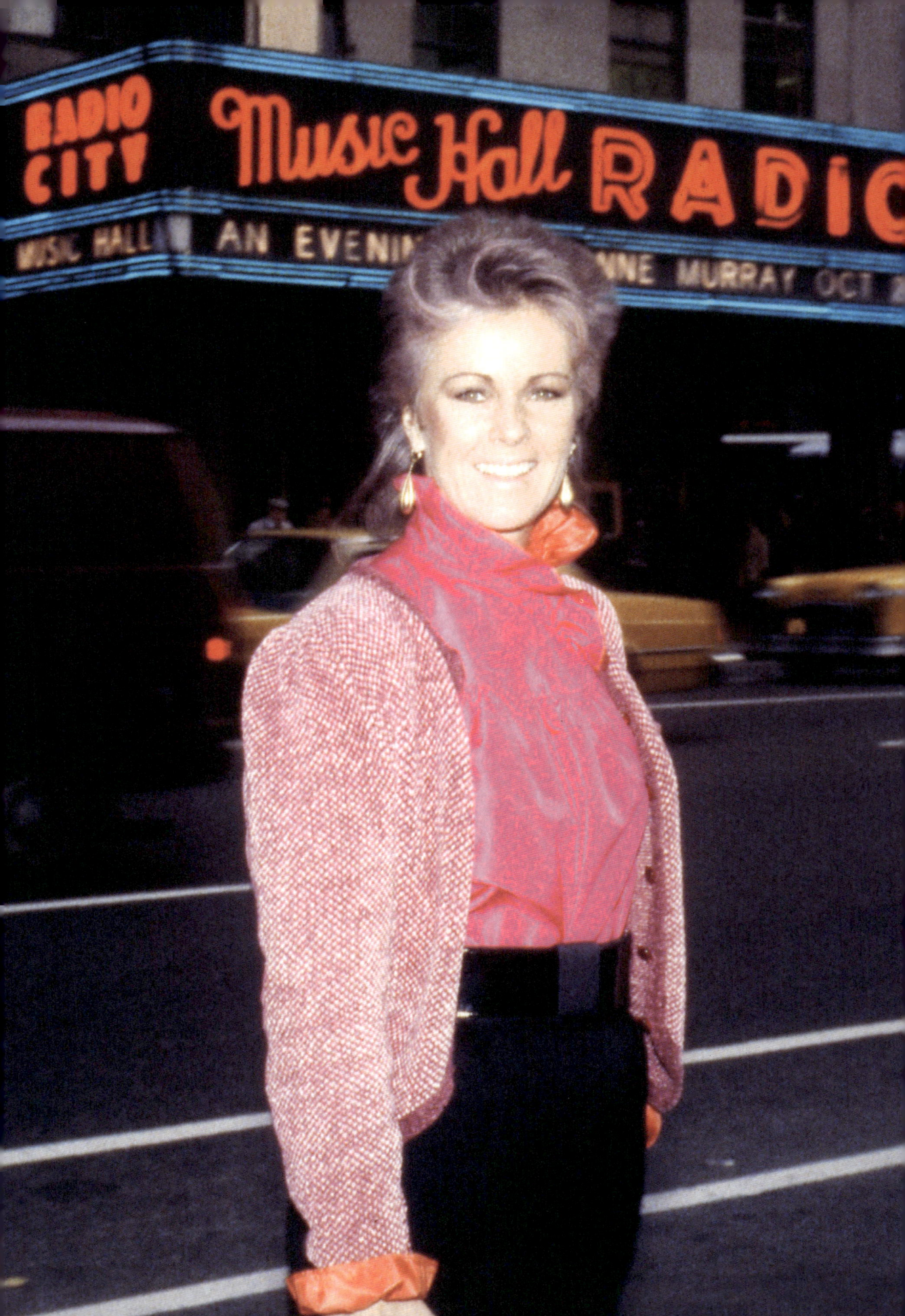

Anni-Frid Lyngstad
New York City, 1982

Everything she did had rhythm, even when standing still.

She was always in motion. Ann-Margret shimmered, purred, span — a performer made of silk and fire.

Oscar tried to pin her down just long enough for a shot. But that was part of the fun. She teased the camera, danced through its frame. The photos buzzed with her rhythm.

There was something untamable about her. Something sweet, too, but never saccharine. She was the showgirl with depth, the ingenue with a grin that spelled trouble.

Ann-Margret Olsson
New York City, 1975

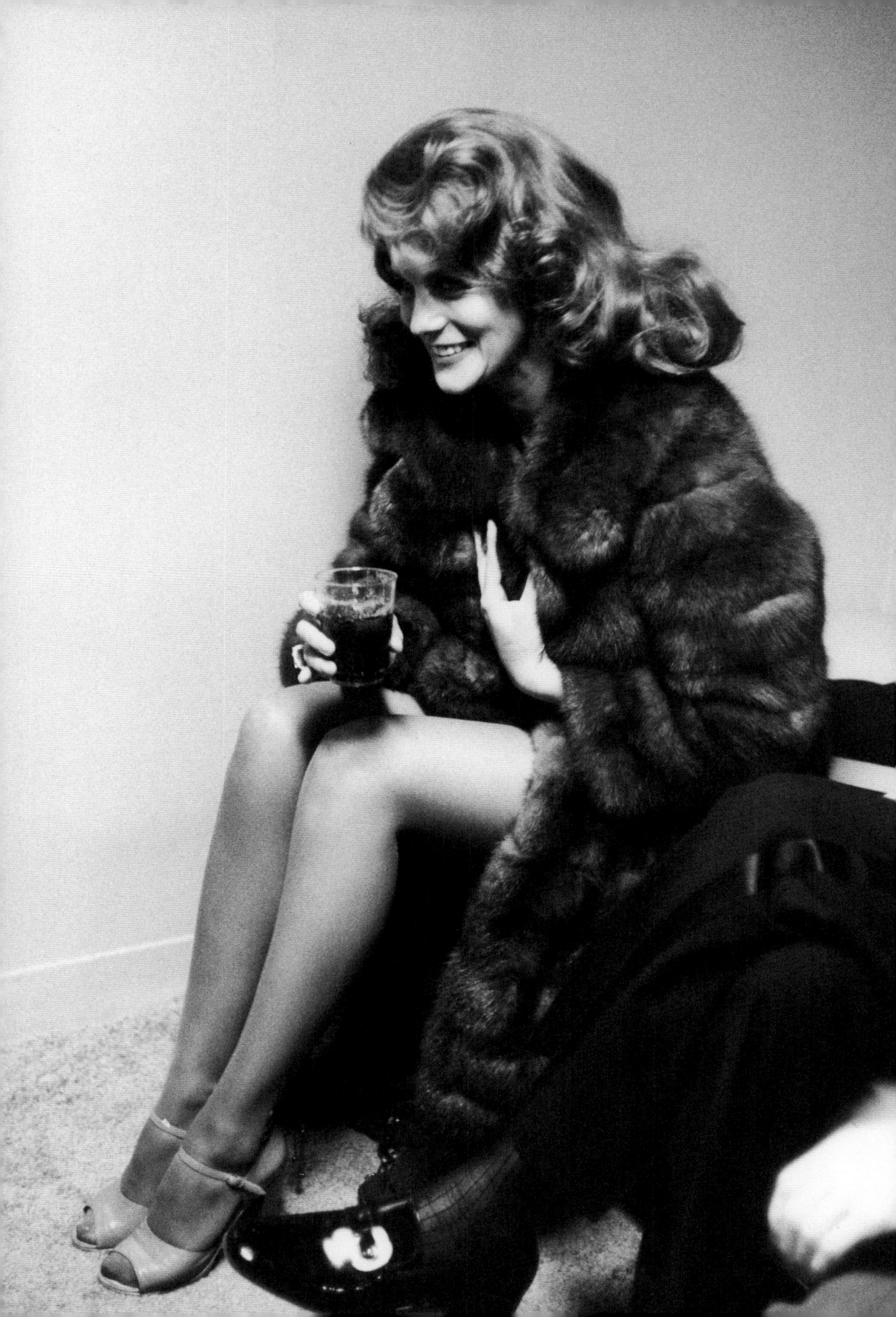

Ann Miller and Ginger Rogers
New York City, 1982

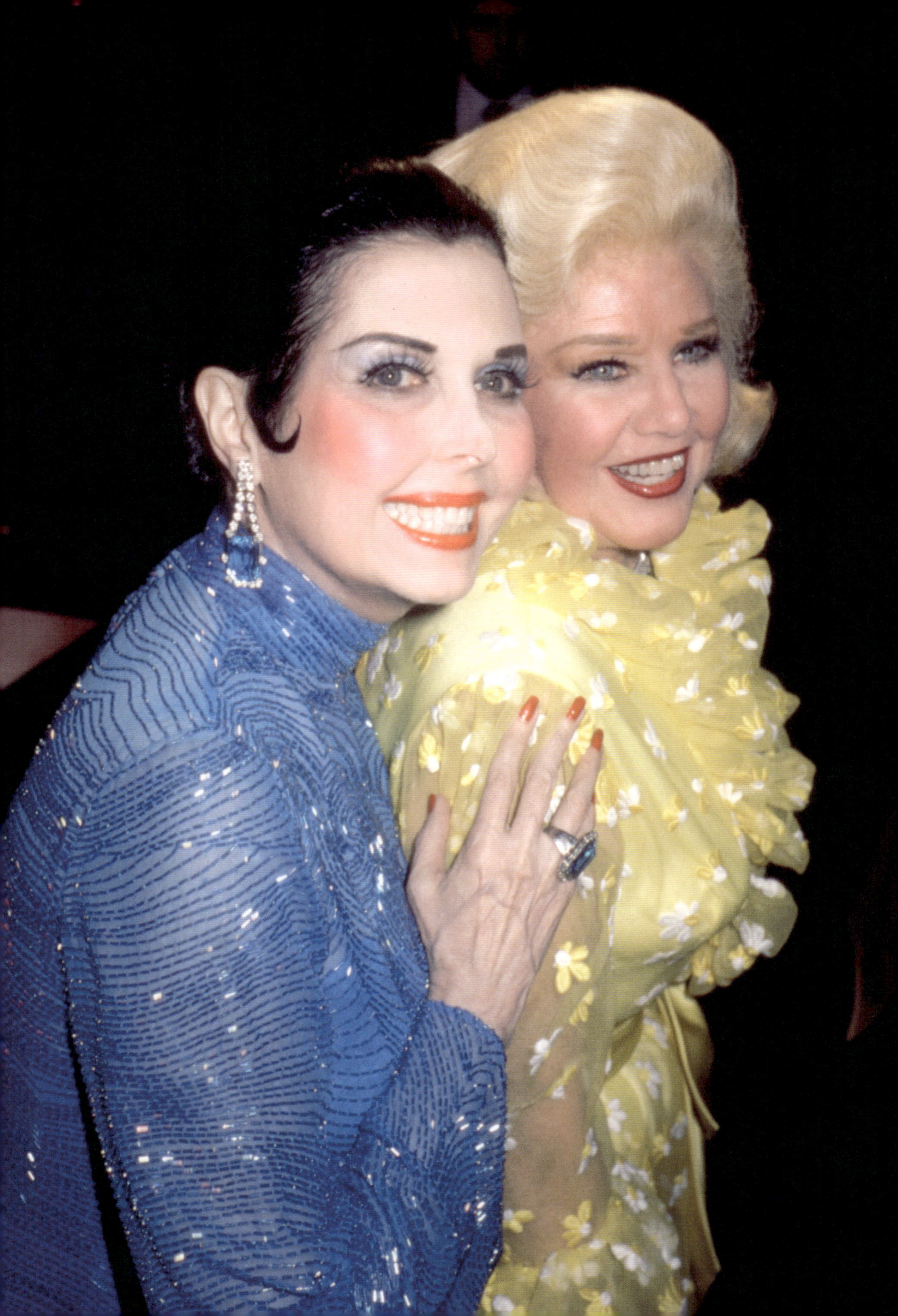

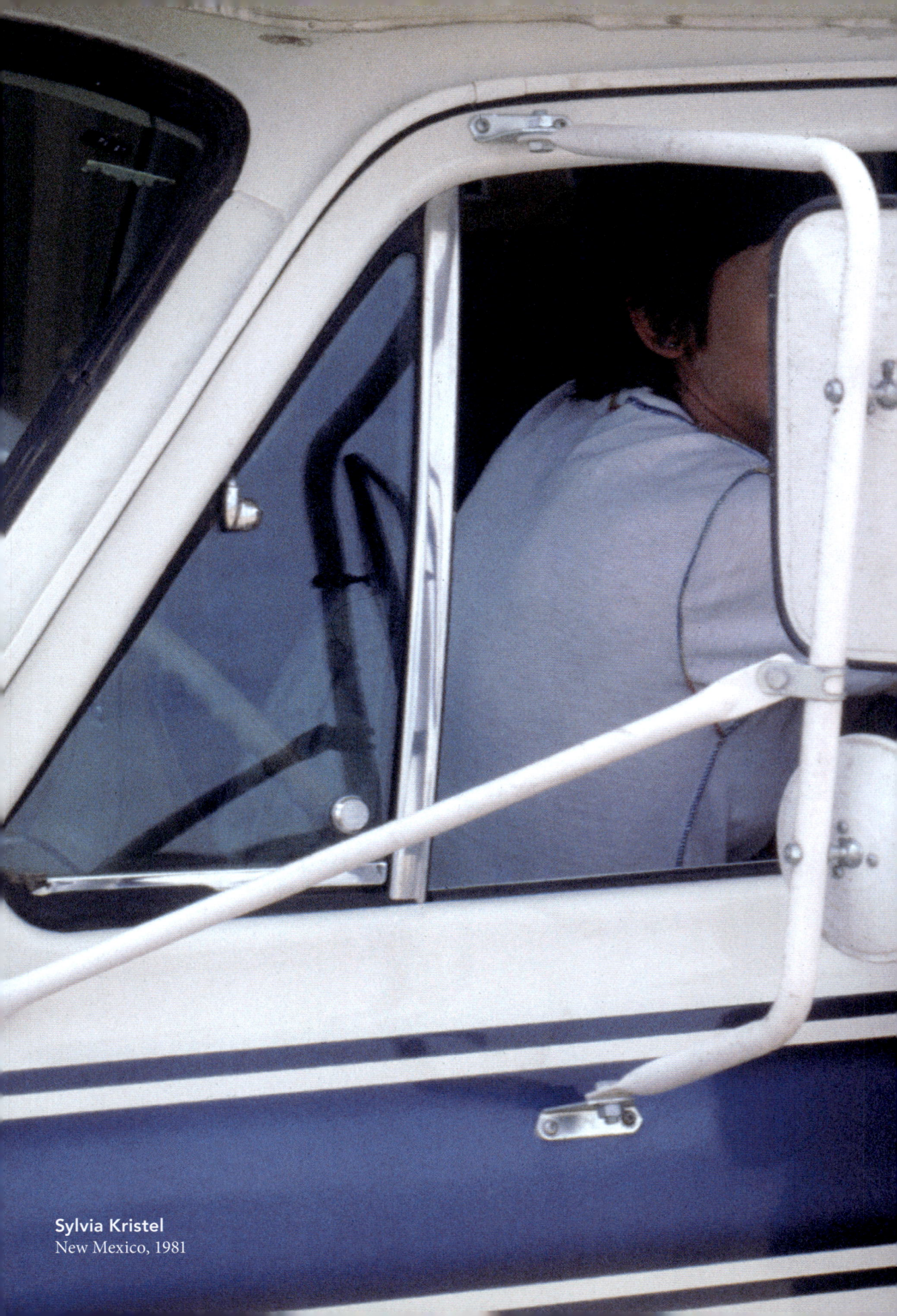

Sylvia Kristel
New Mexico, 1981

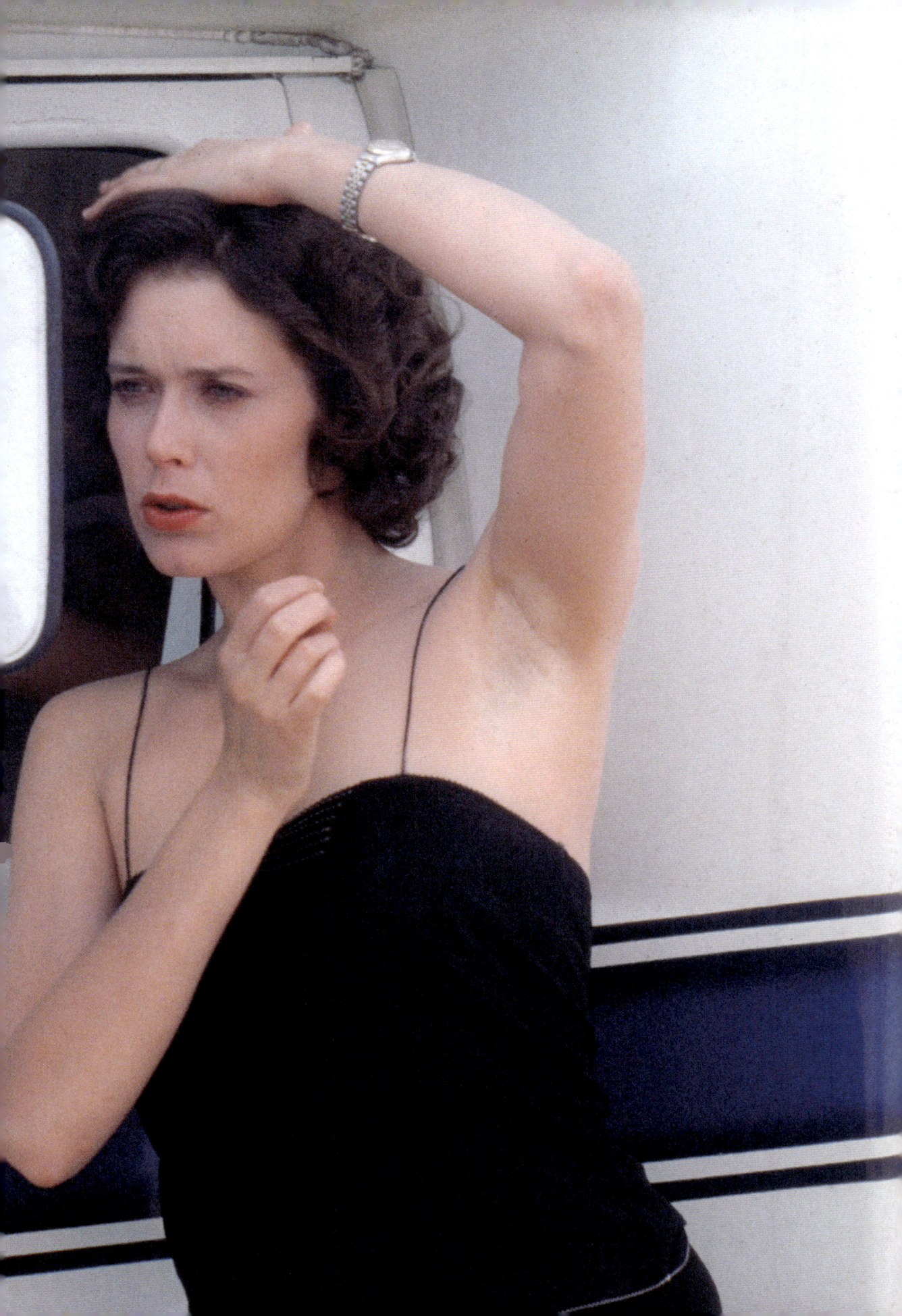

Aretha Franklin
New York City, 1967

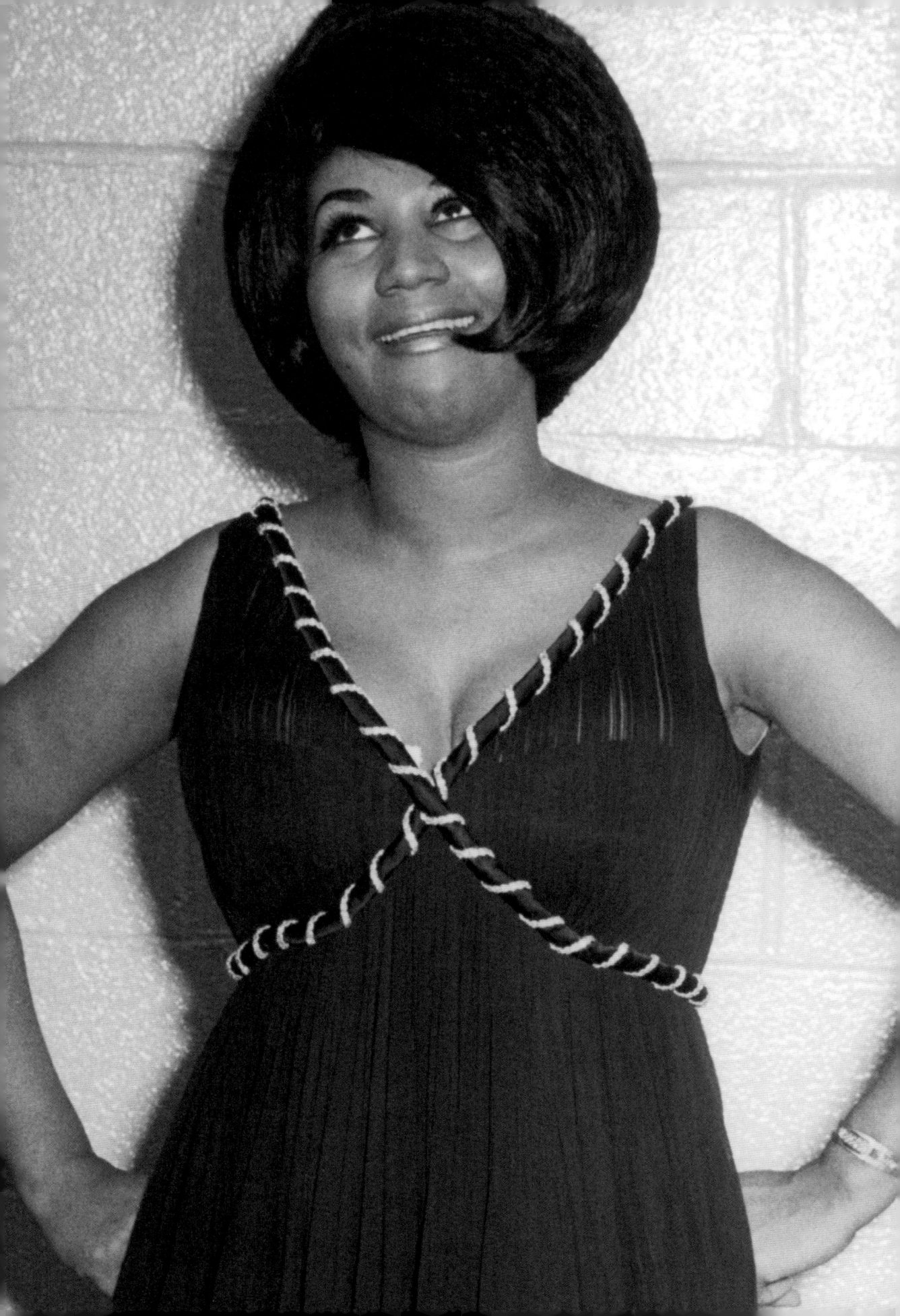

Arlene Dahl
New York City, 1983

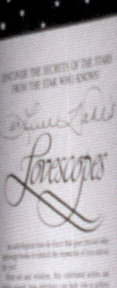

Naomi Campbell
New York City, 1991

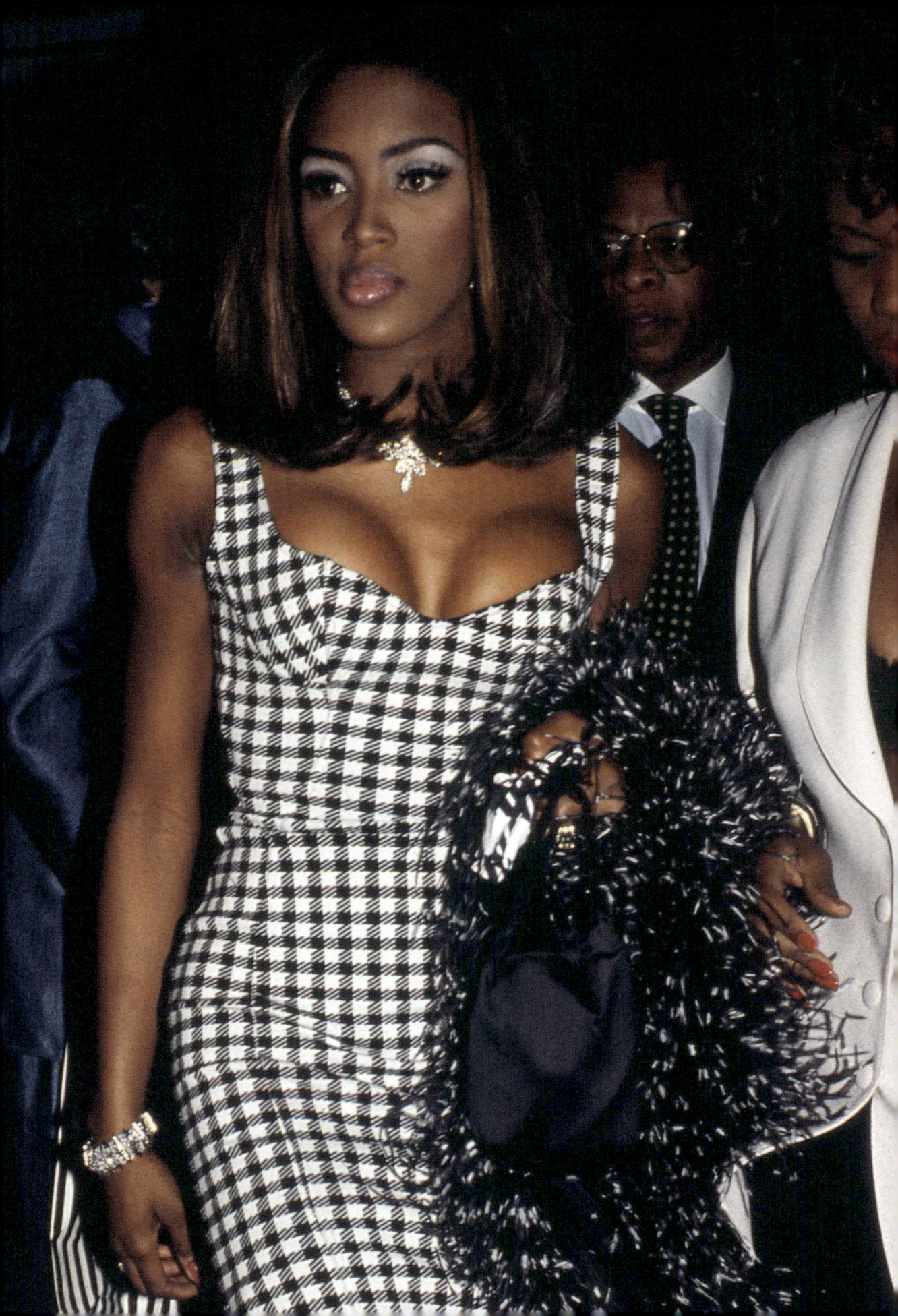

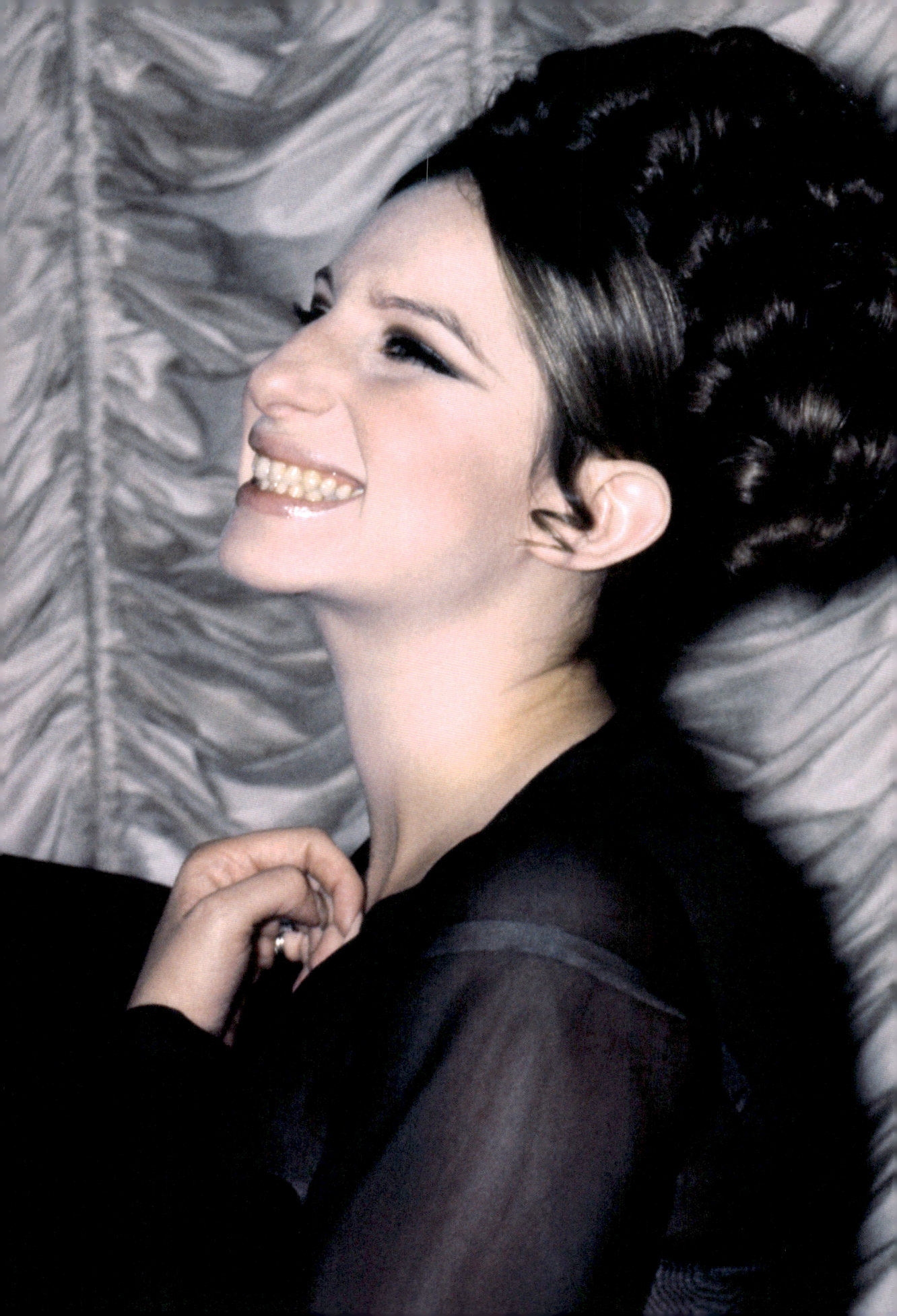

"Life's too short. Start with dessert."

Barbra Streisand
New York City, ca. 1970

Light didn't fall on her — it radiated from within.

There was nothing loud about Audrey Hepburn, yet she always stood out against the background.

She brought an inner stillness to everything — as if the noise of the world had no business around her. Oscar admired that. When he photographed her, it wasn't about finding the perfect light. Audrey was the light.

The lens didn't reveal her so much as reflect her. Her presence was calm, clear, and quietly revolutionary.

Audrey Hepburn
New York City, 1982

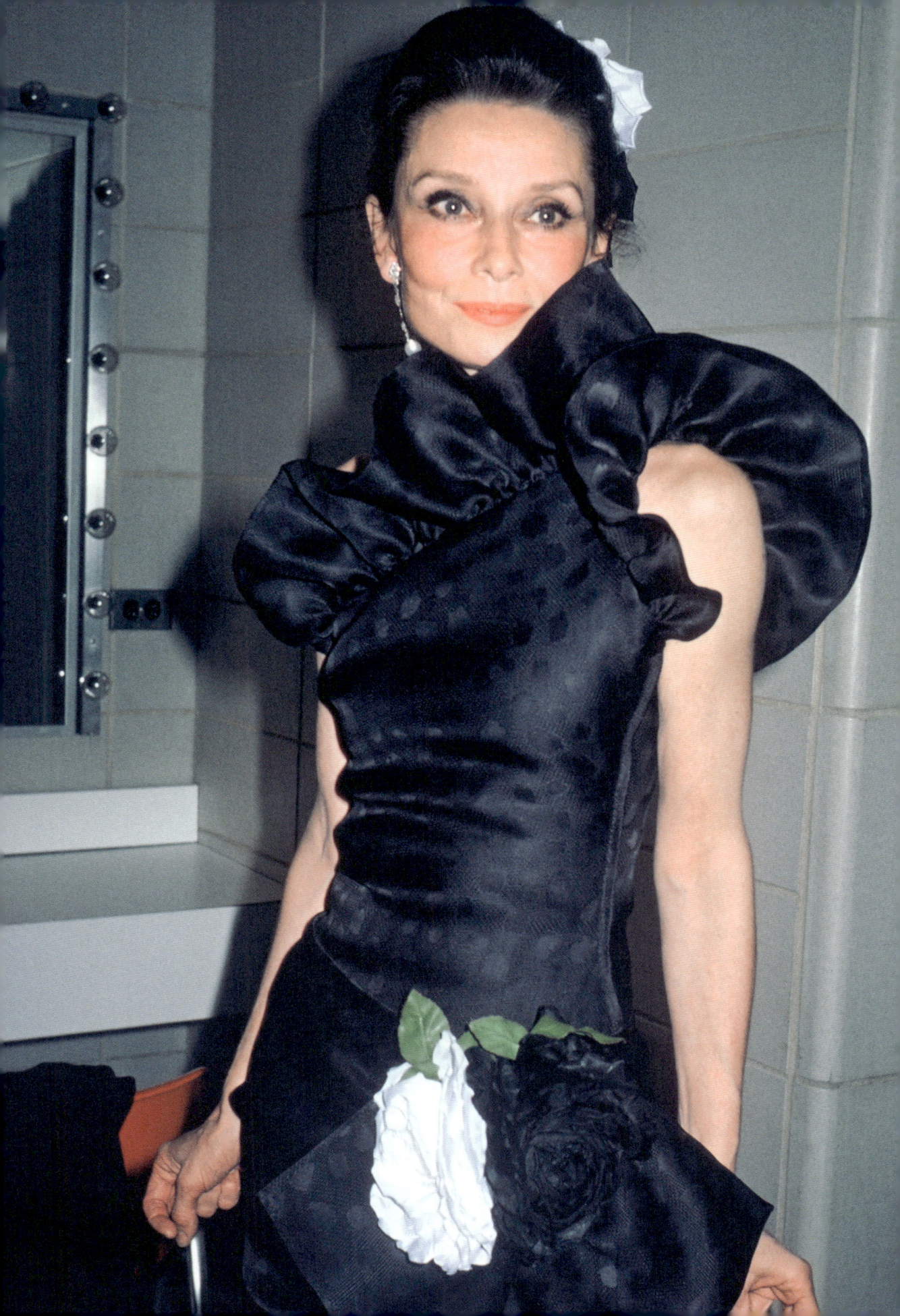

Mia Farrow
New York City, 1968

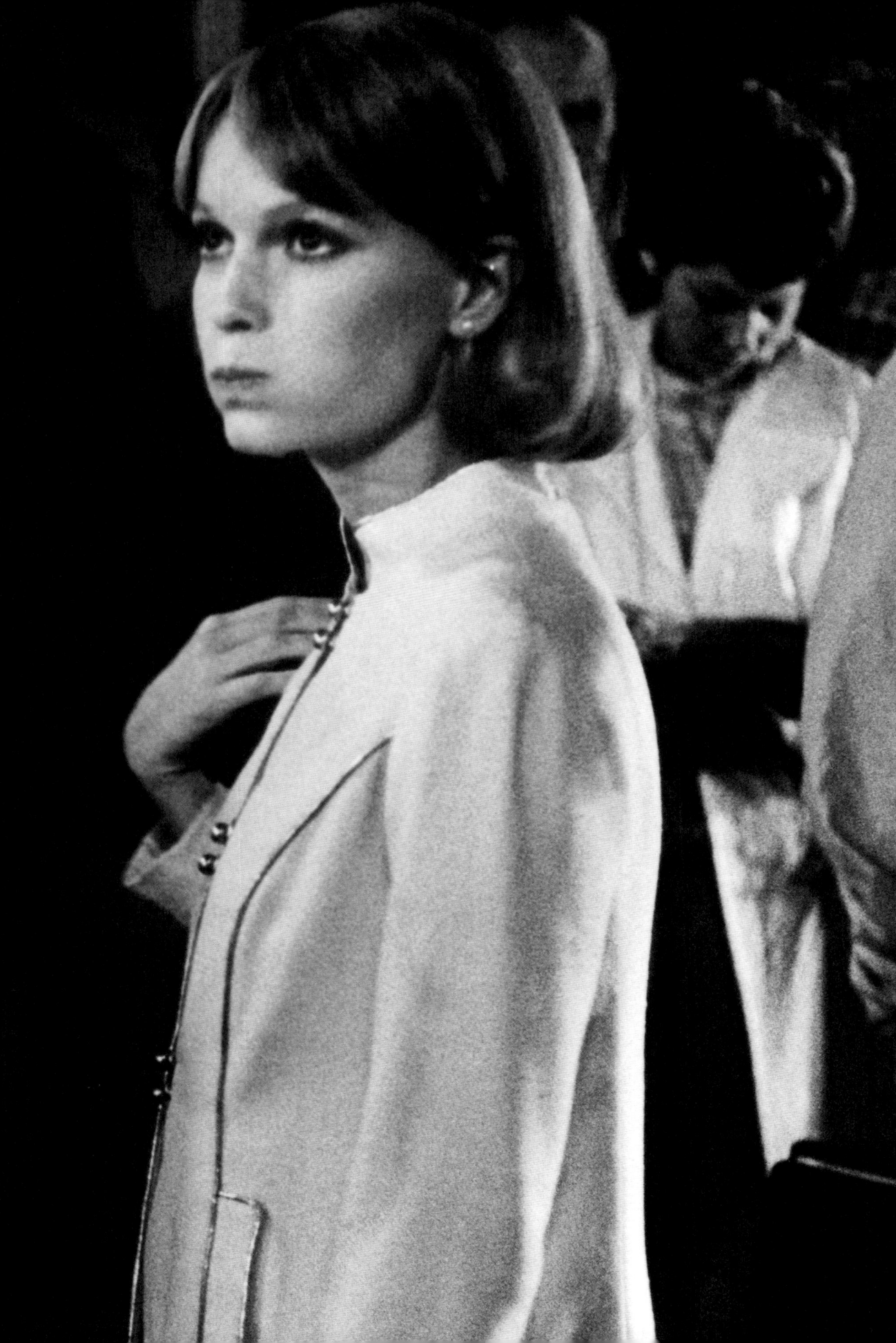

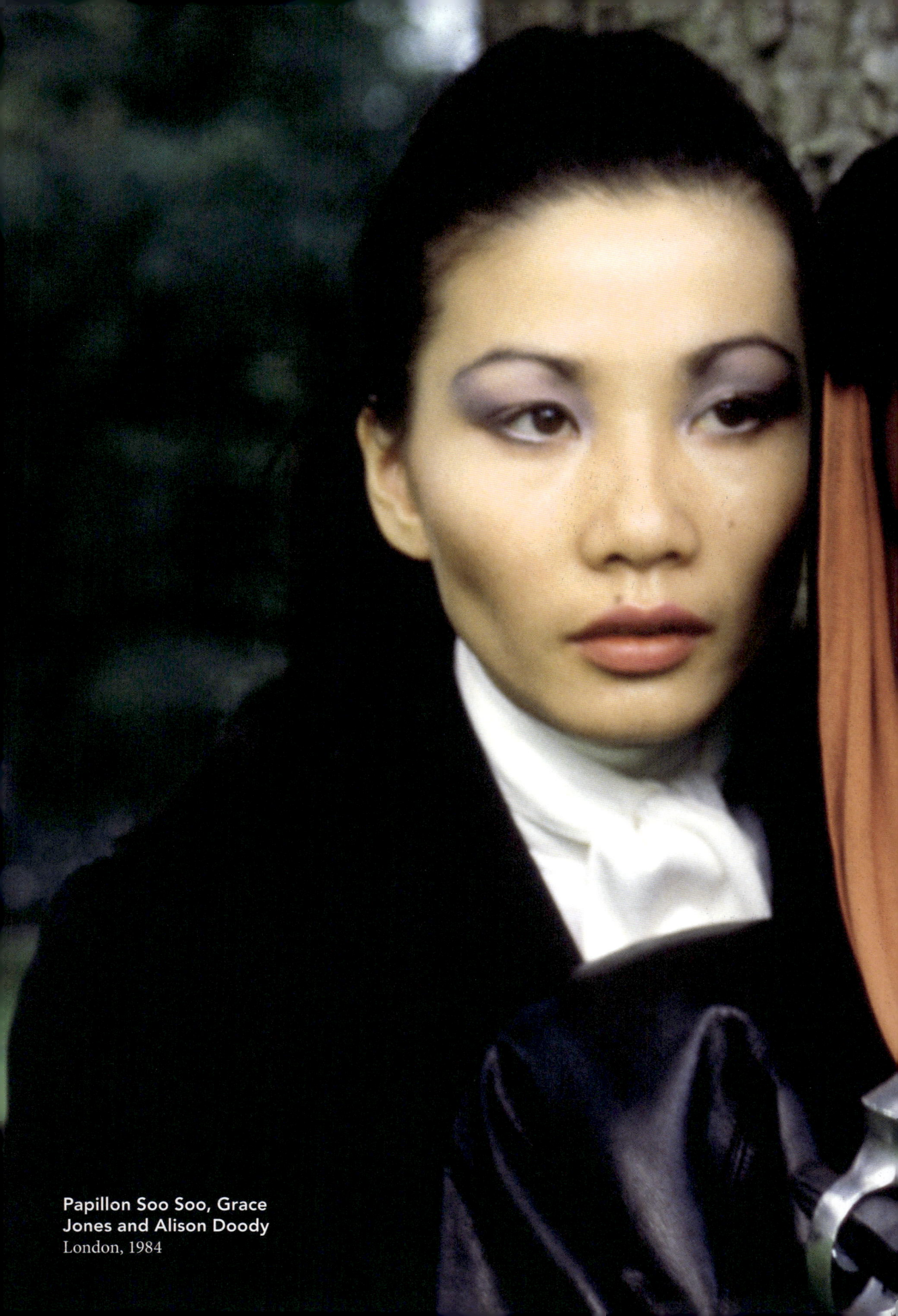

Papillon Soo Soo, Grace
Jones and Alison Doody
London, 1984

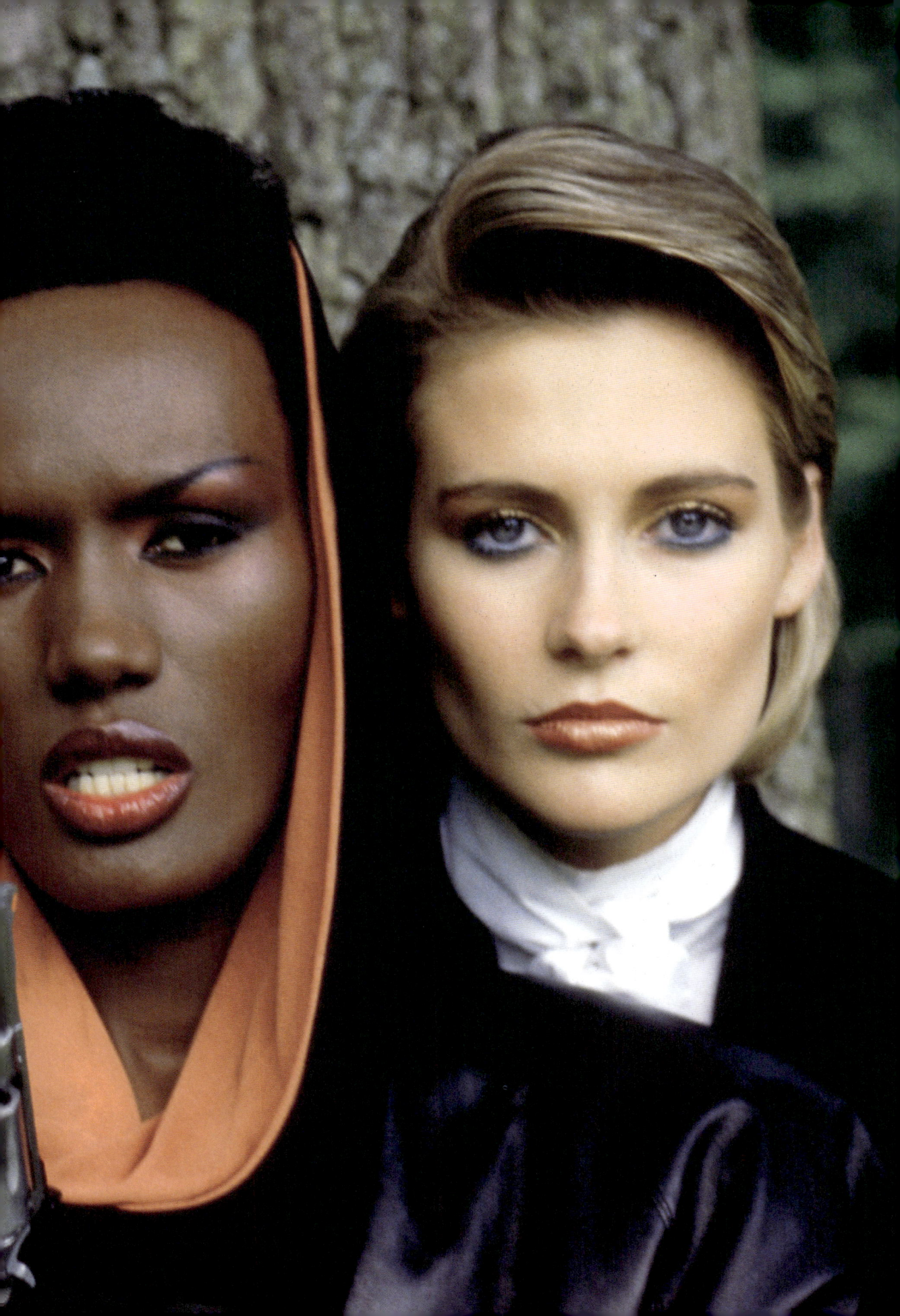

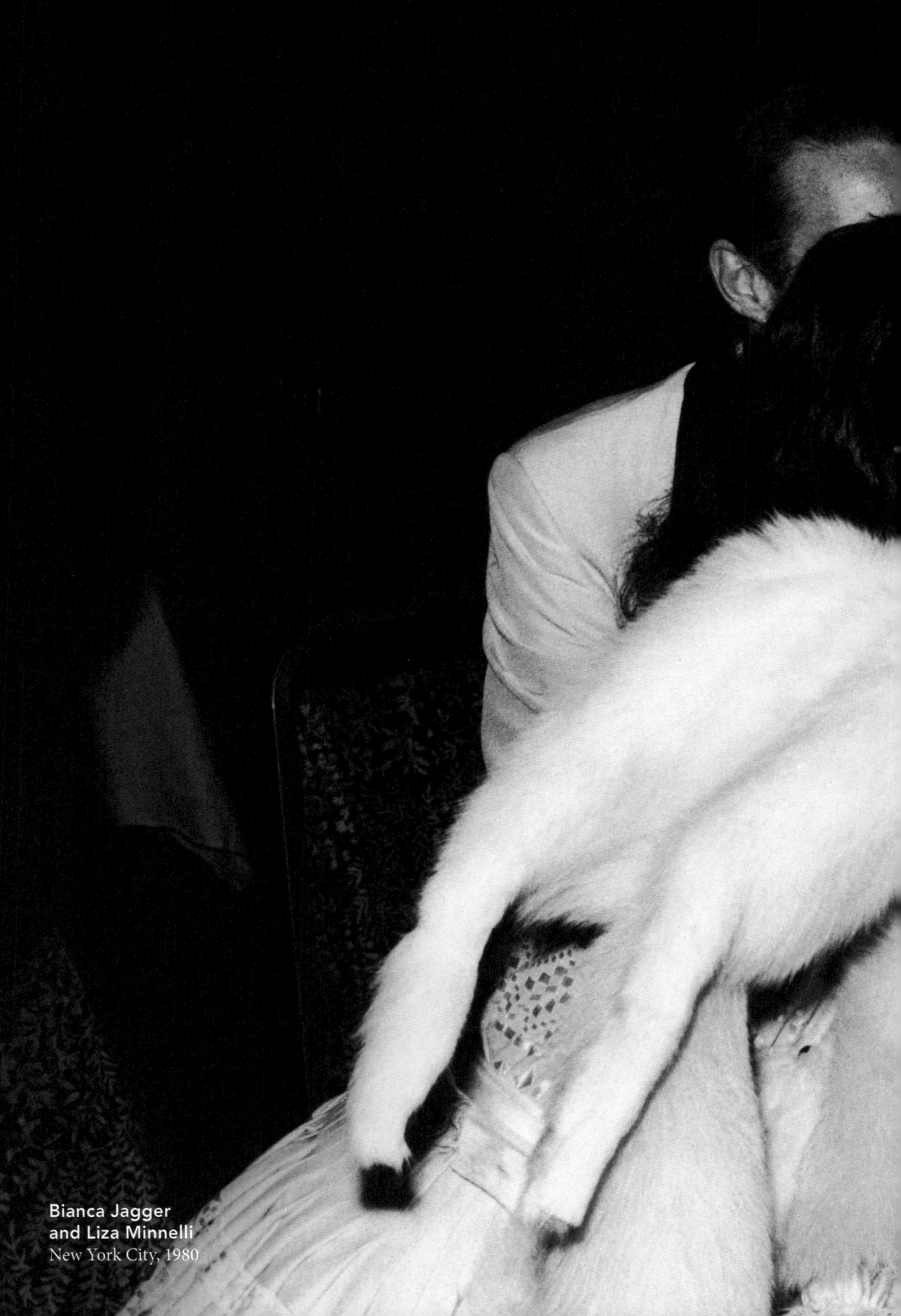

**Bianca Jagger
and Liza Minnelli**
New York City, 1980

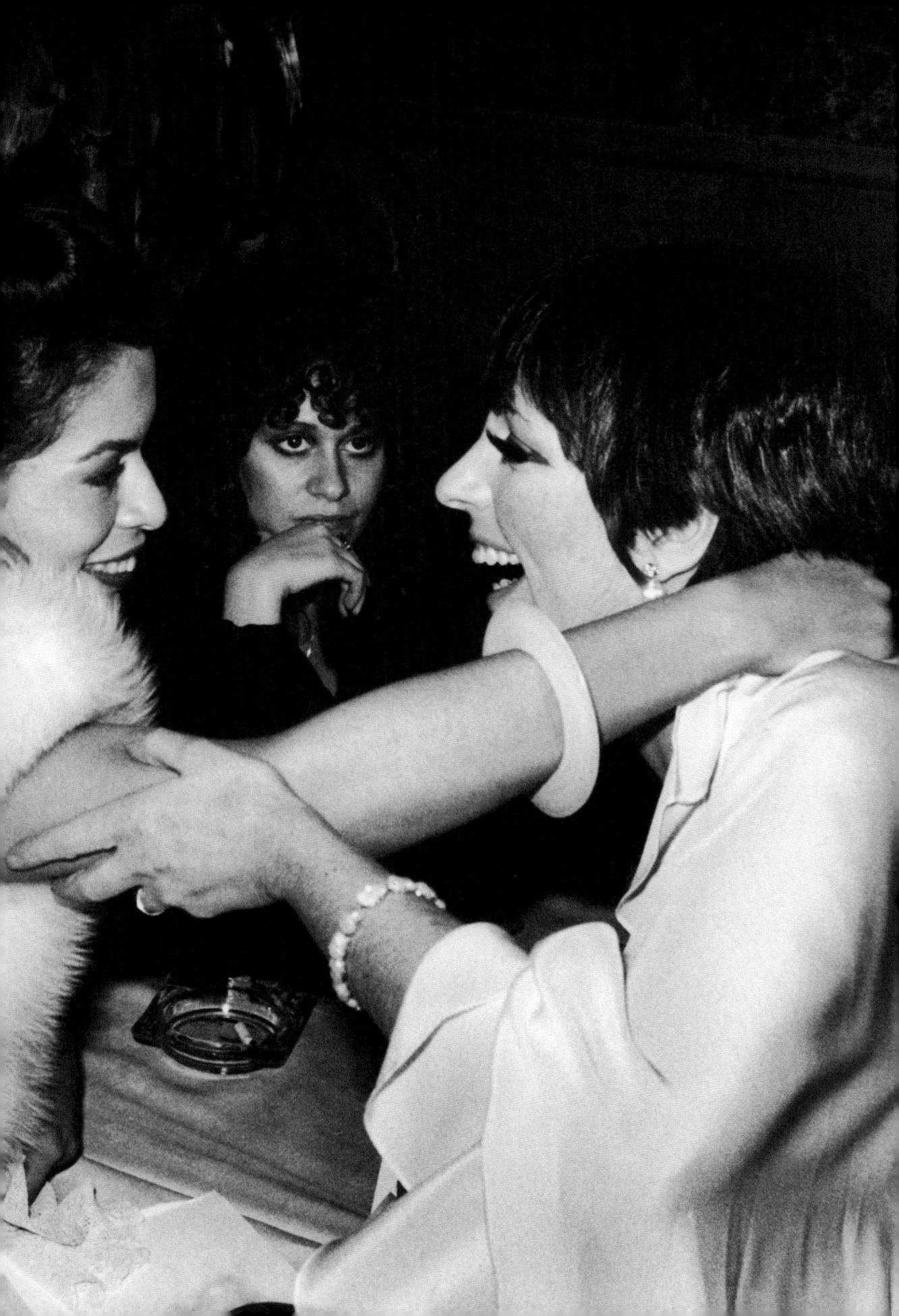

Roberta Flack
New York City, ca. 1980

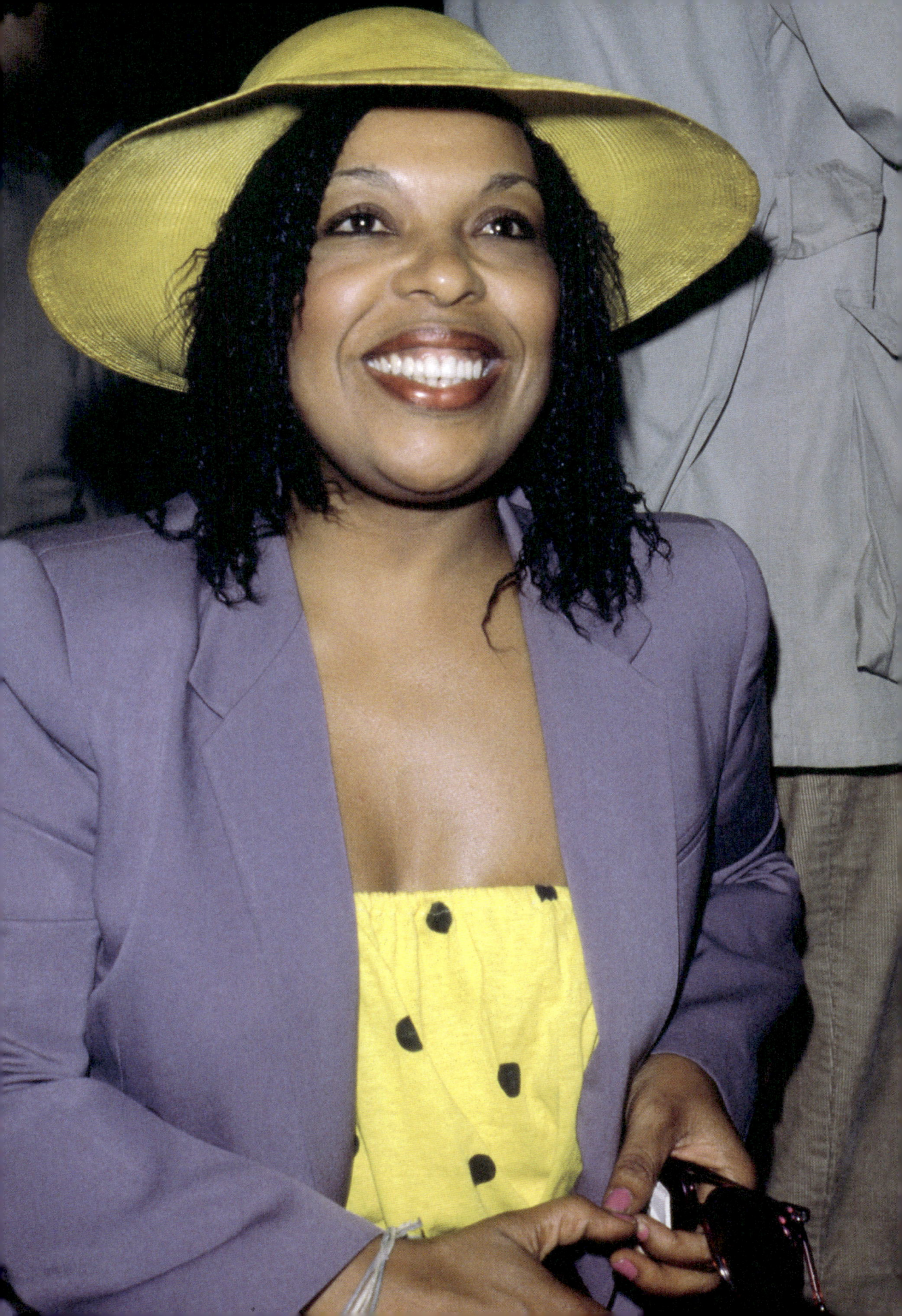

Carol Channing
New York City, 1968

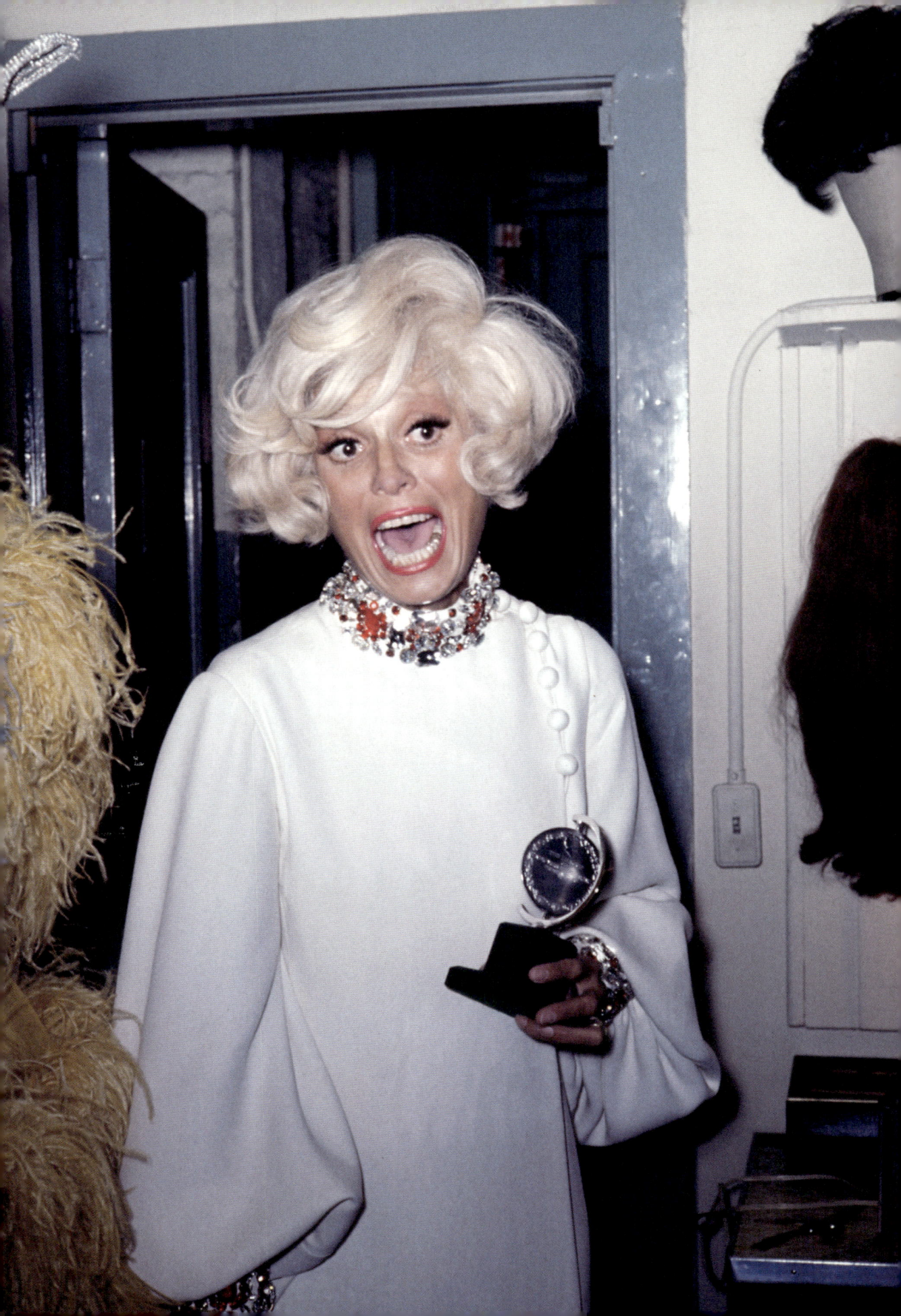

Every glance was a scene, every gaze a story.

She had already burned through decades of spotlights by the time Oscar photographed her.

Bette Davis didn't smile for the camera. She didn't need to. Her face — etched with power, elegance, and weariness — charted the life of a woman who had fought her way through an industry that underestimated her.

Oscar took the shot knowing she wouldn't pose, wouldn't pretend, wouldn't perform. And that's exactly why it worked.

Bette Davis
New York City, 1973

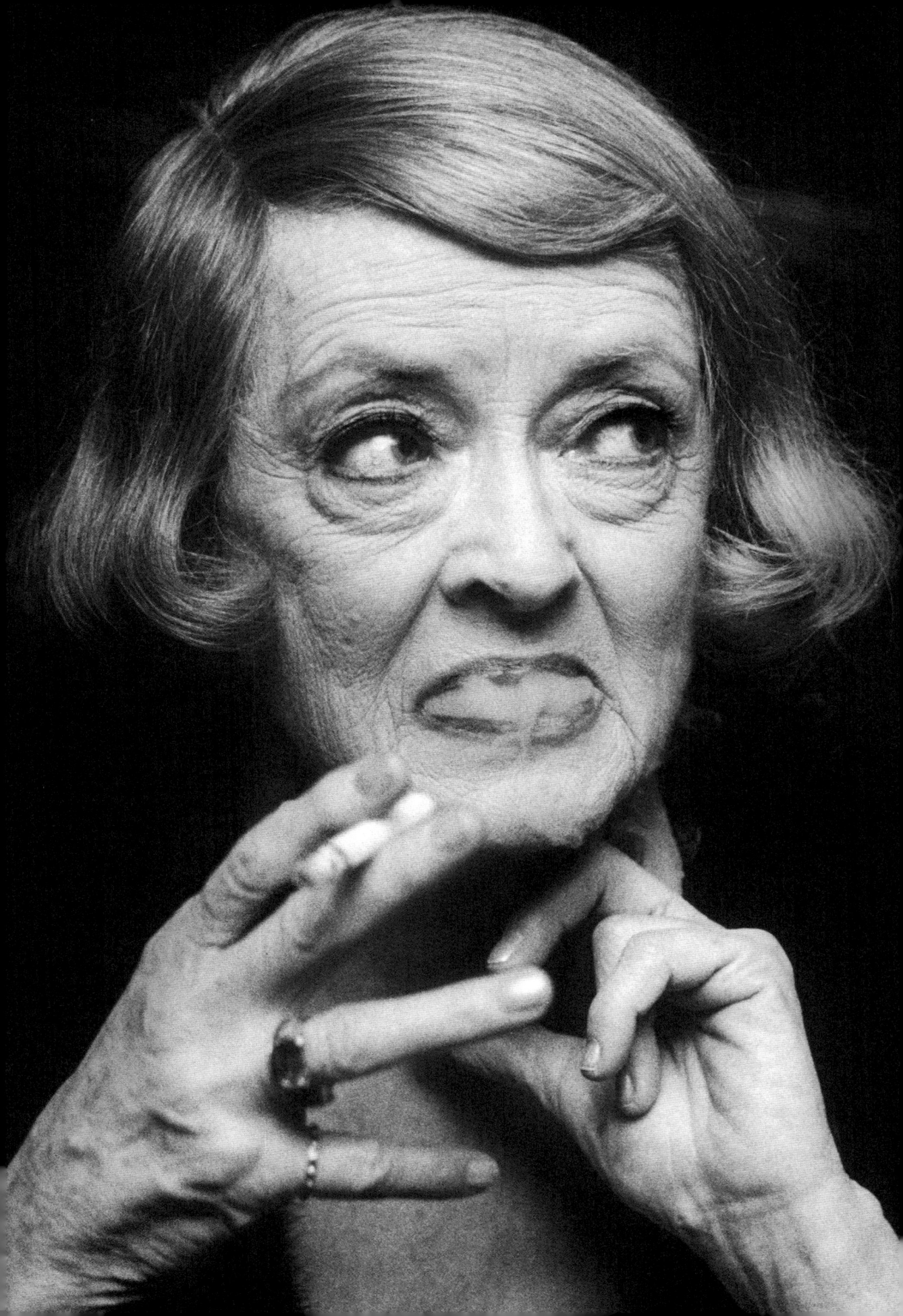

Catherine Deneuve
New York City, 1983

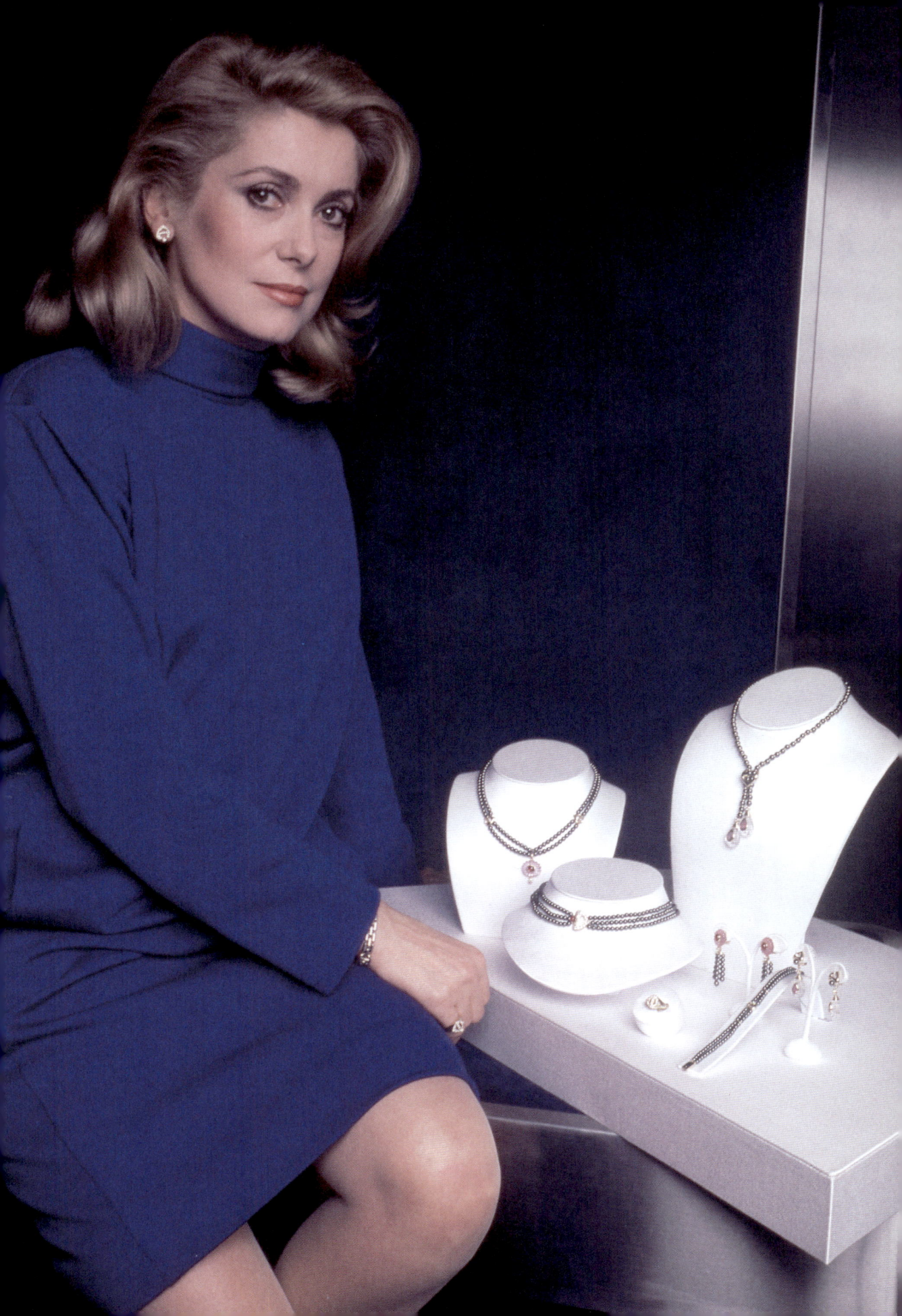

Mia Farrow
New York City, 1969

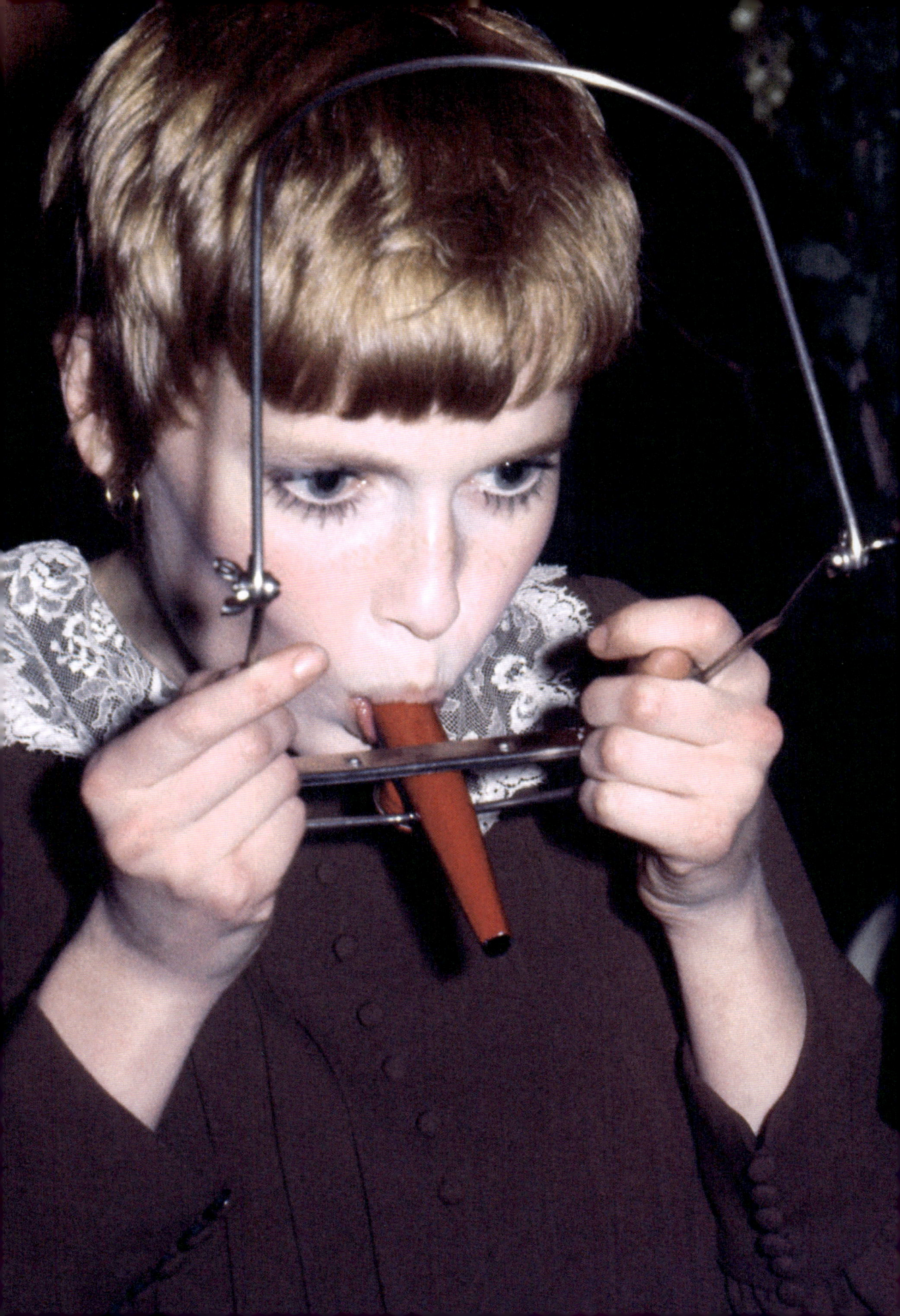

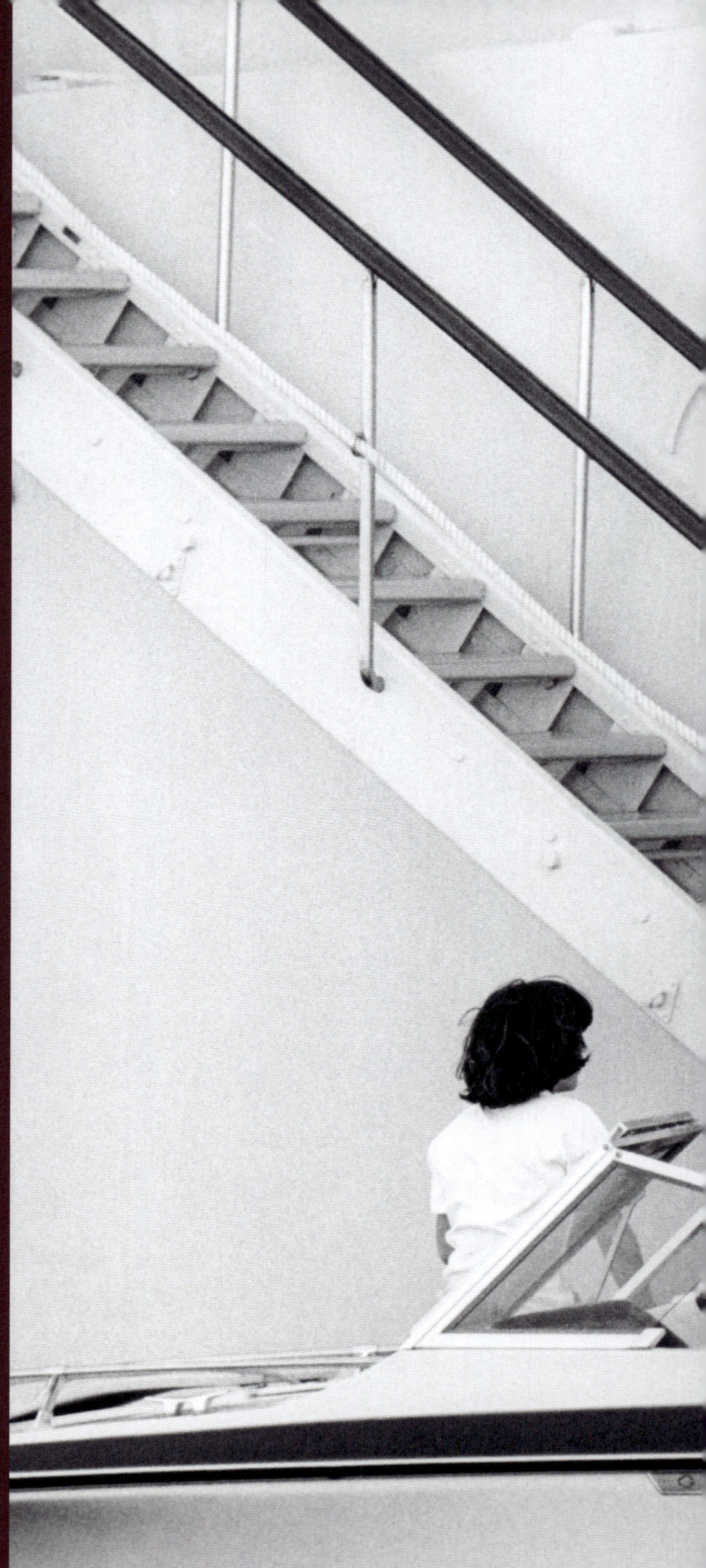

Jackie Kennedy Onassis
Palm Beach, 1972

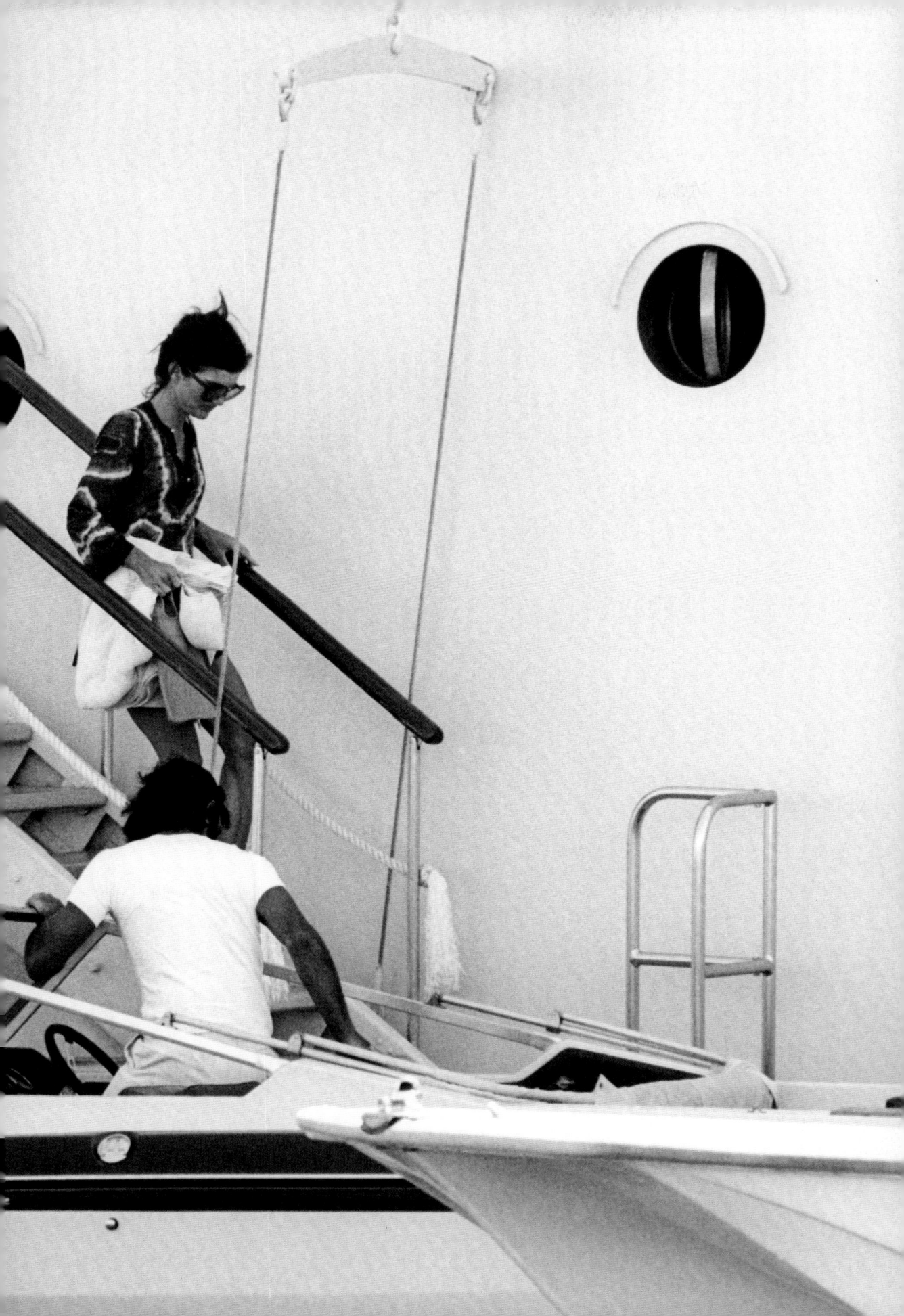

Charo
New York City, ca. 1975

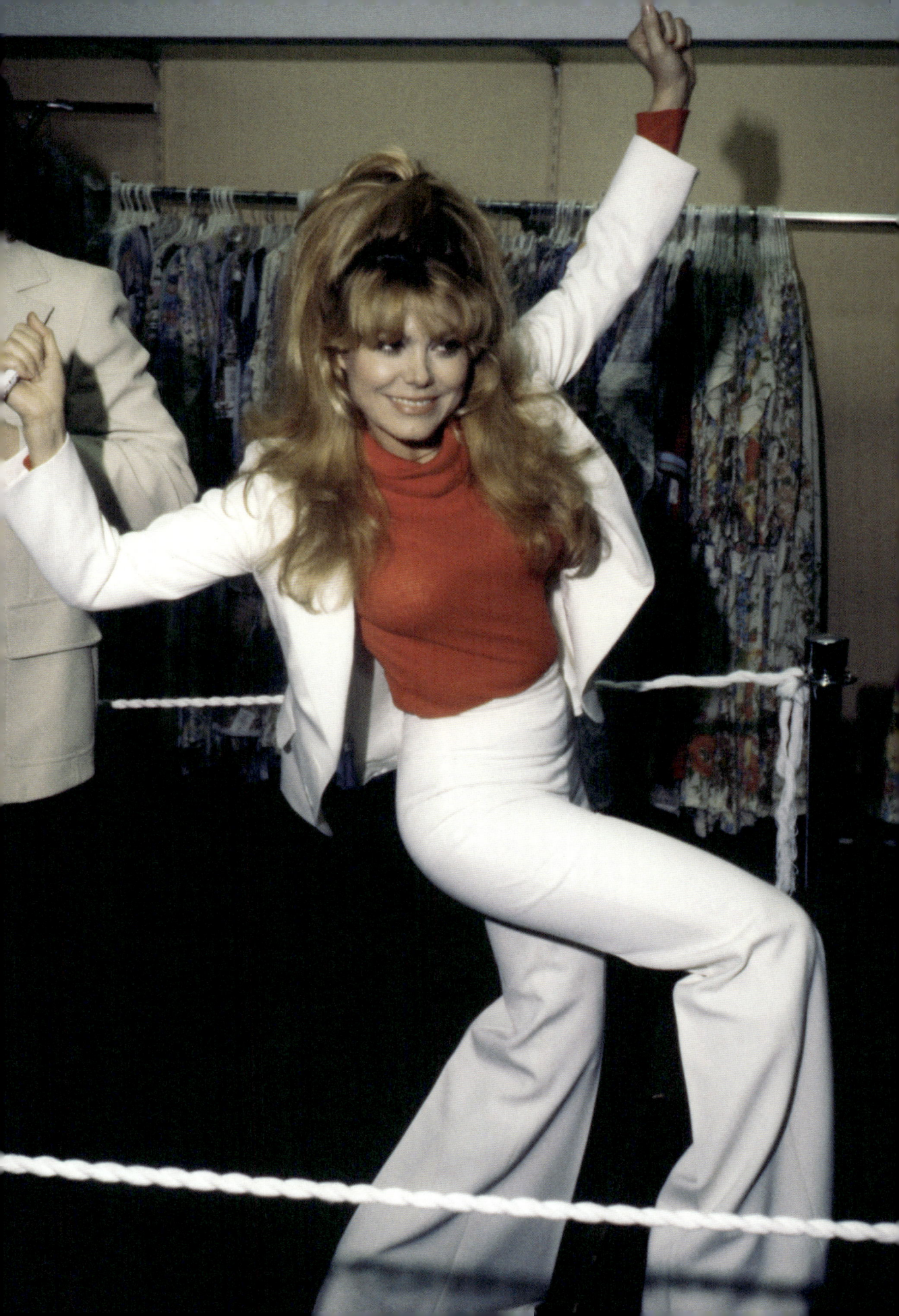

Cher
New York City, 1968

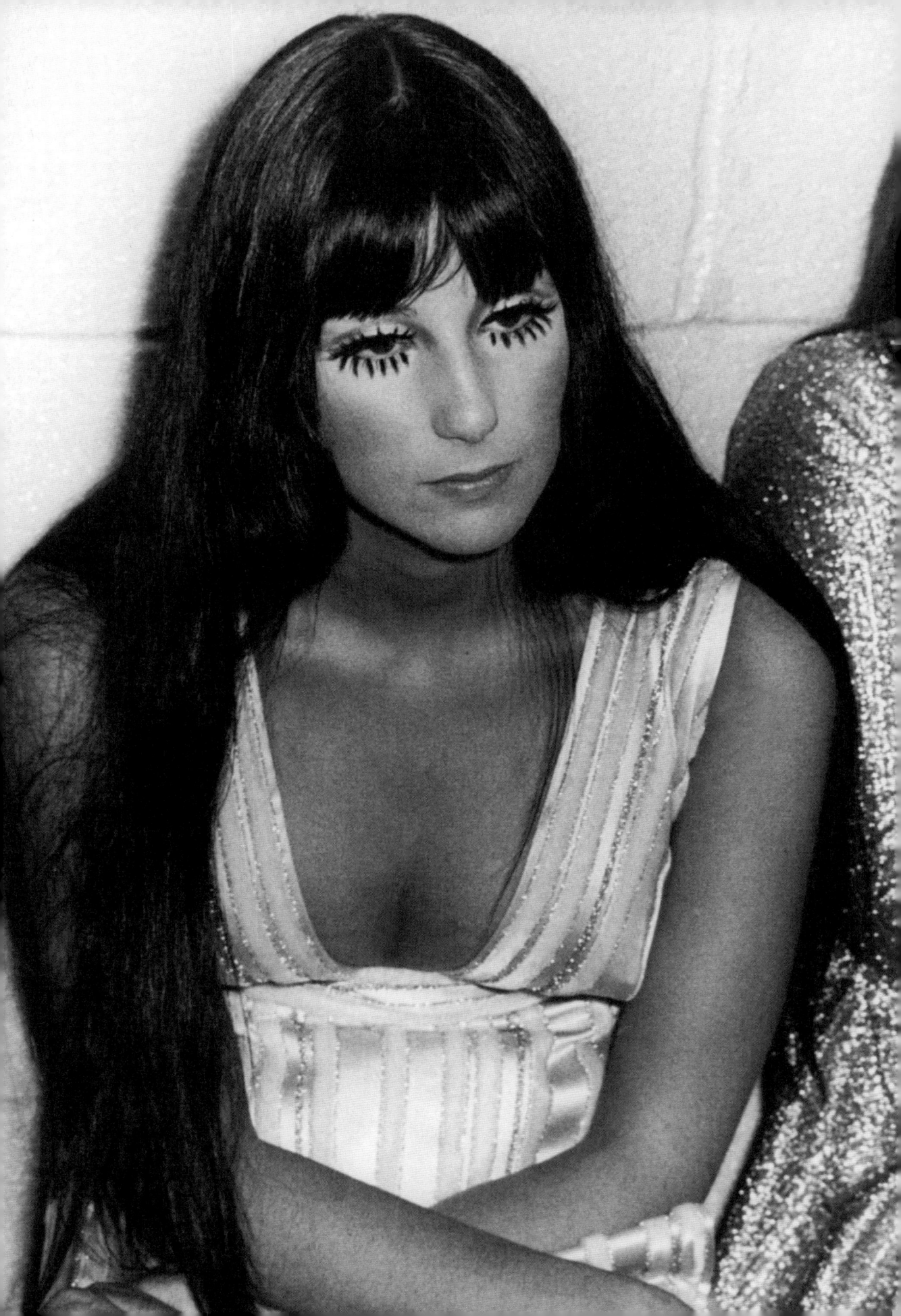

Christina Onassis
Palm Beach, 1972

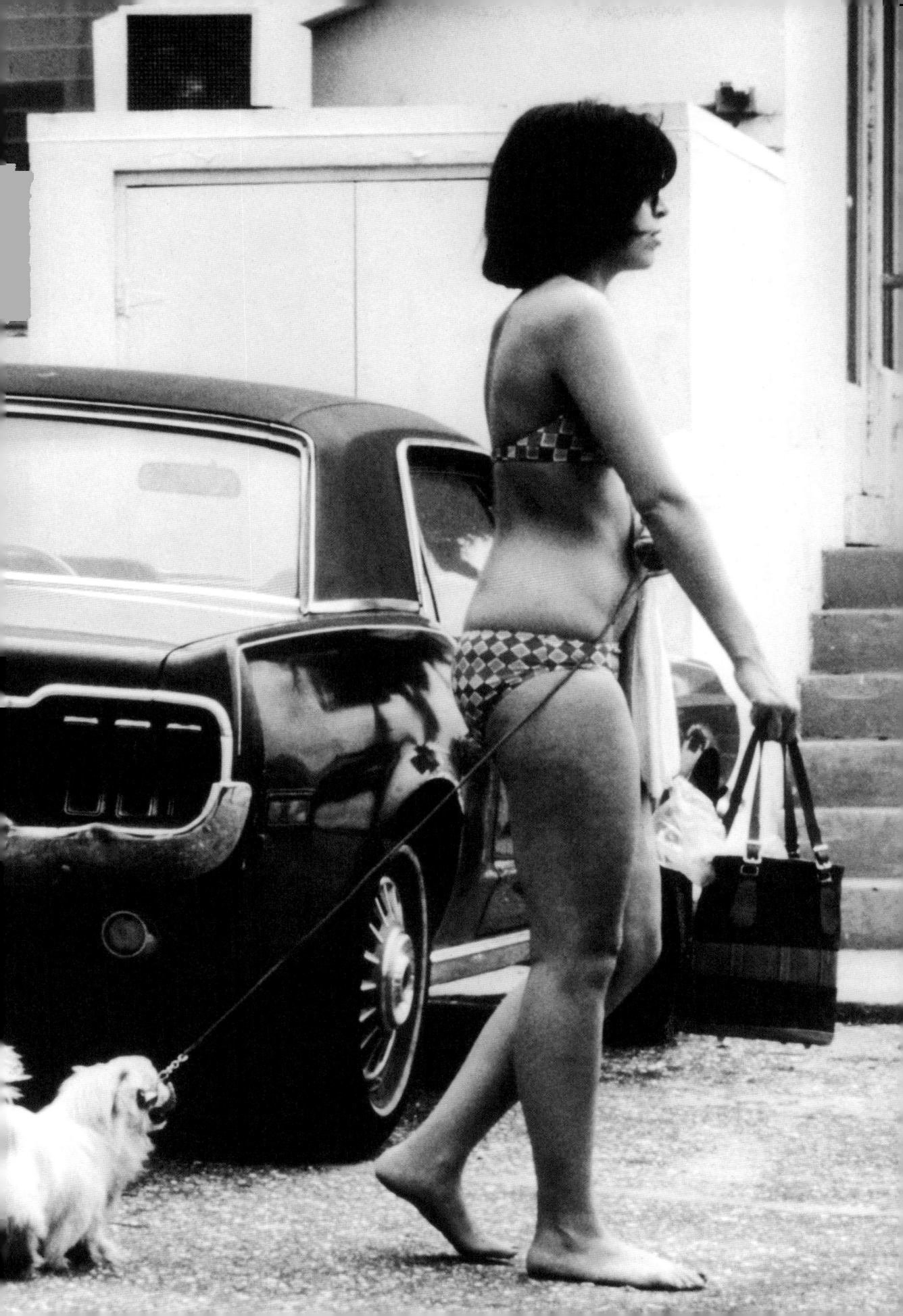

Claudette Colbert
New York City, ca. 1980

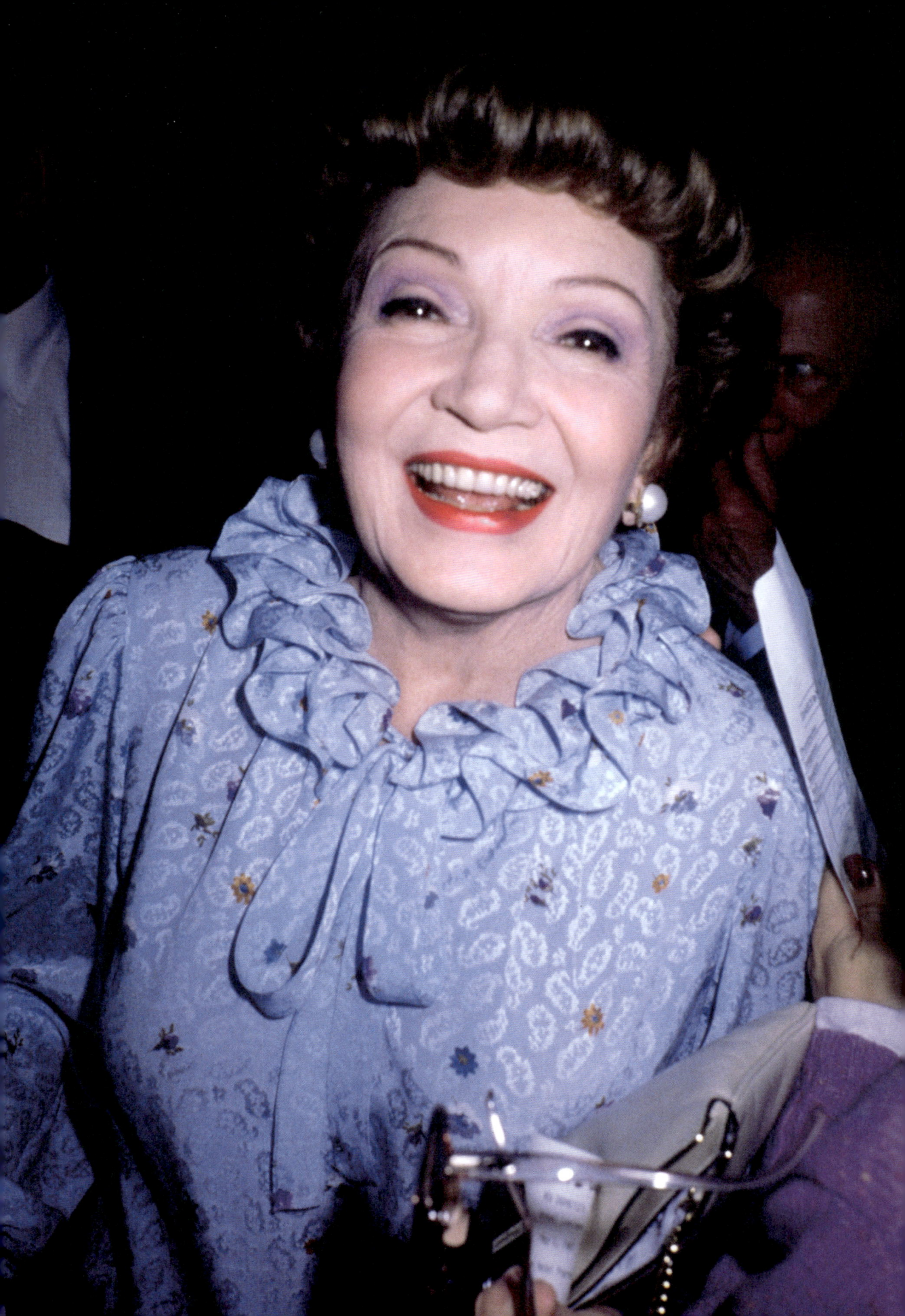

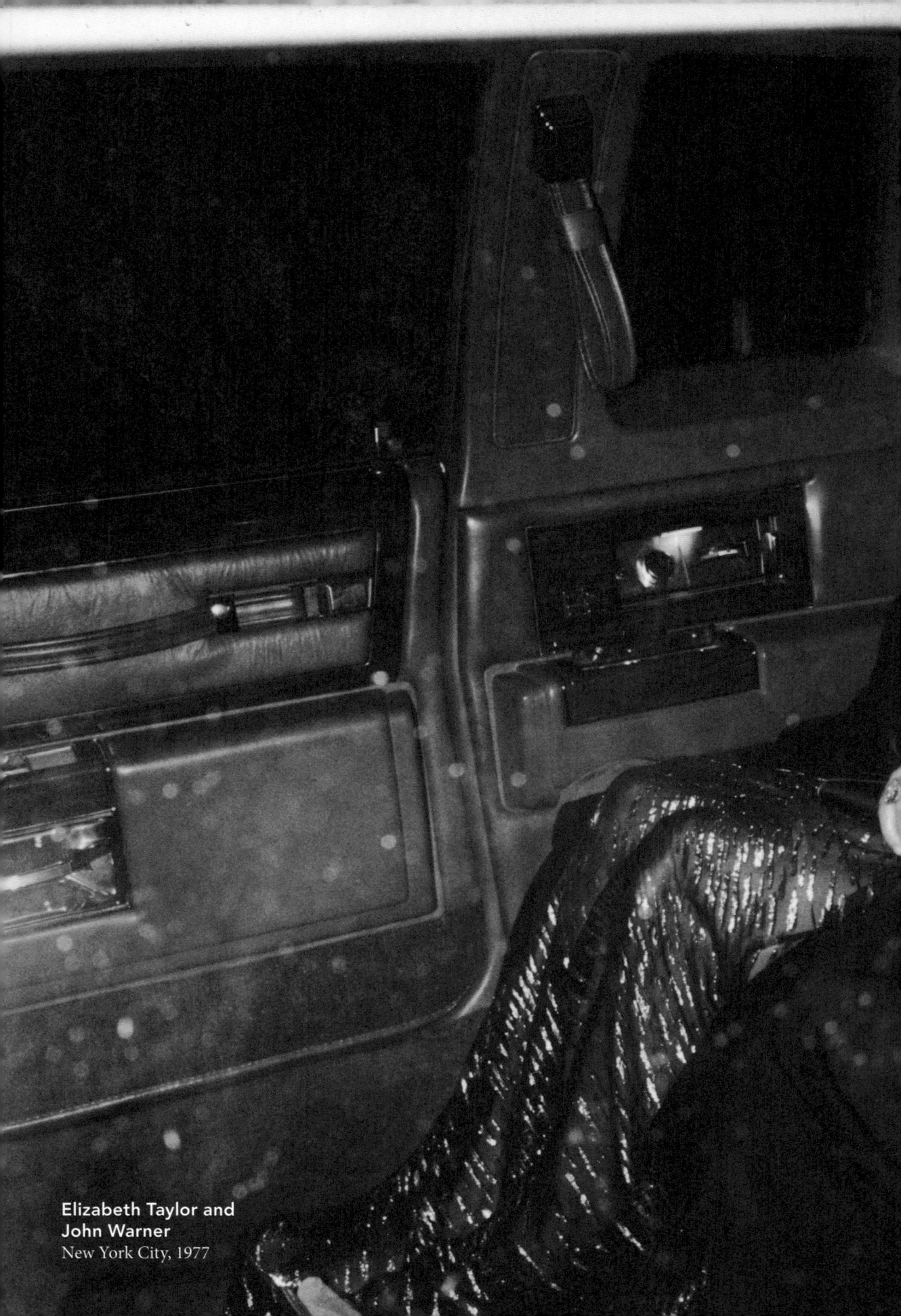

**Elizabeth Taylor and
John Warner**
New York City, 1977

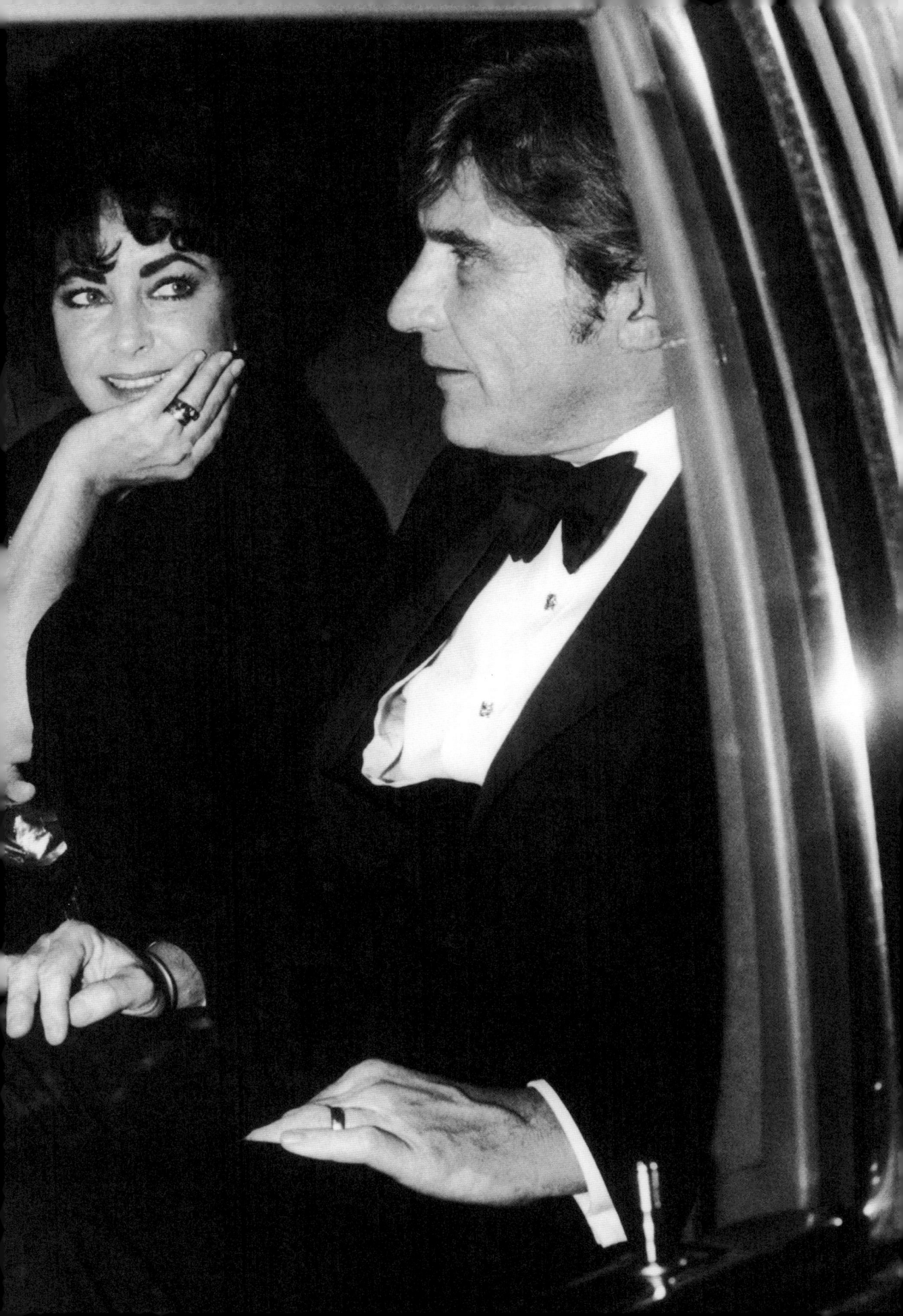

Behind the poster, there was a woman few really knew.

For most, she would always be the woman in the red swimsuit — the smile, the hair, the 12 million pin-ups.

But there was more depth to Farrah Fawcett than the image revealed. Oscar saw it. The California sunshine was real, yes, but so was the weariness underneath. She laughed easily but didn't fake it. She knew the power of performance — and the price she paid for being adored.

He caught her in a moment that felt like neither posing nor hiding. Just Farrah, breathing.

Farrah Fawcett
Los Angeles Beach, 1977

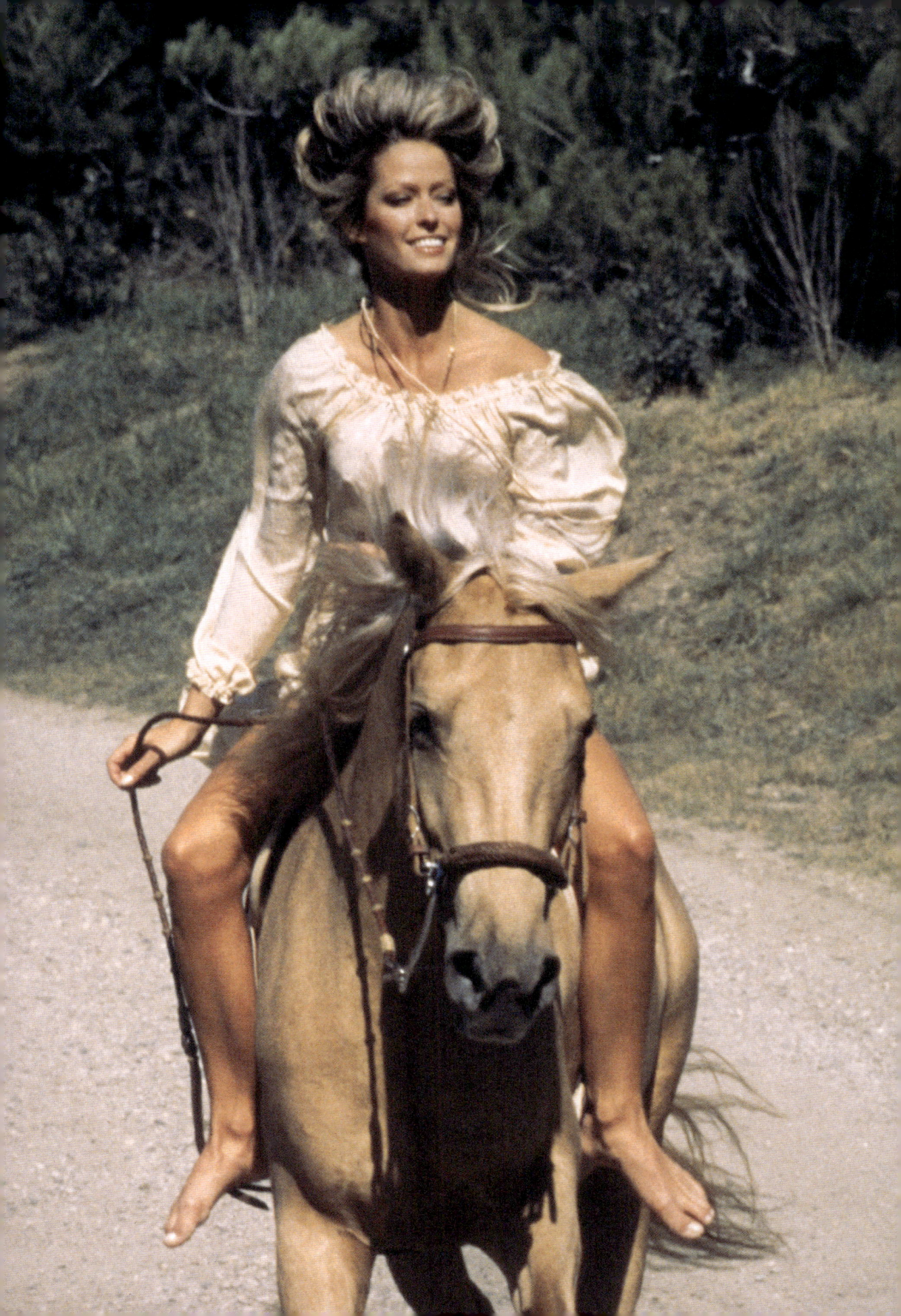

Cyndi Lauper
New York City, ca. 1988

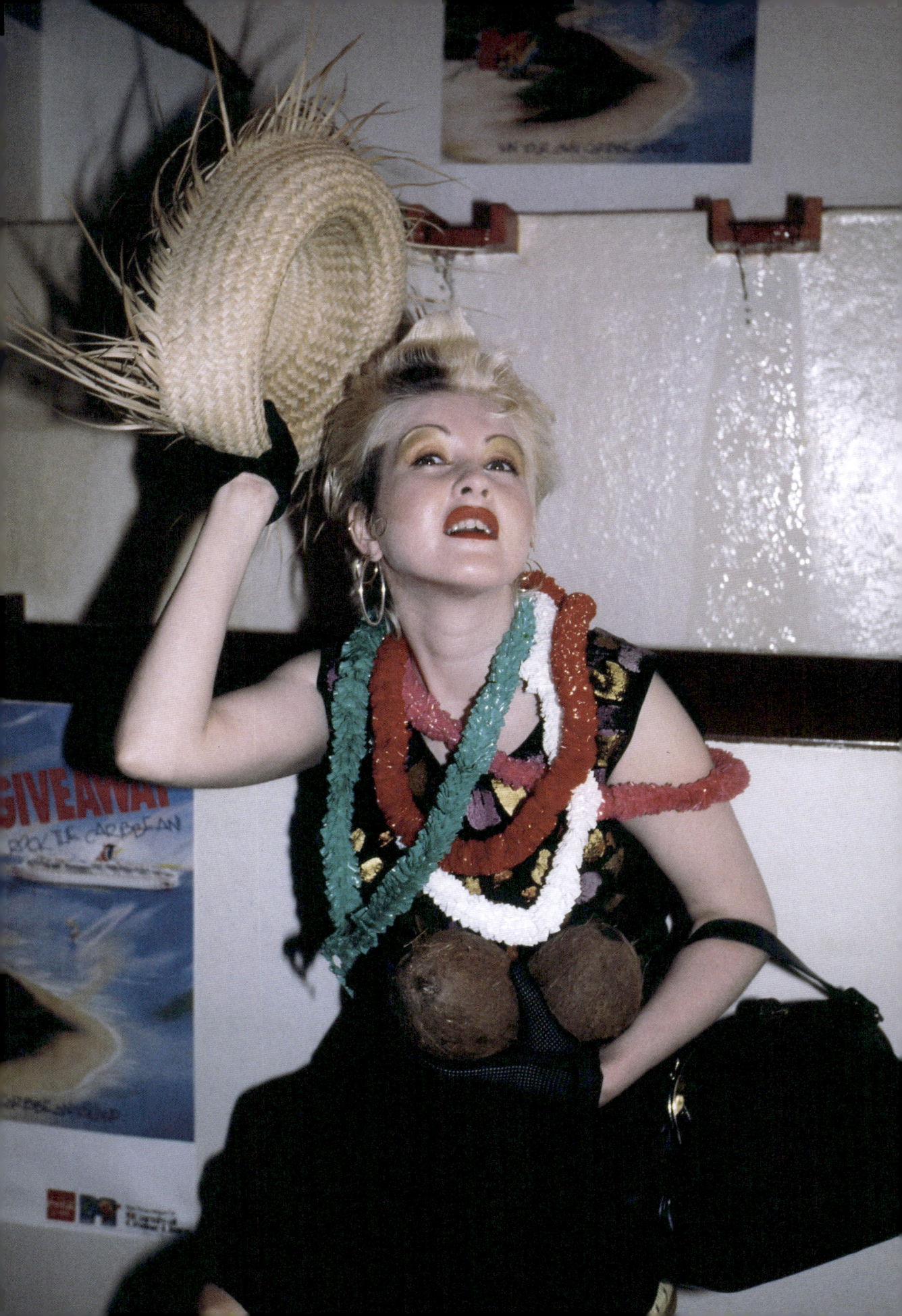

Debbie Harry
New York City, 1987

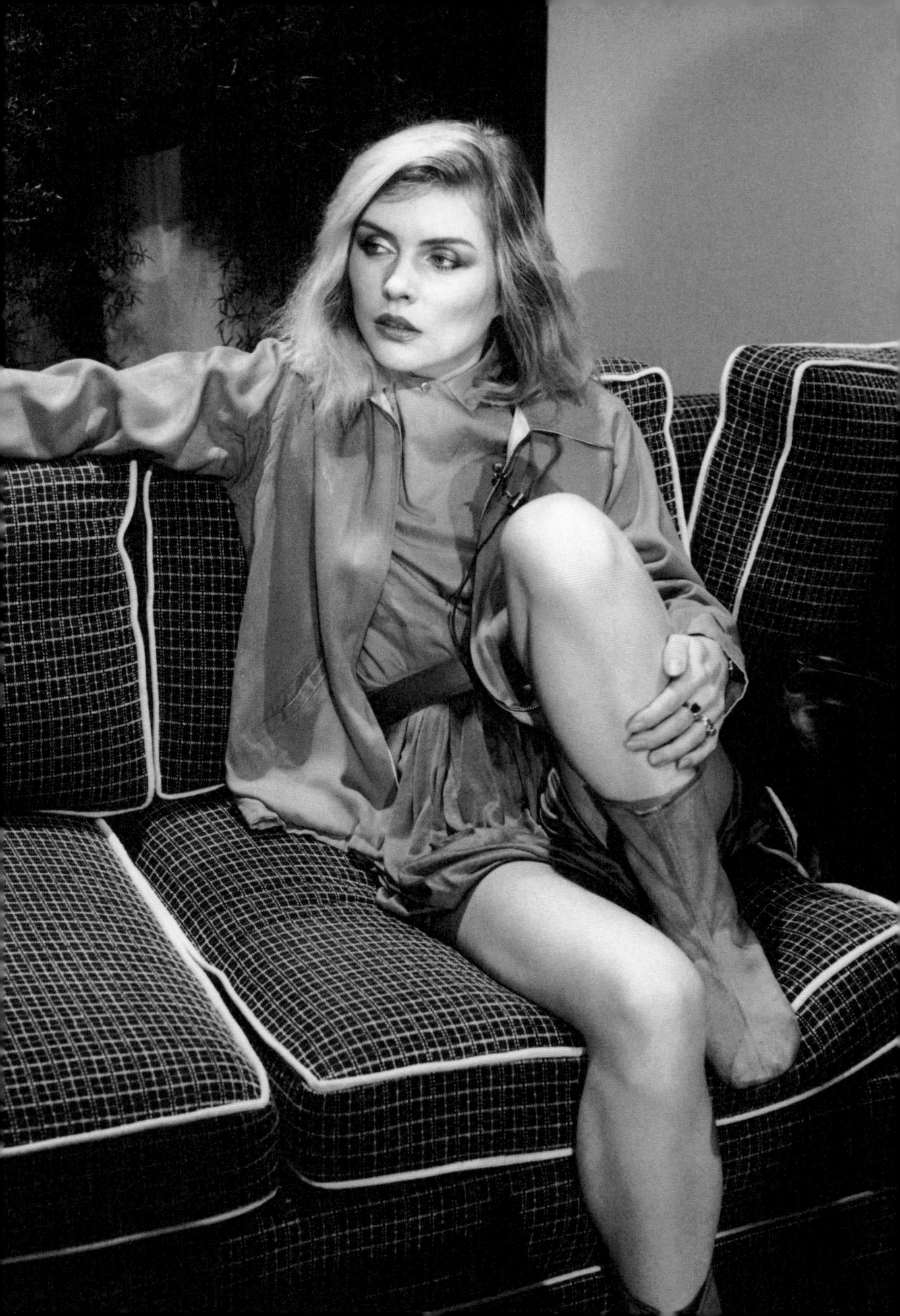

To look at her was to witness art in motion.

She burst into the world like a design object brought to life: all edges, energy, and an unapologetic stare. She didn't ask to be looked at. She dared you to keep looking.

Oscar didn't try to contain her. He let her spill into the frame — genderless, genre-less, and in absolute control. In a world of soft filters, she was a hard truth.

Grace Jones
New York City, 1981

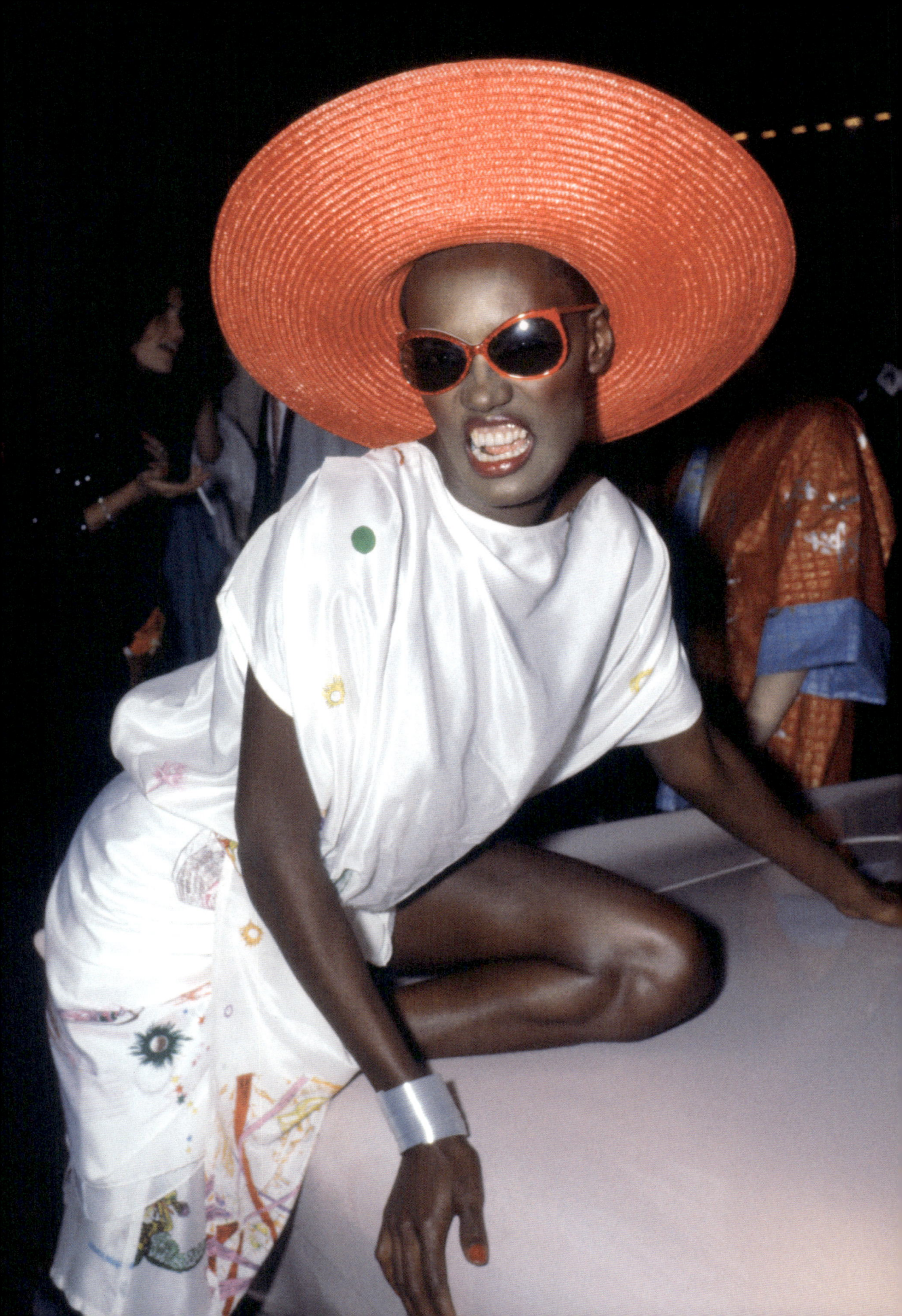

Diana Ross
New York City, 1982

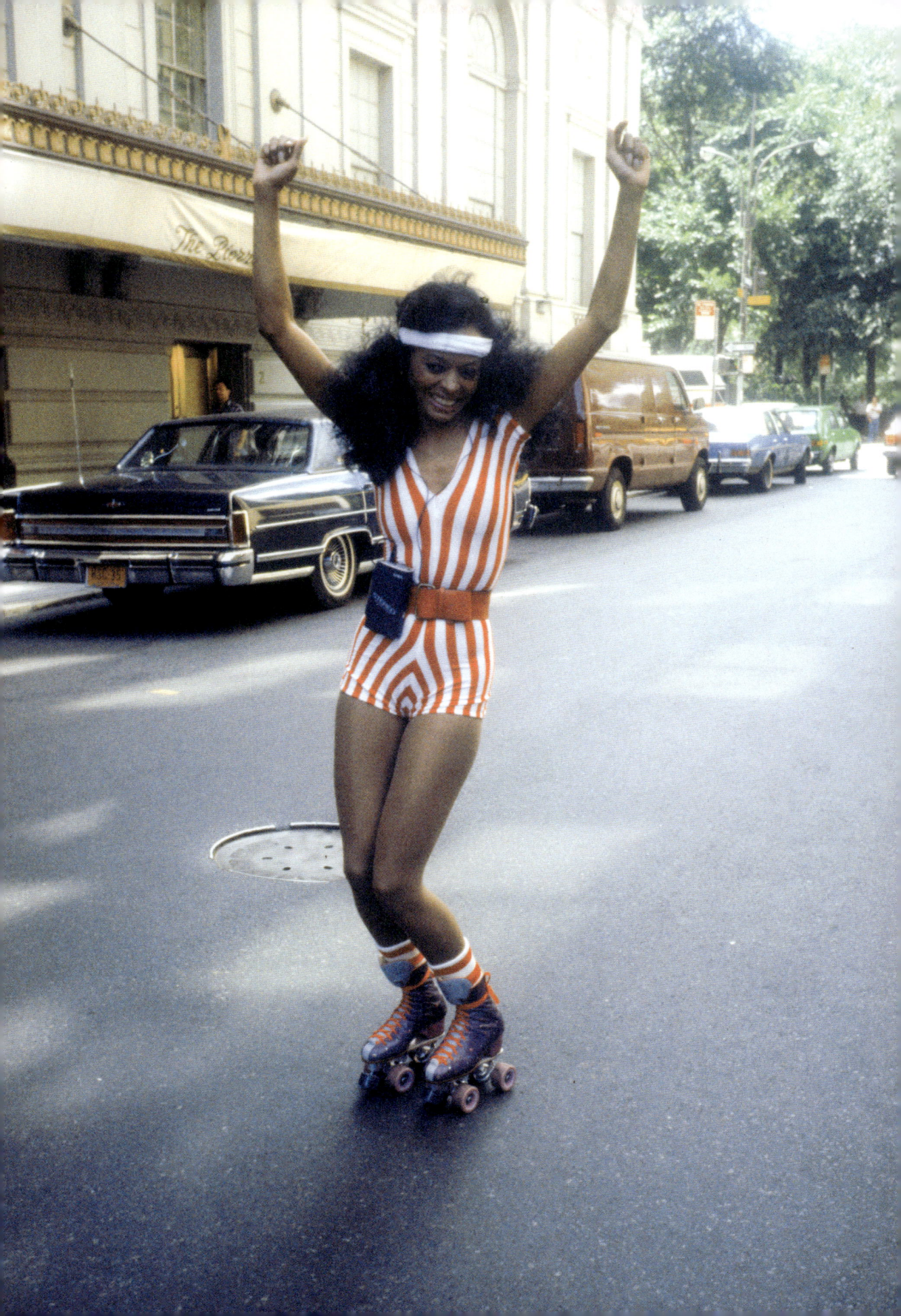

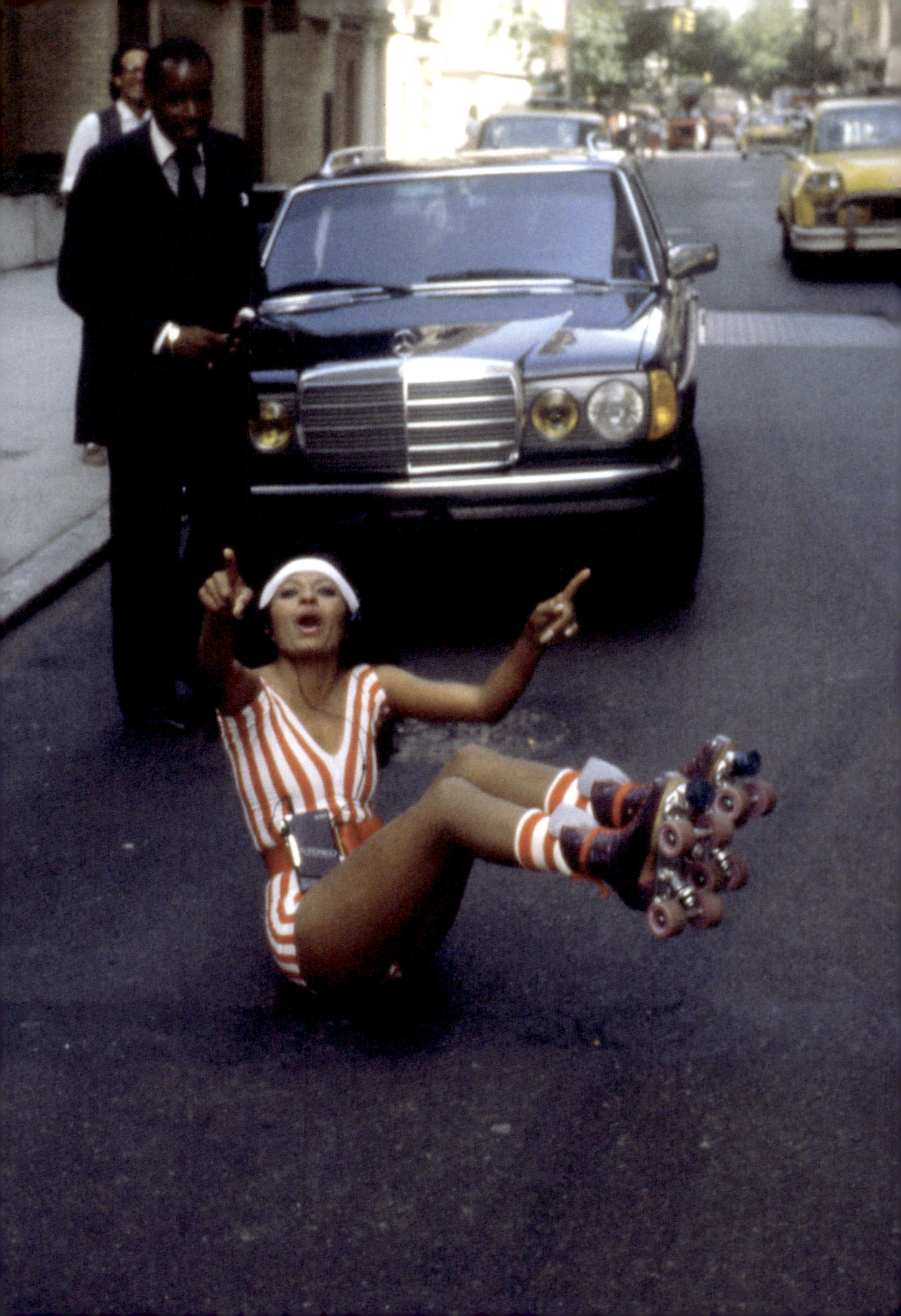

Diana Ross
New York City, 1982

Priscilla Presley
Dallas, 1983

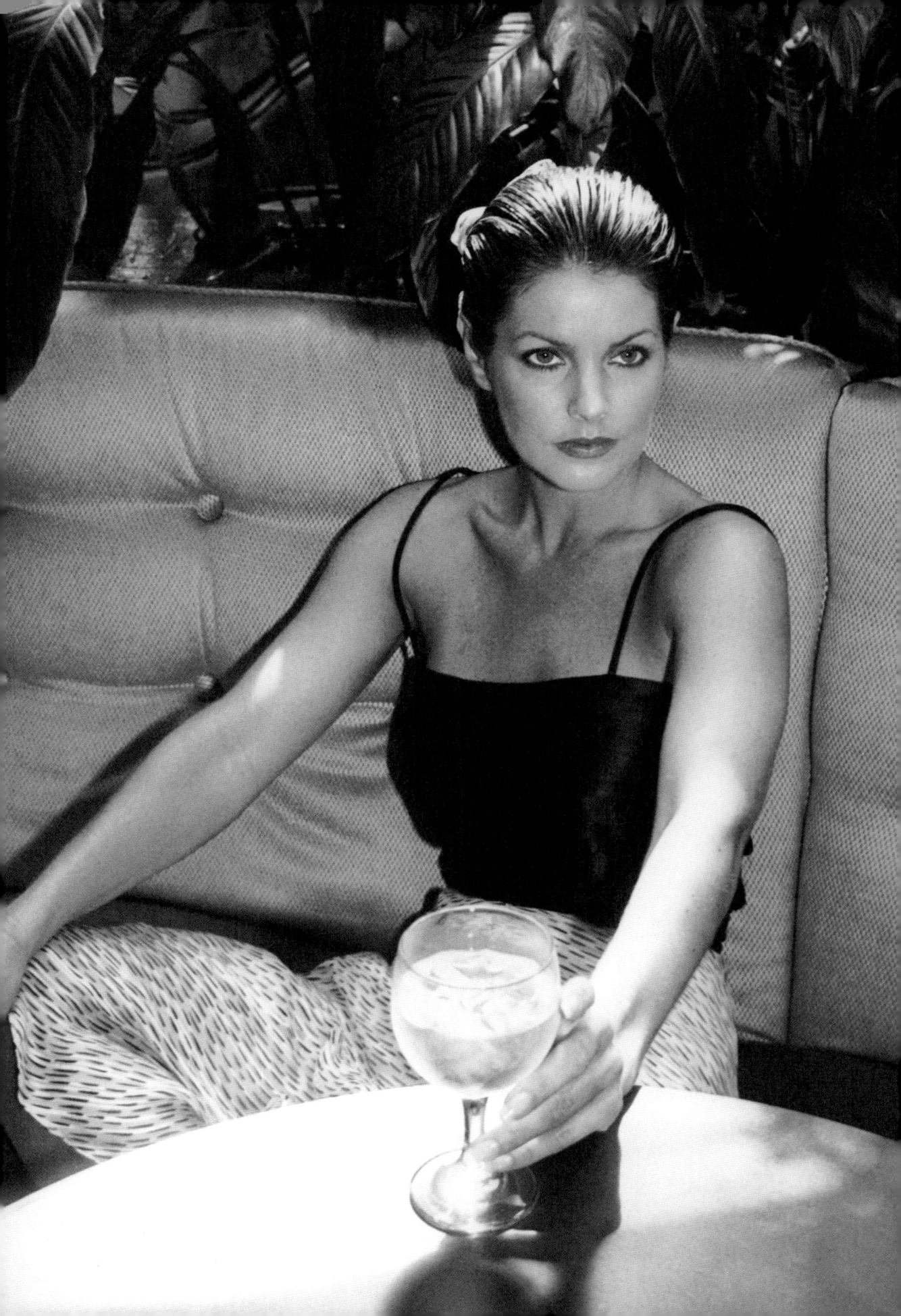

Sylvia Kristel
New York City, 1980

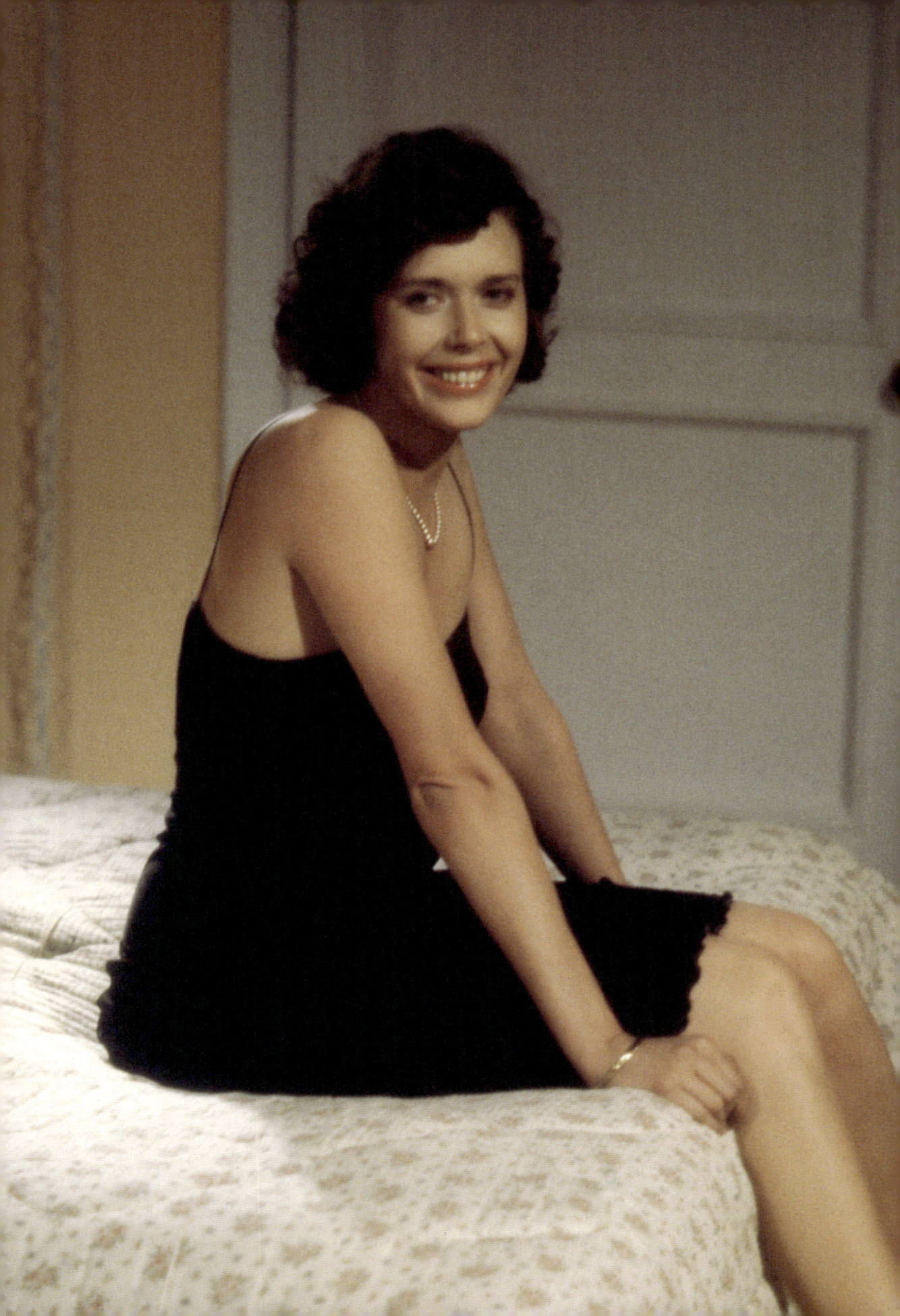

Diana Vreeland
New York City, 1975

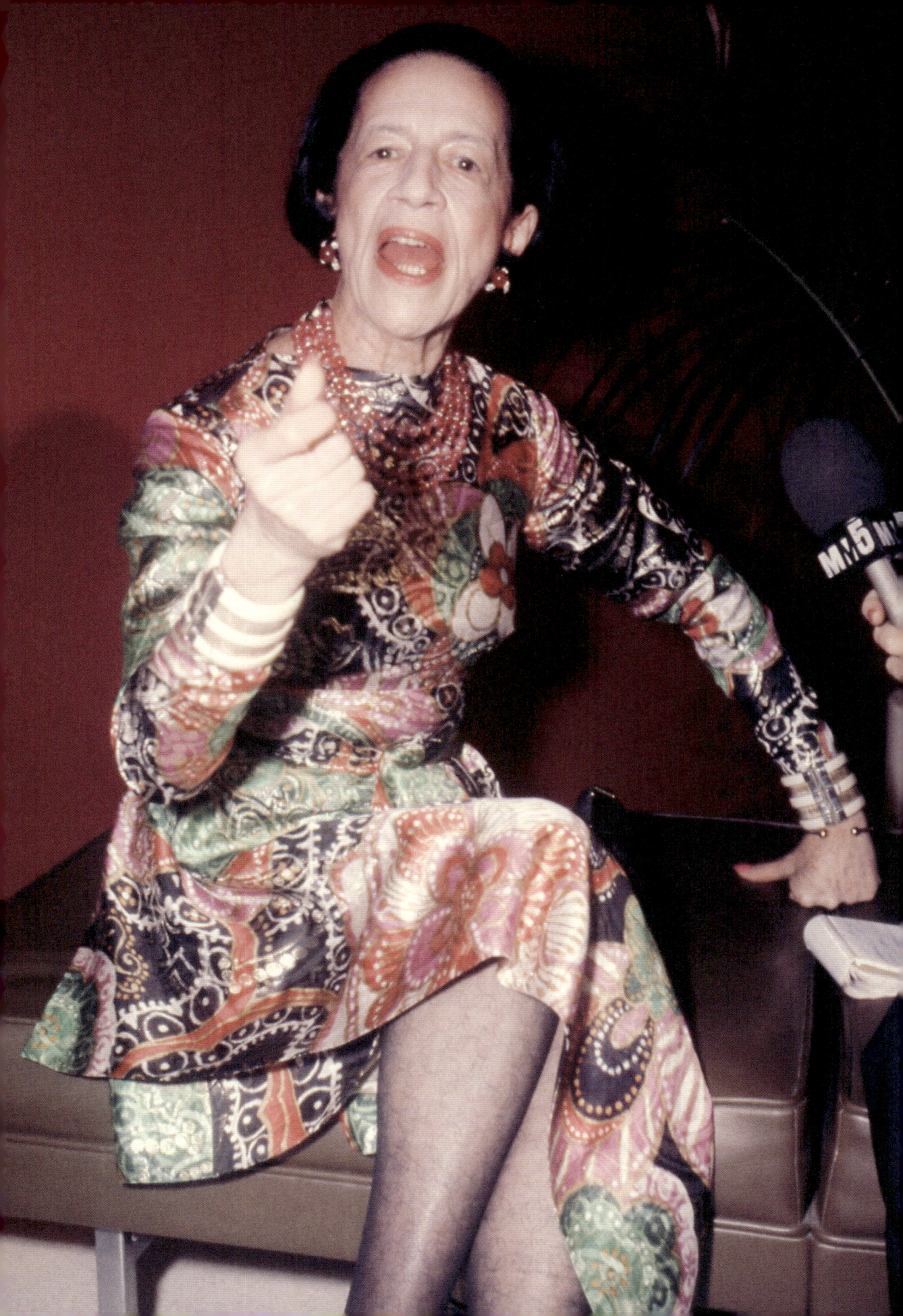

Divine
(Harris Glenn Milstead)
New York City, 1978

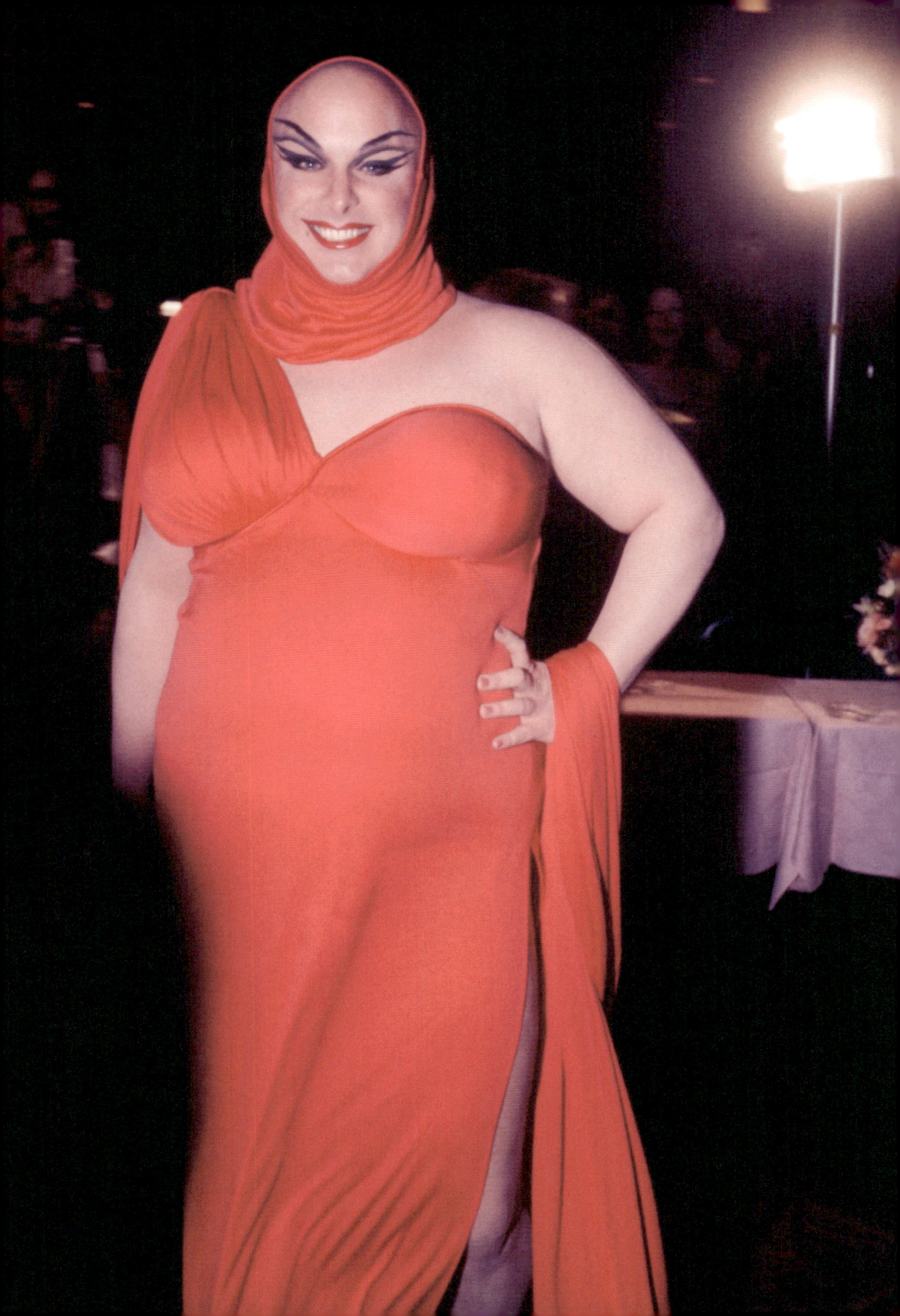

Donna Summer
New York City, 1989

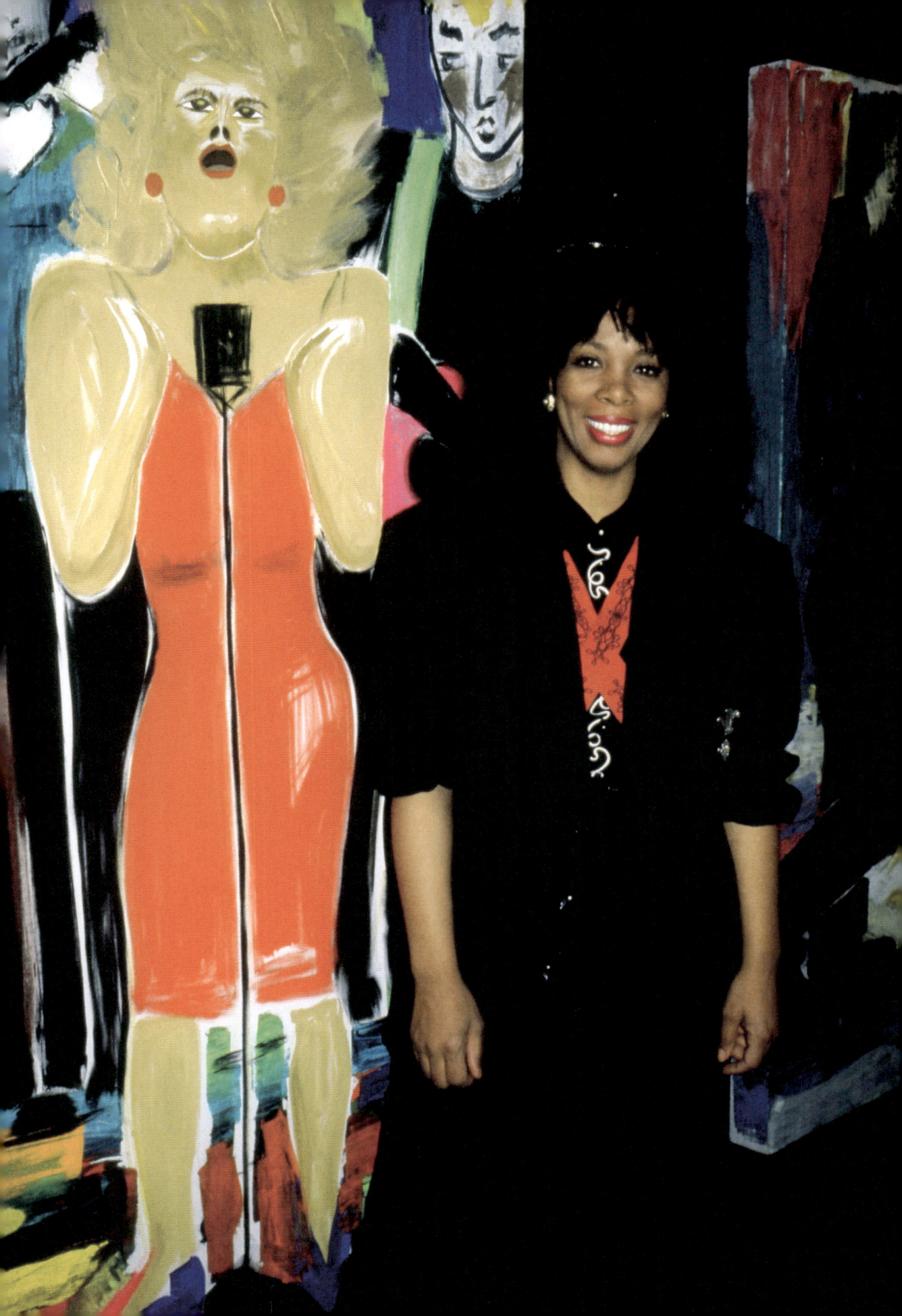

Elizabeth Taylor didn't just walk into a room — she possessed it.

With violet eyes that could stop conversations in mid-sentence and a life that blurred the line between screen legend and tabloid myth, Liz was more than a star — she was an era. She made opulence look effortless, scandal feel glamorous, and vulnerability seem like strength.

Oscar photographed her not as Cleopatra, not as the eight-time bride, but as a woman who had seen it all — and still knew exactly how to hold your gaze. Because Liz knew: being looked at was power. But being seen? That was something else entirely.

Elizabeth Taylor
New York City, 1967

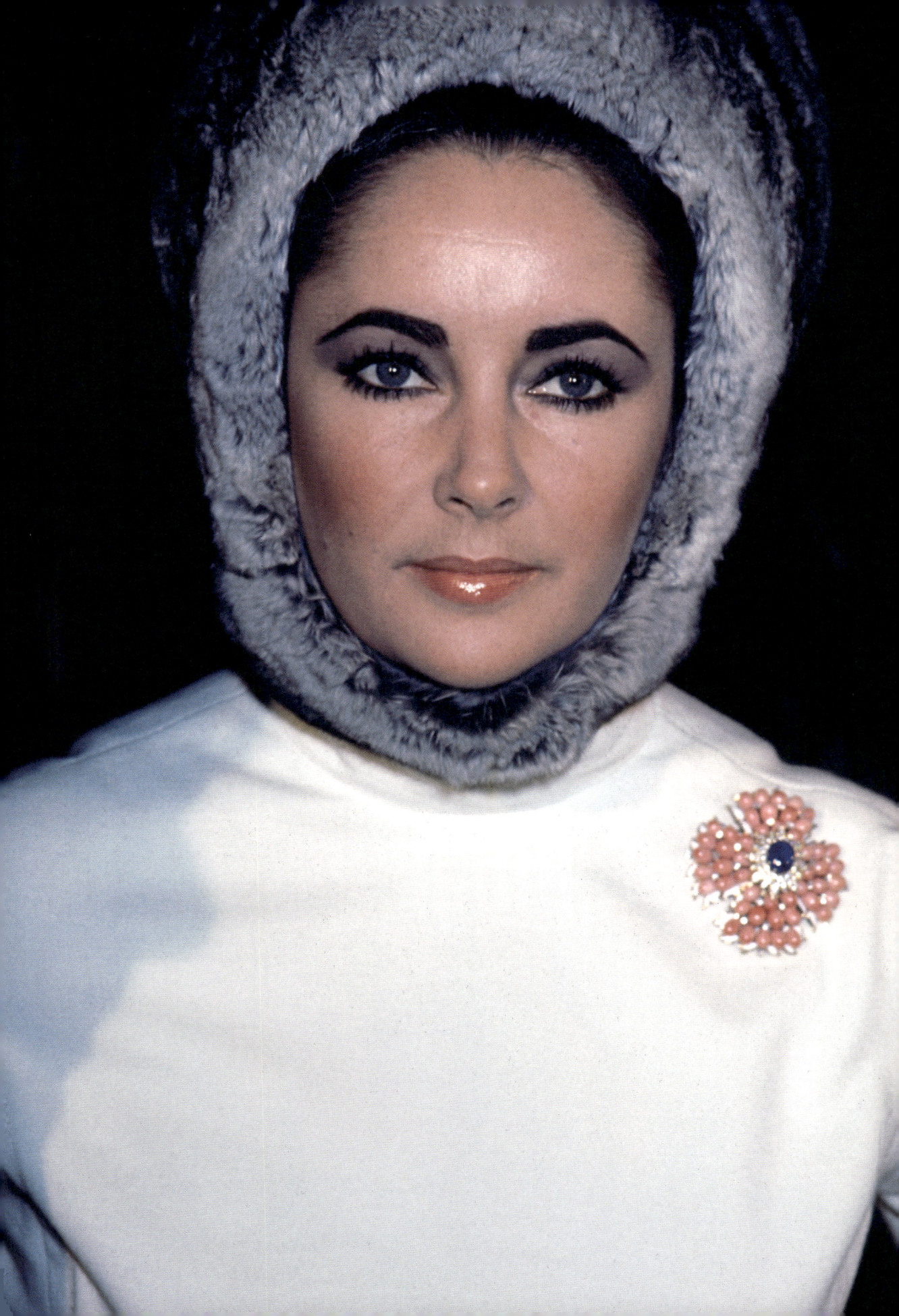

Goldie Hawn
New York City, ca. 1970

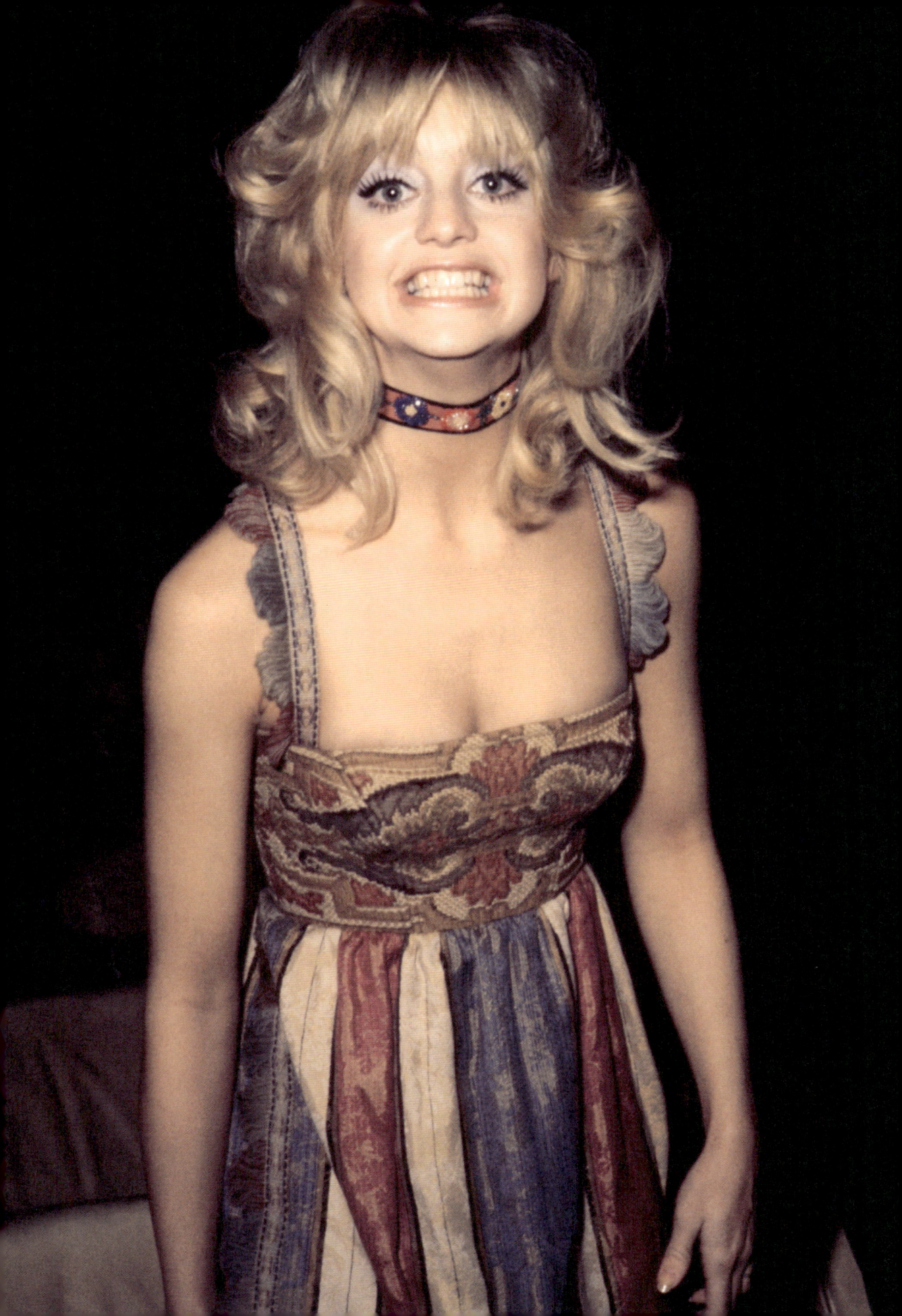

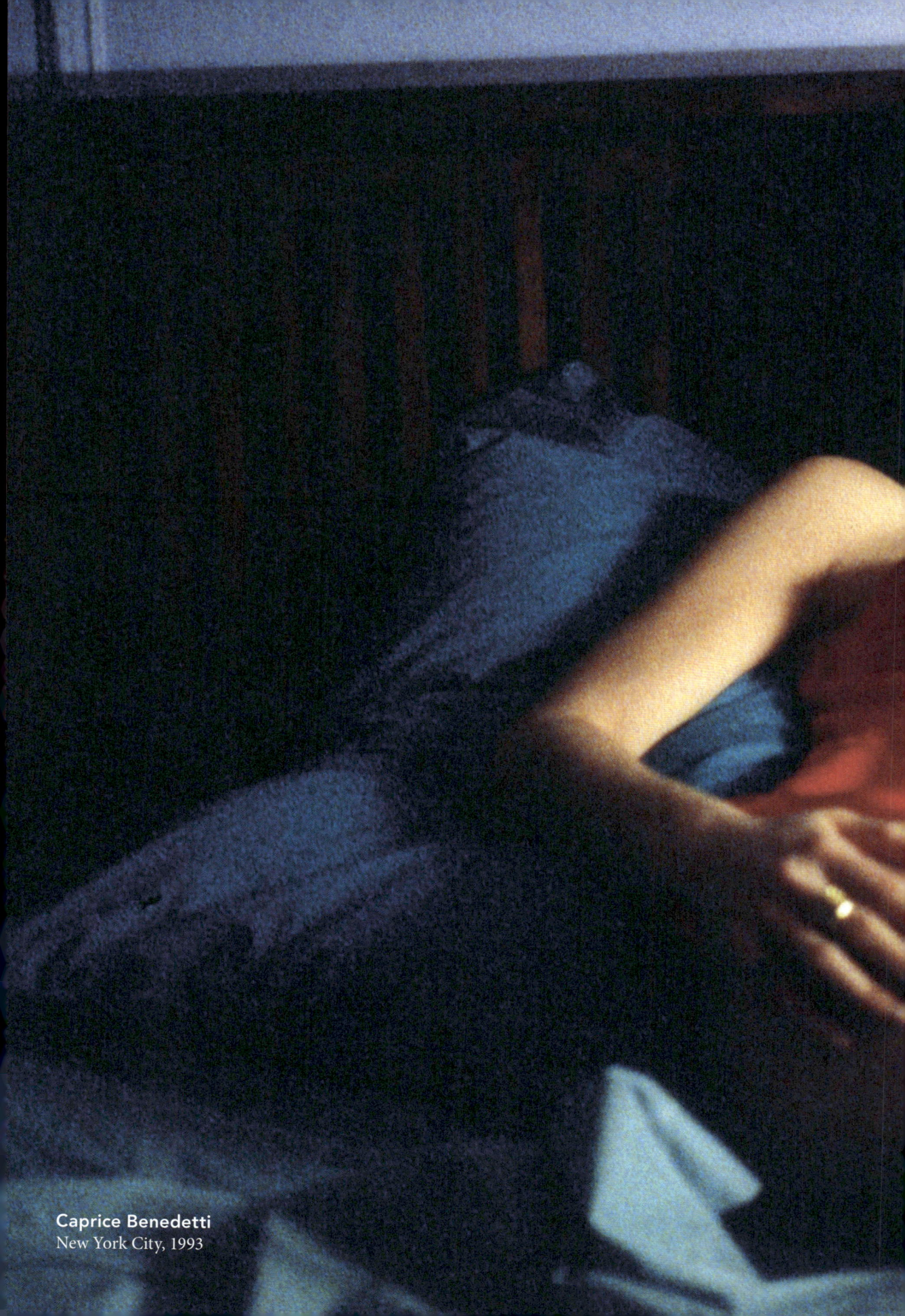

Caprice Benedetti
New York City, 1993

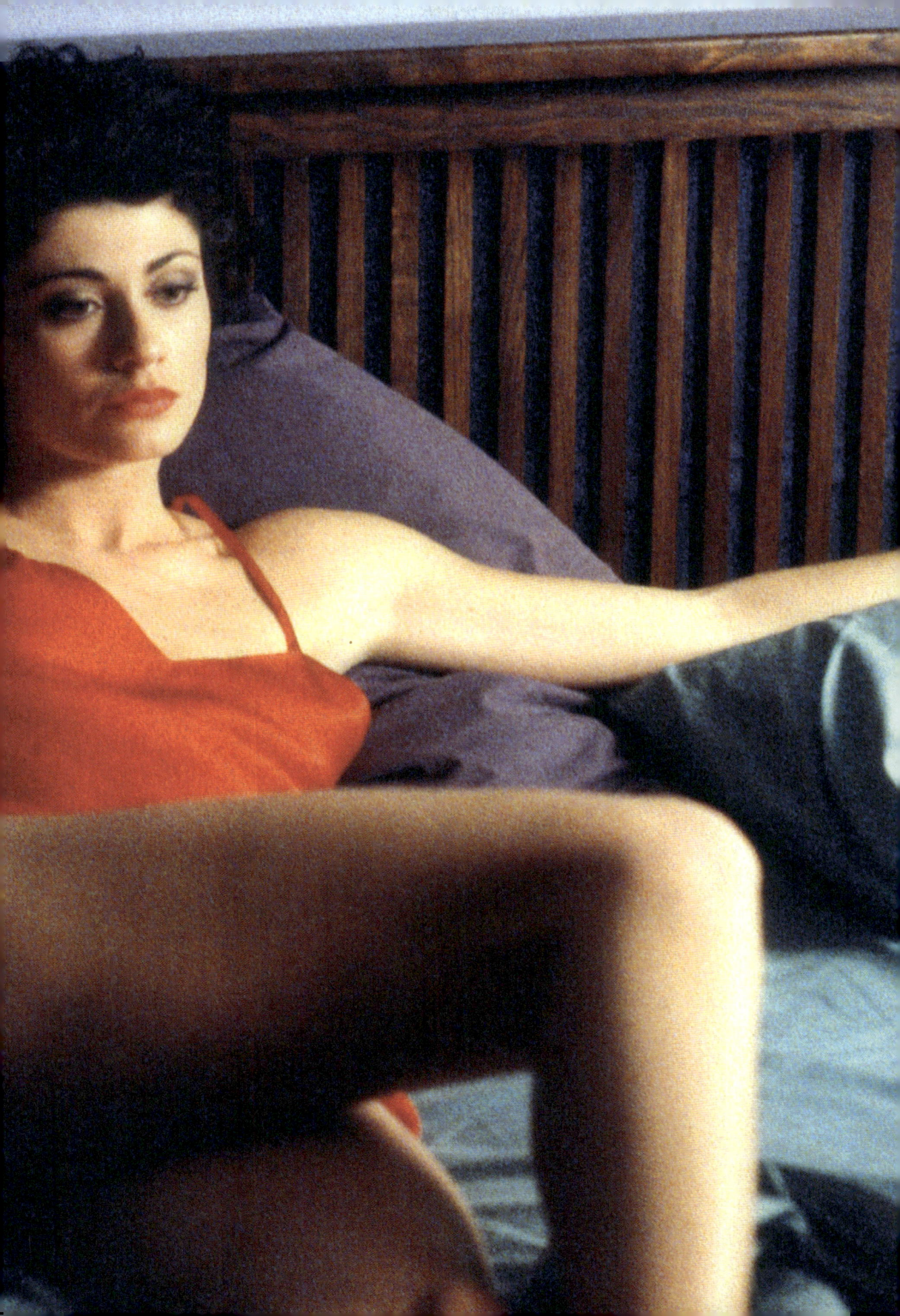

Esther Rolle
New York City, ca. 1980

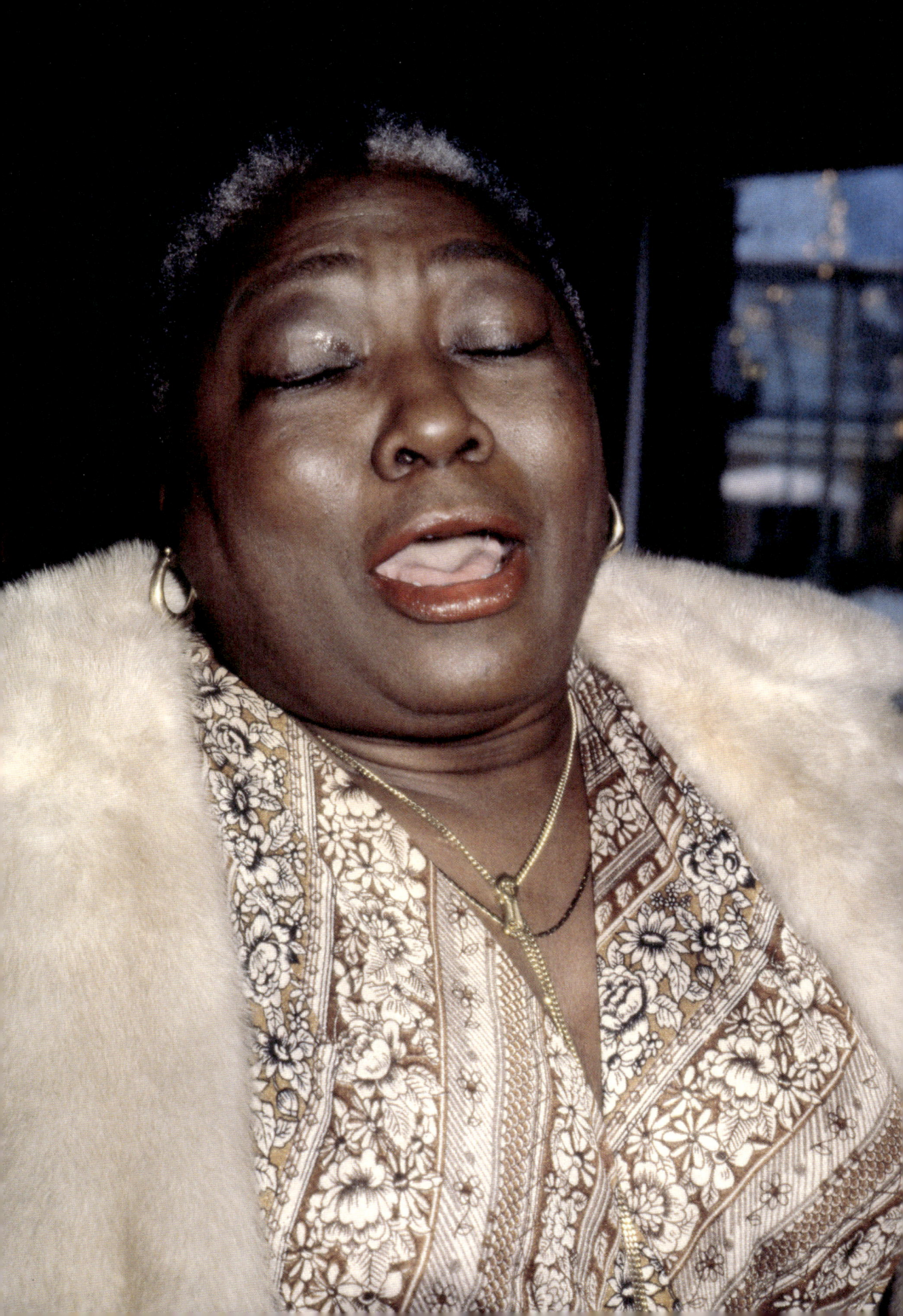

Ginger Rogers
New York City, 1970

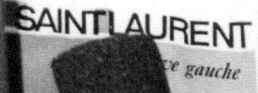

A master of poise.

To the world, she was elegance incarnate: the First Lady of style, grace, and mystery. But to photographers like Oscar, she was a moving target — not just elusive, but wary. She knew the cost of being watched all too well.

Their relationship was… complicated. She knew his camera, and didn't always welcome it. And Oscar? He respected her presence, even when she turned away. He knew some portraits are made not in closeness, but in distance — when the subject refuses to perform, and insists on her own terms.

Jackie didn't need the spotlight. She had already shaped history — and didn't owe it another pose.

Jackie Kennedy Onassis
New York City, 1975

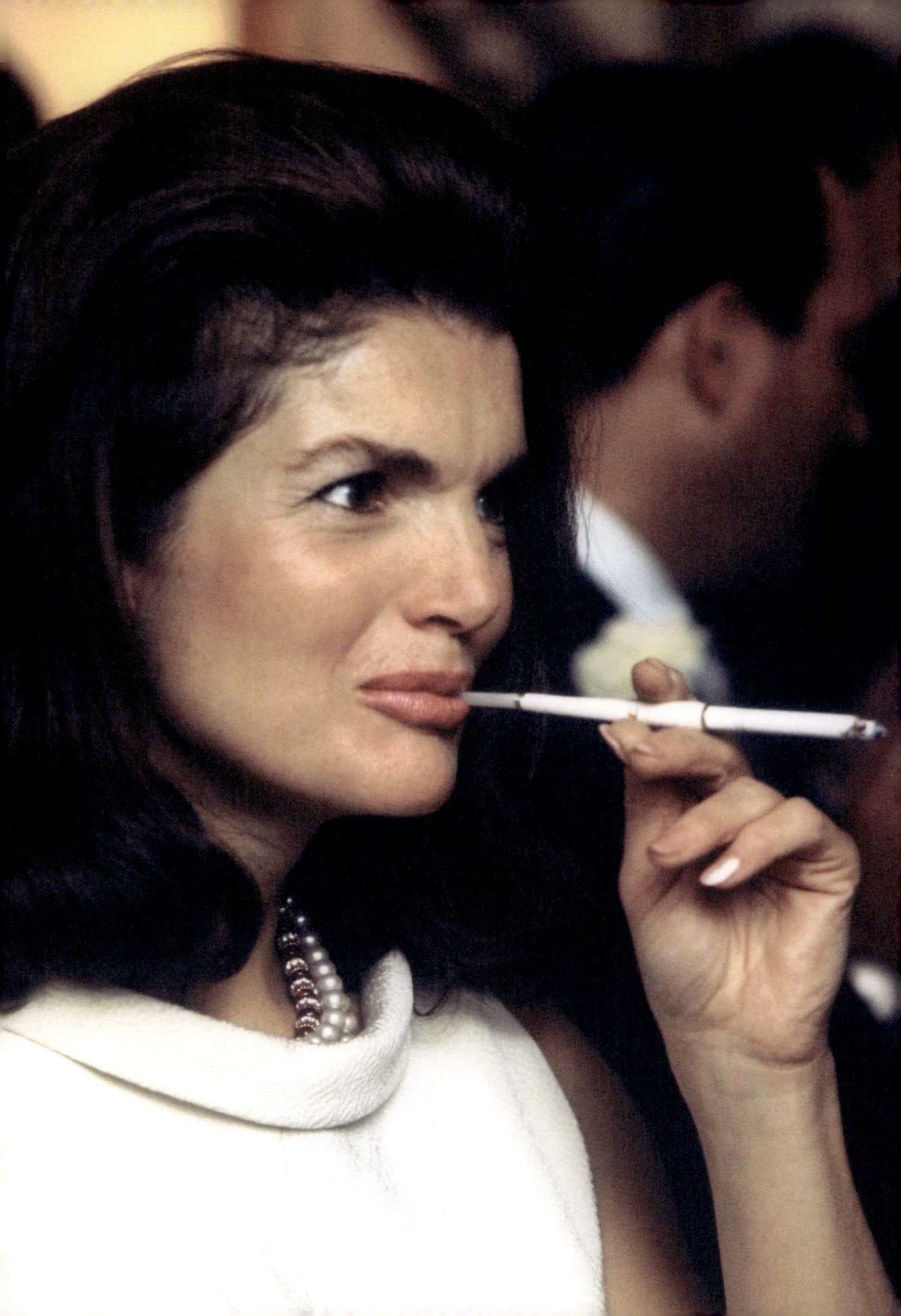

Helen Hayes
New York City, ca. 1975

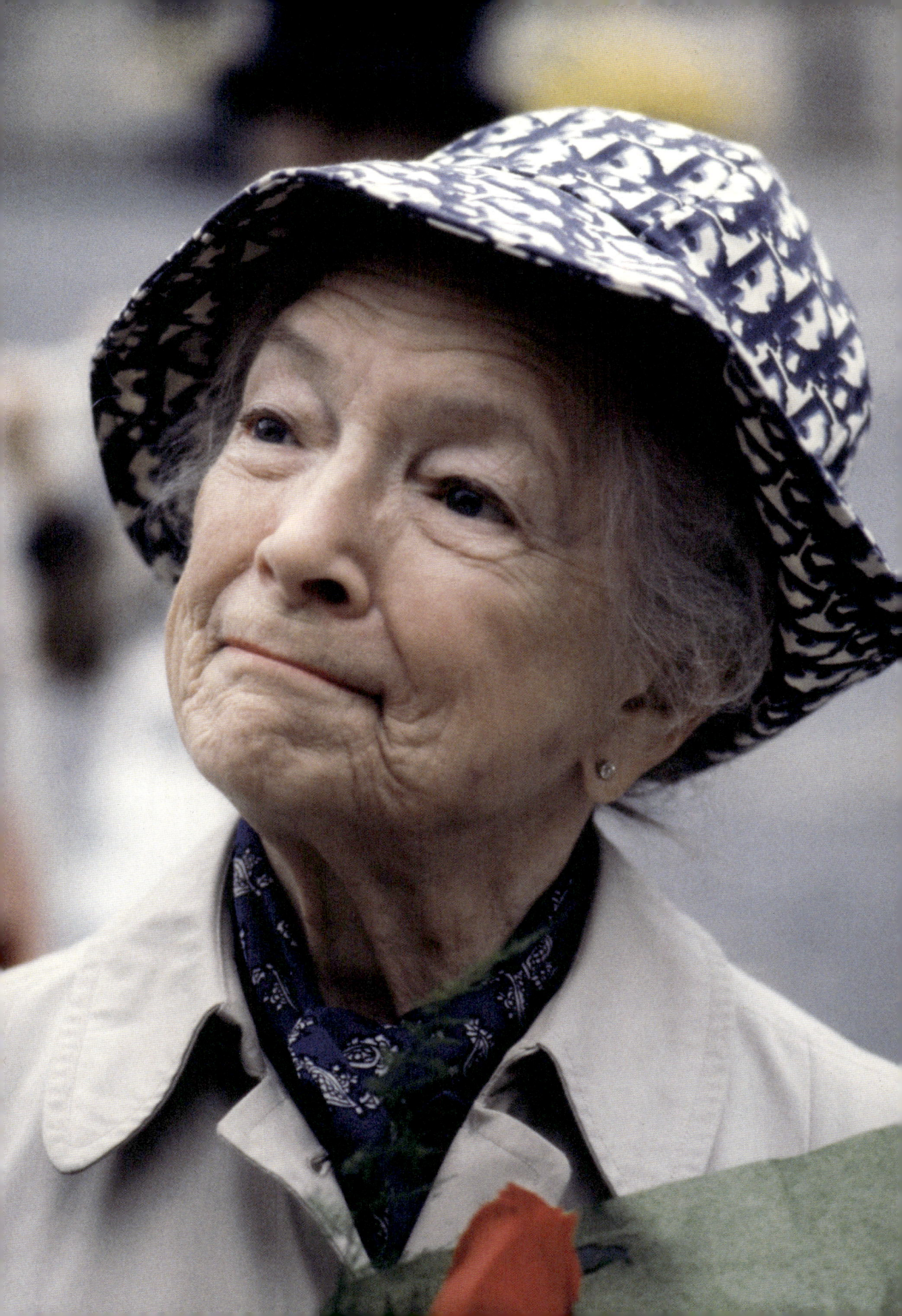

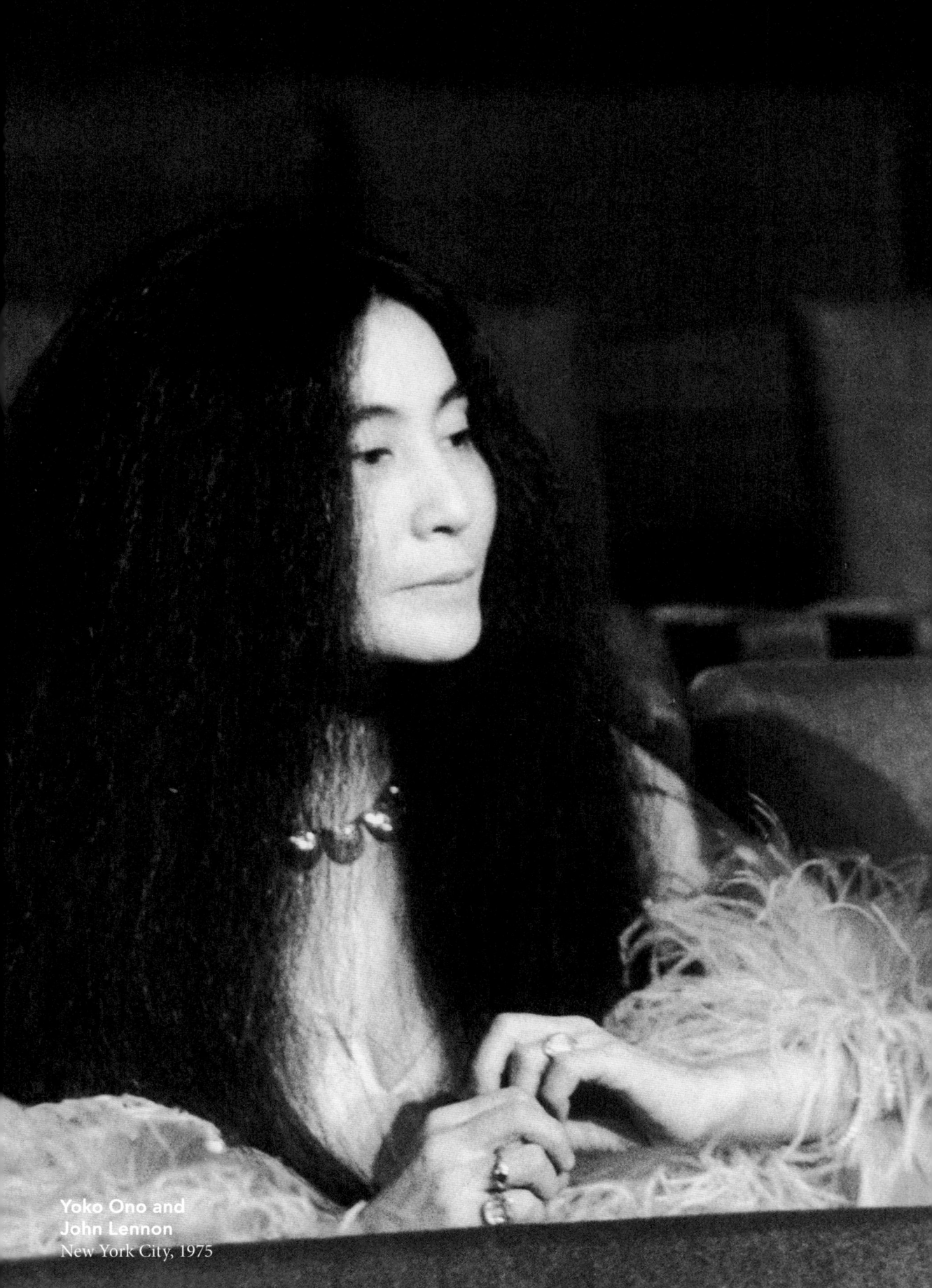

Yoko Ono and
John Lennon
New York City, 1975

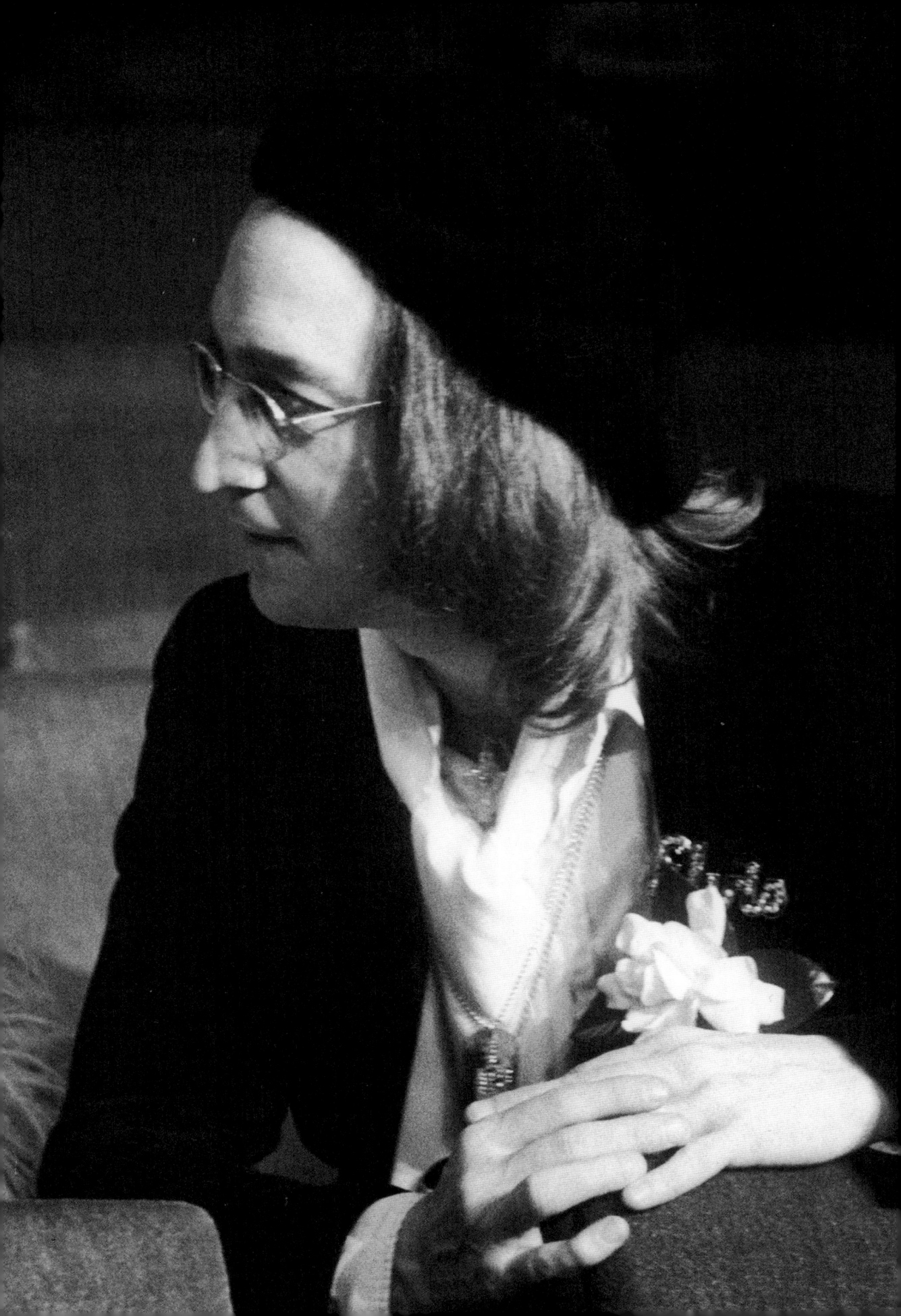

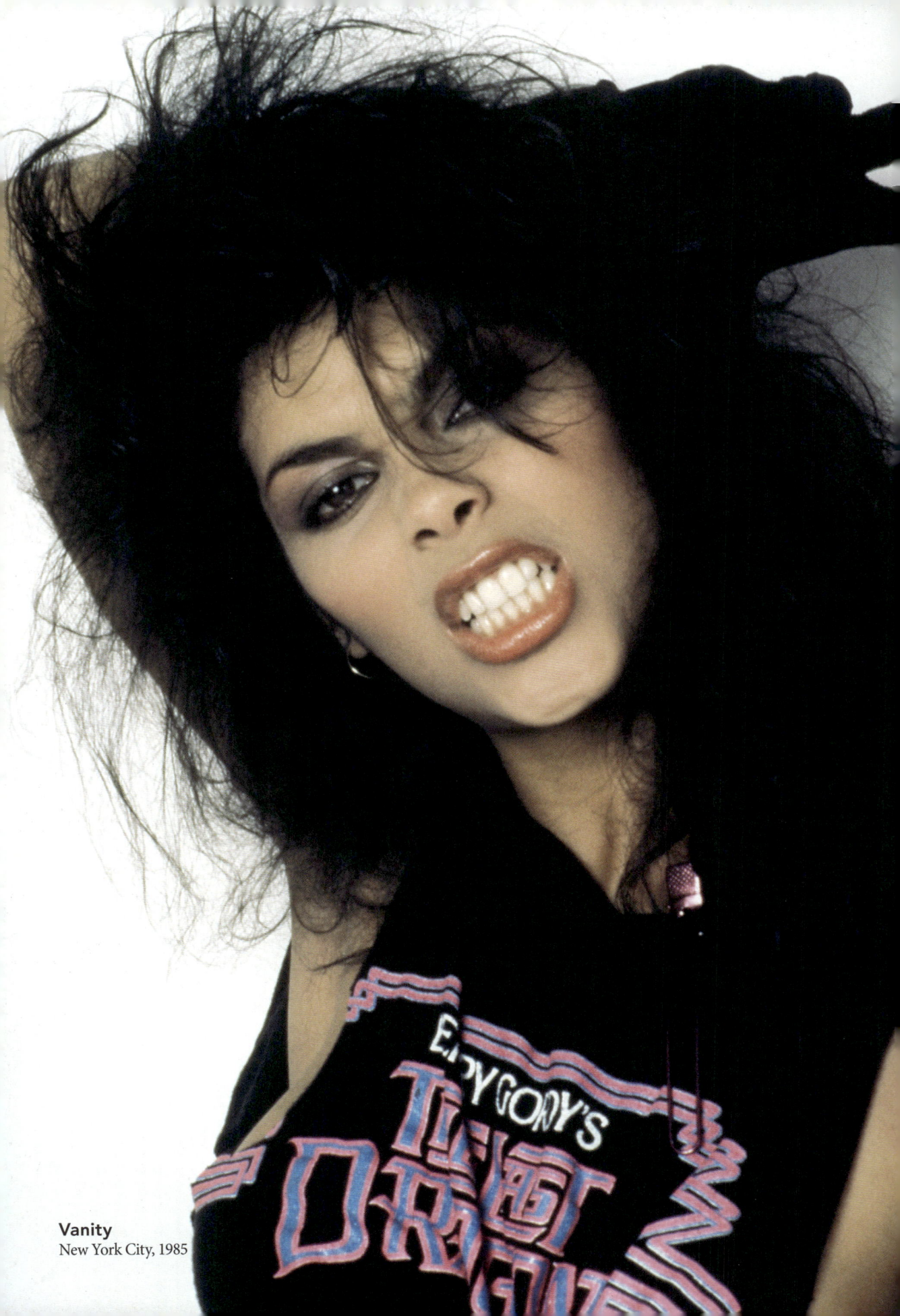

Vanity
New York City, 1985

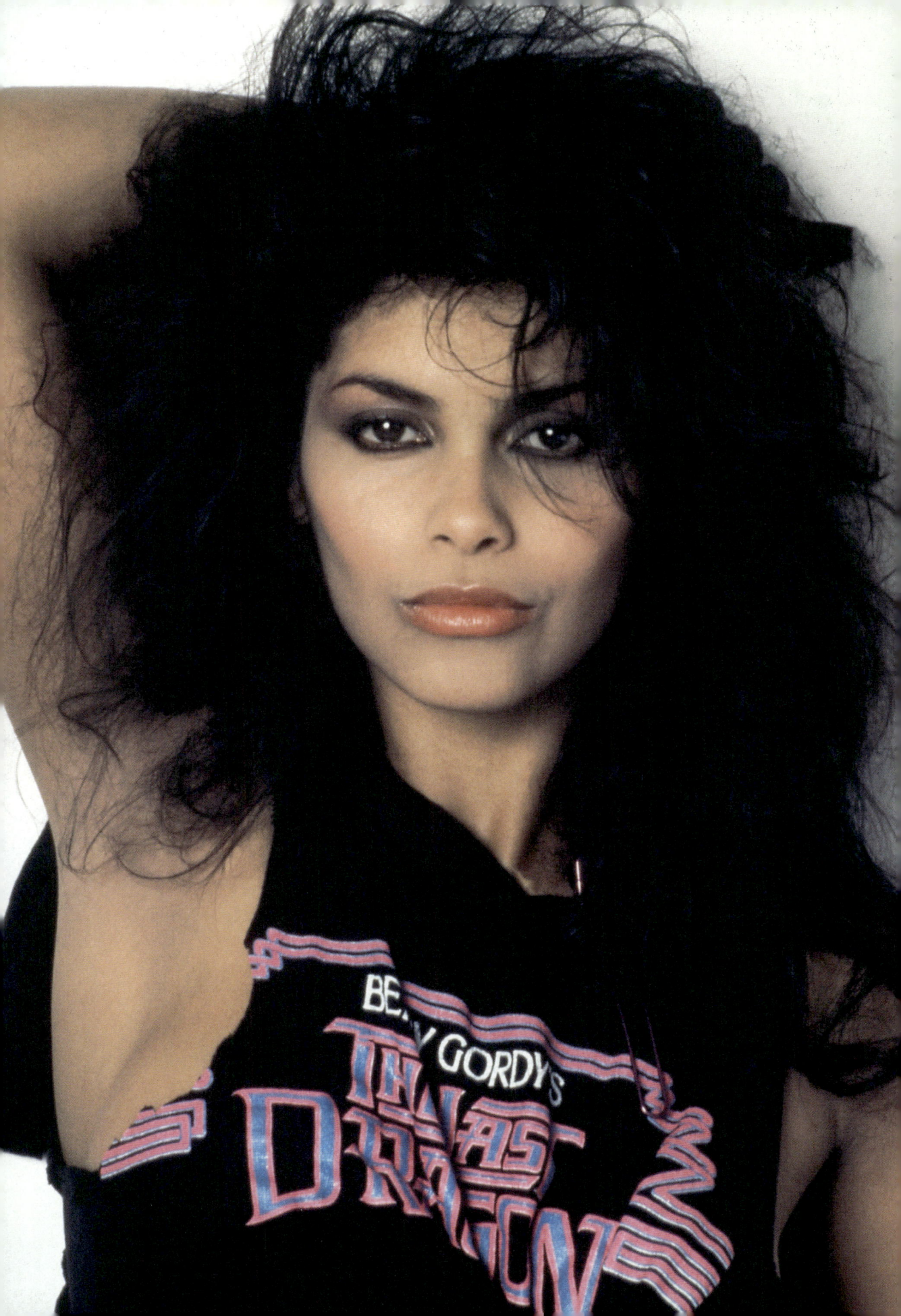

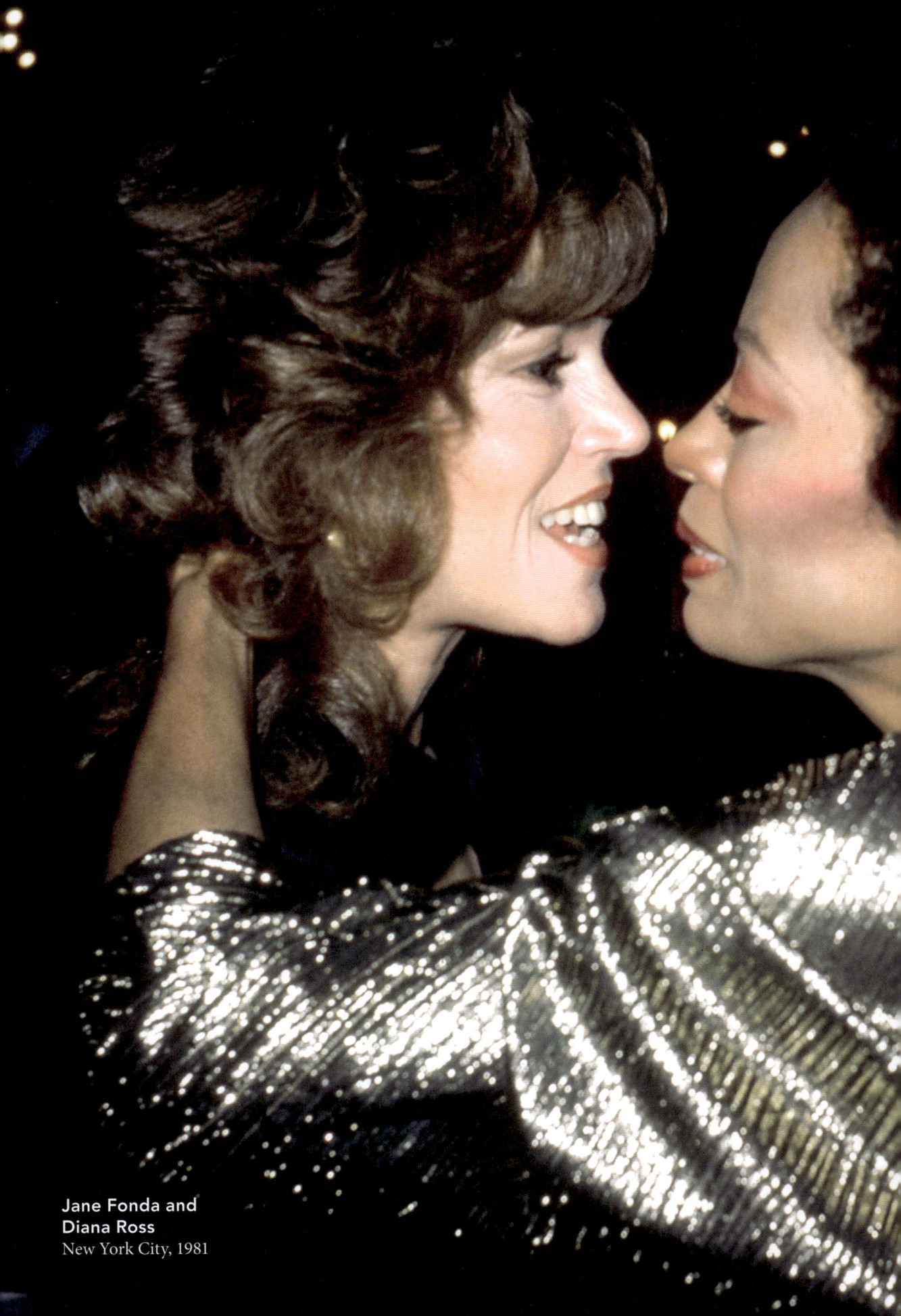

**Jane Fonda and
Diana Ross**
New York City, 1981

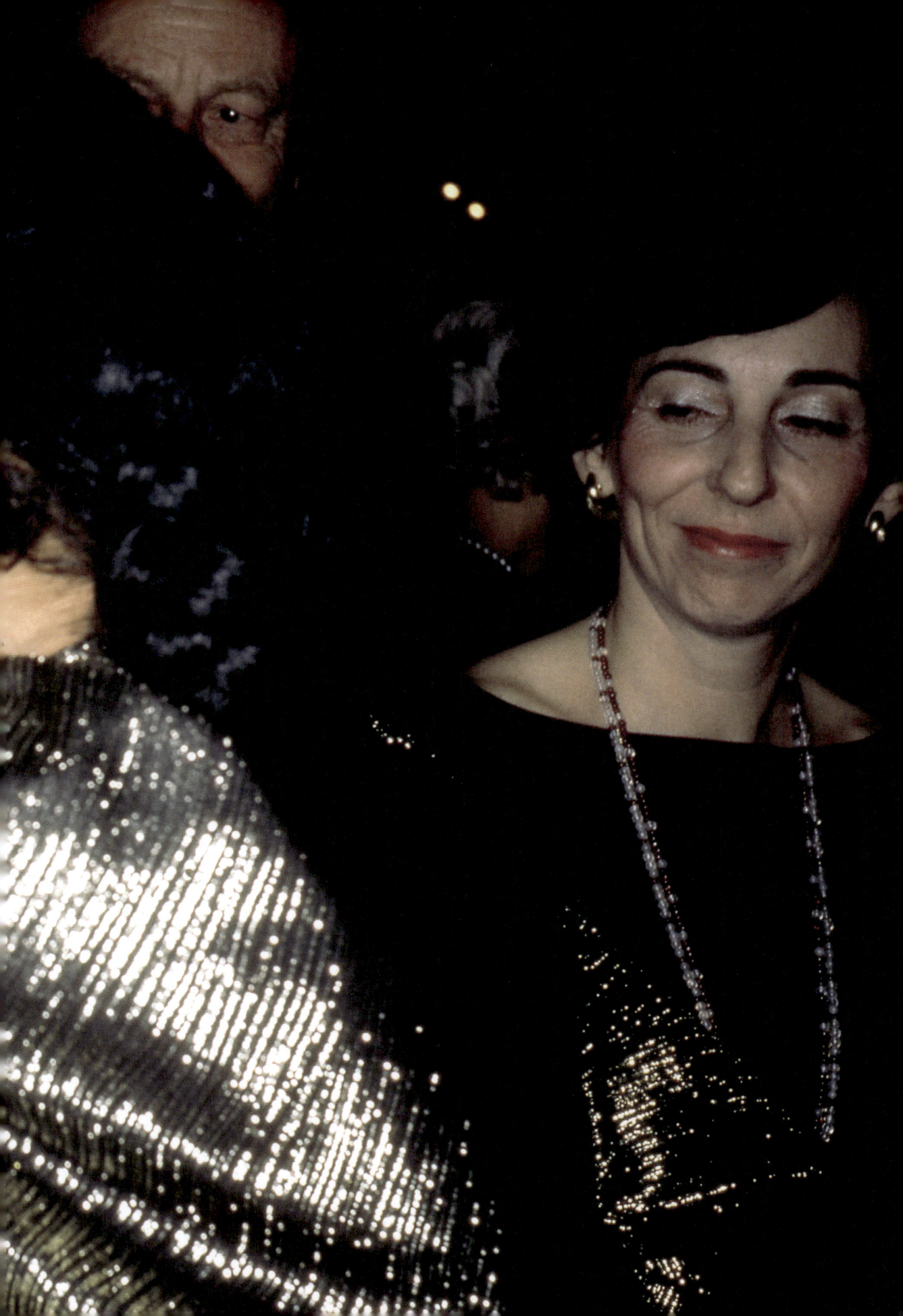

Janis Joplin
New York City, 1969

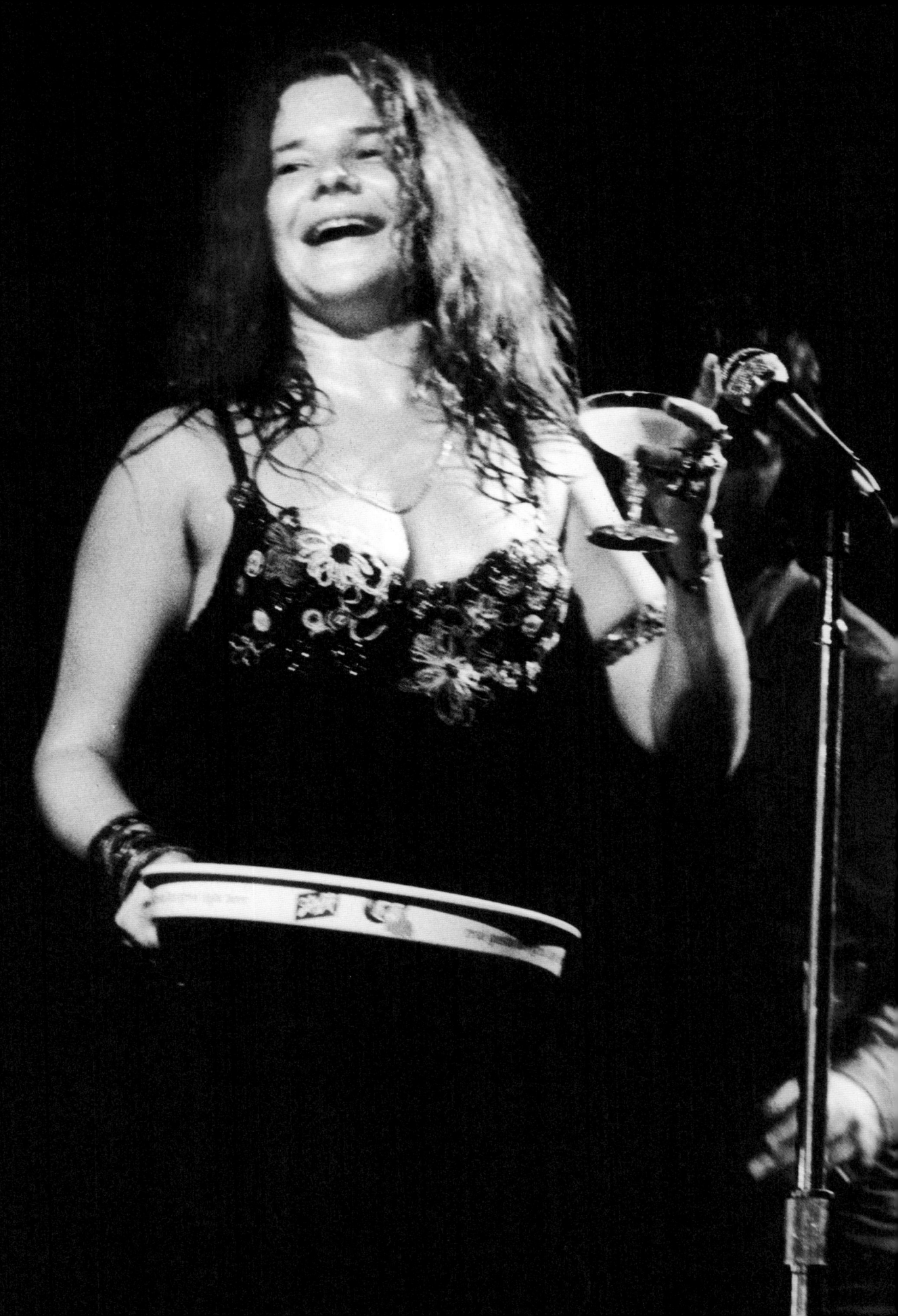

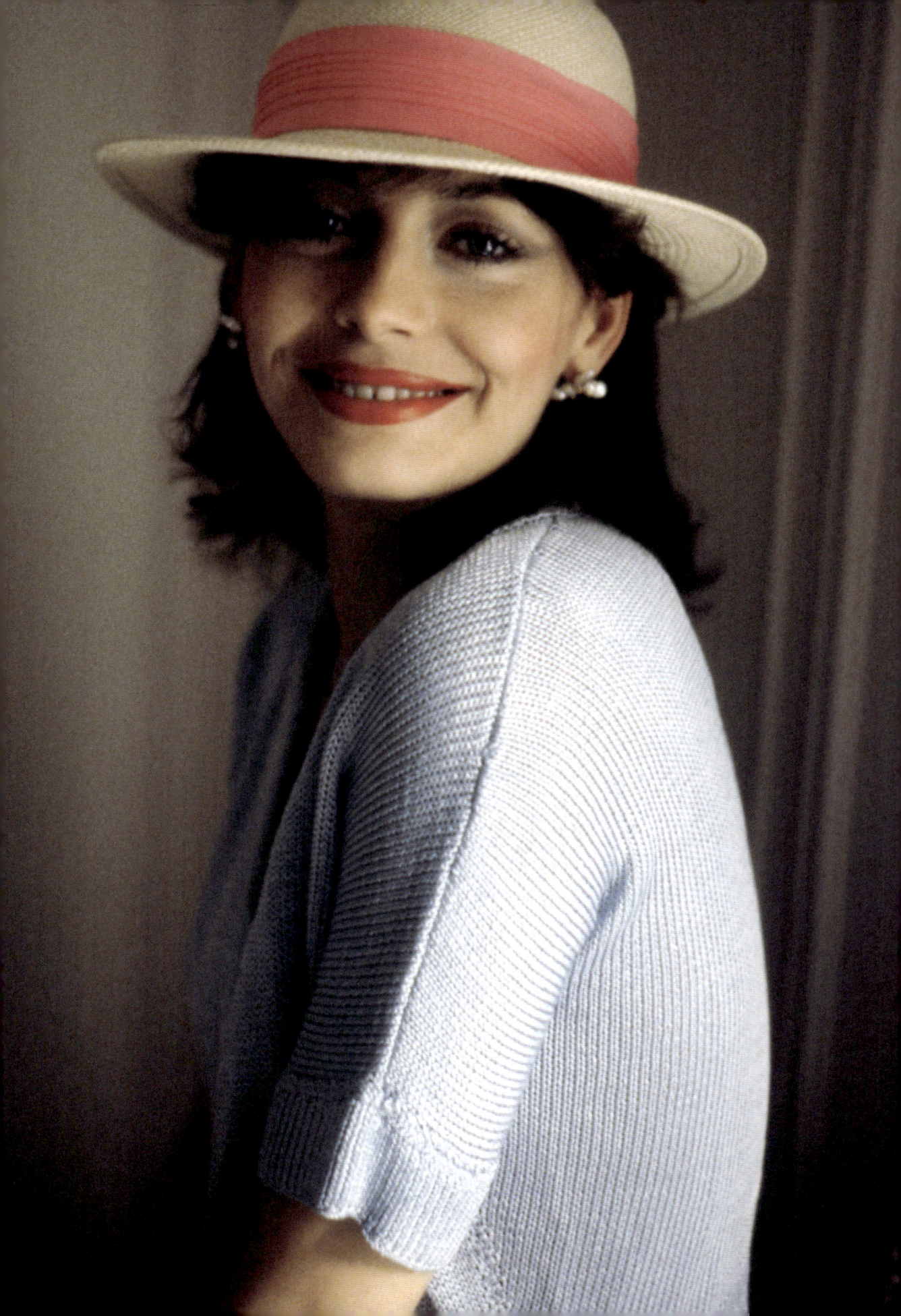

Lesley-Anne Down
New York City, 1979

"The secret of staying young is to live honestly, eat slowly, and lie about your age."

Lucille Ball
New York City, 1974

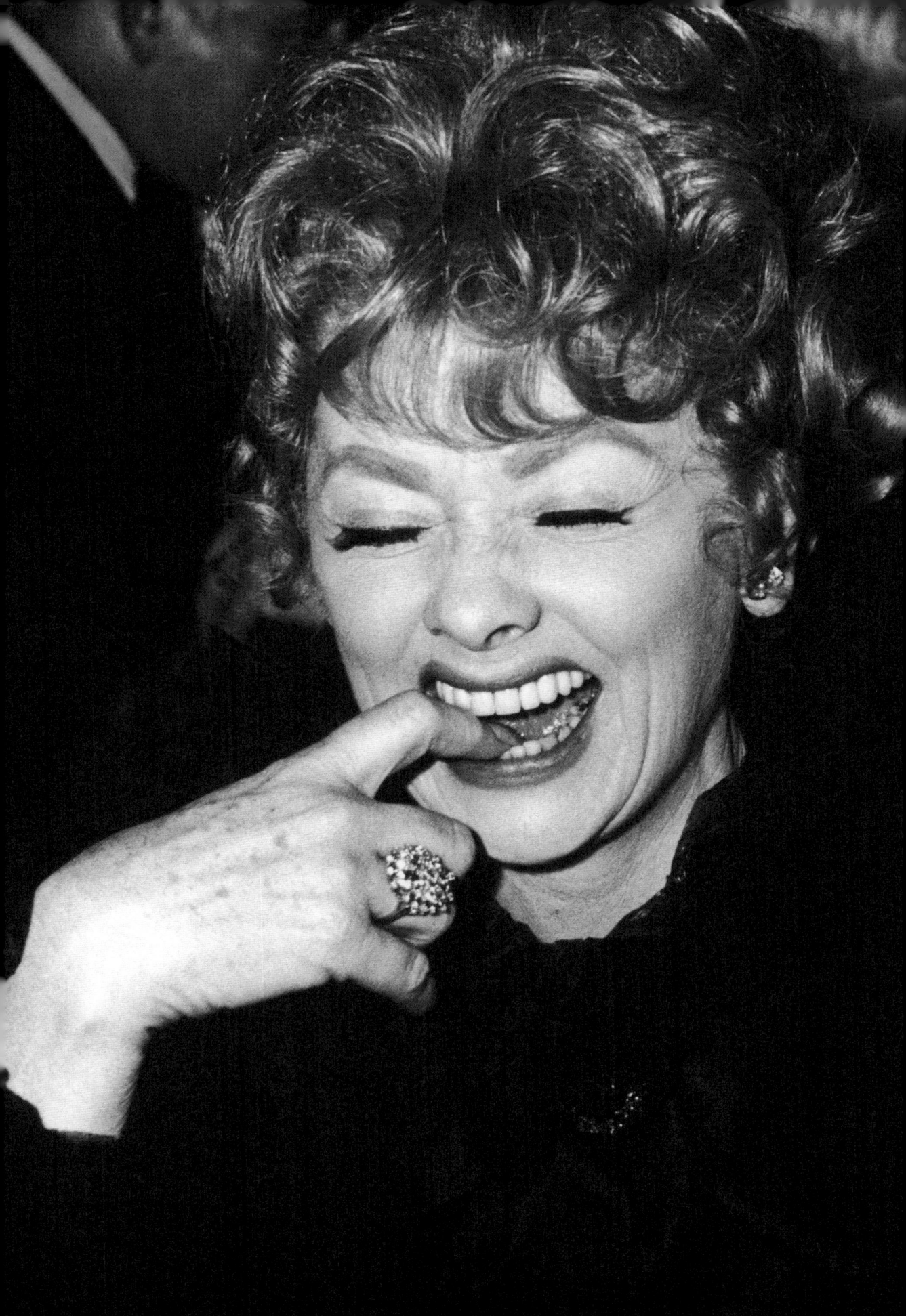

Bianca Jagger
New York City, 1975

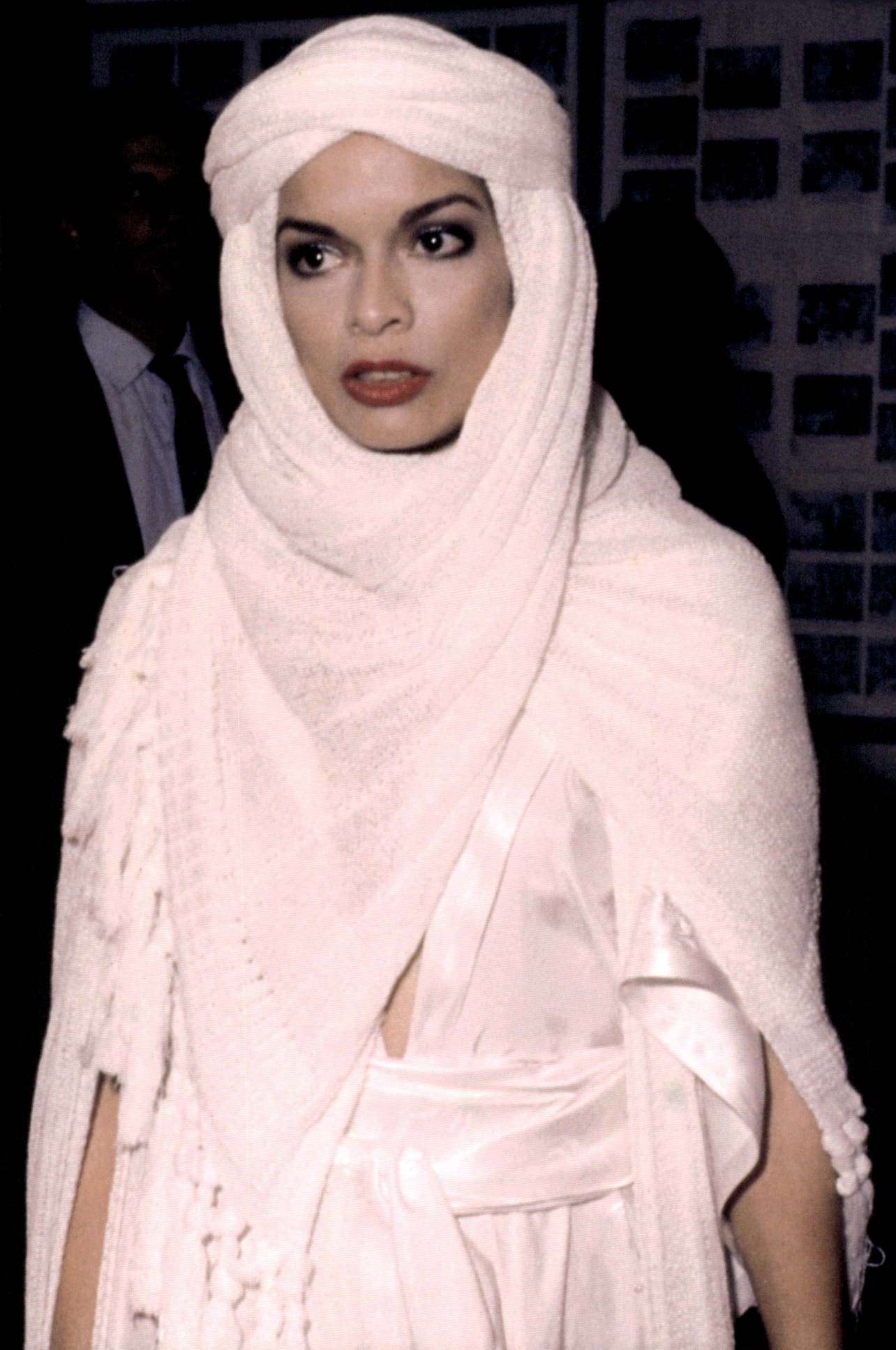

Ann-Margret Olsson
New York City, 1975

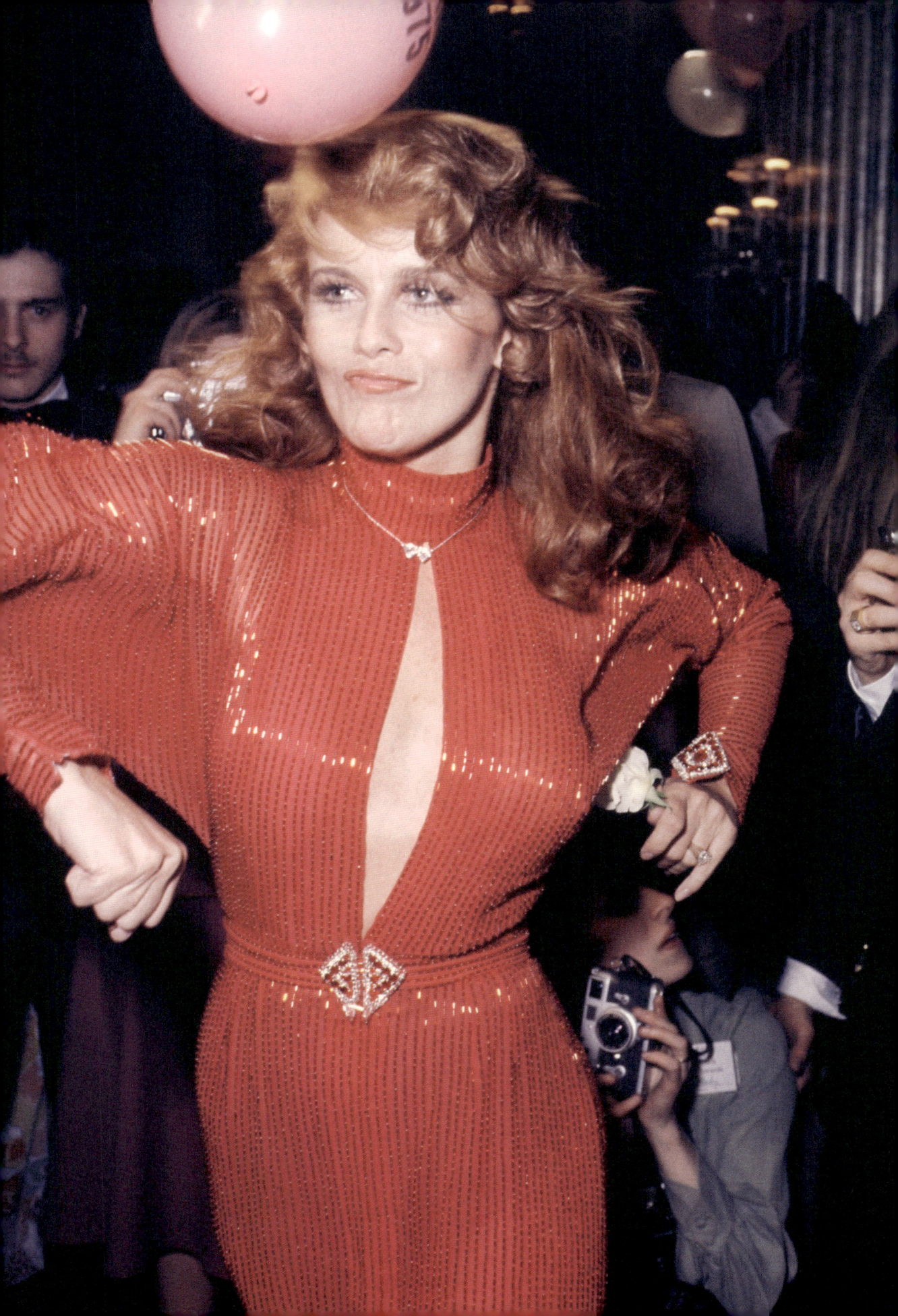

Agnetha Fältskog
New York City, ca. 1977

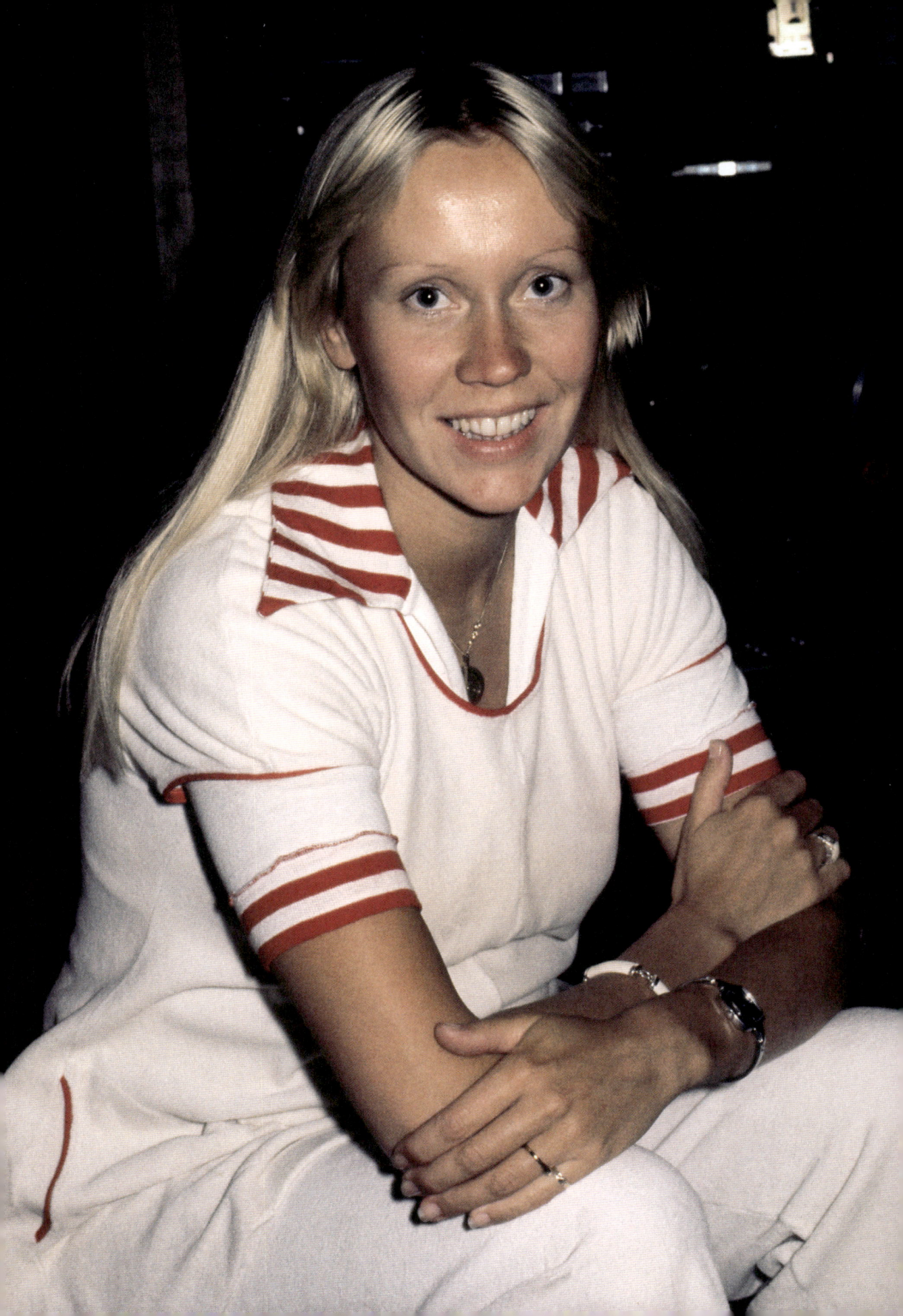

Josephine Baker
New York City, ca. 1970

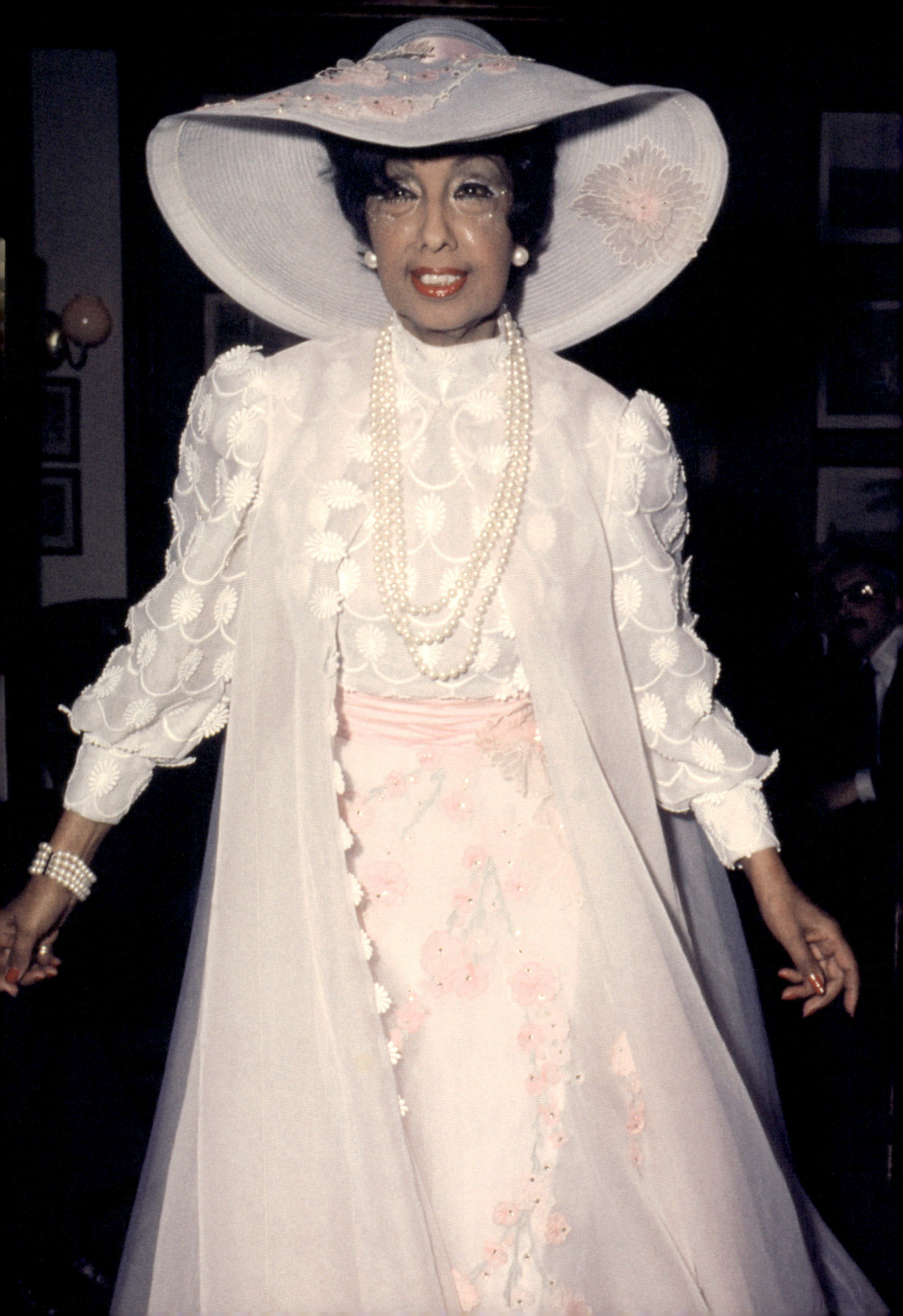

"I have the same goal I've had ever since I was a girl: I want to rule the world."

Madonna
New York City, 1986

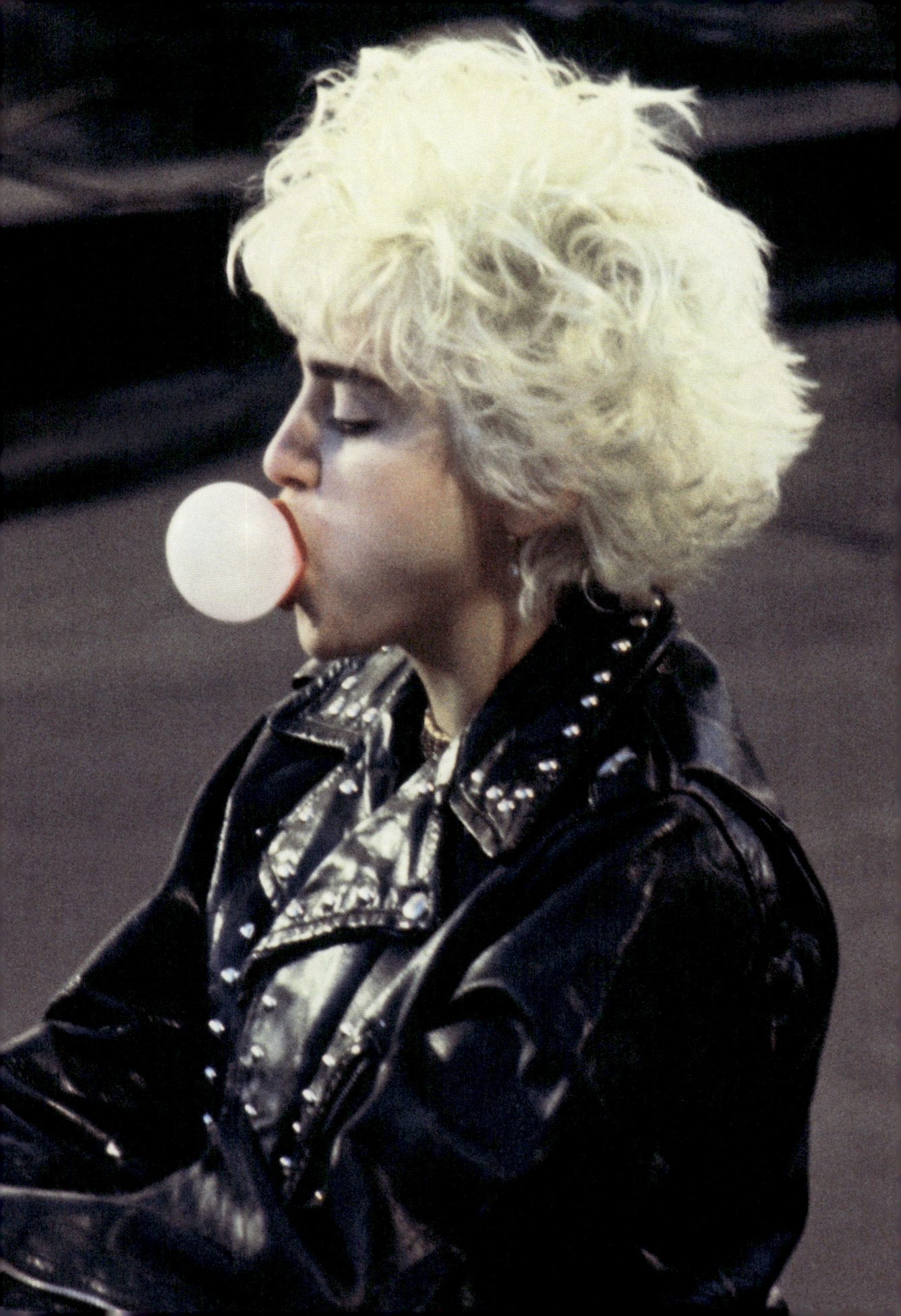

Martina Navratilova
New York City, 1979

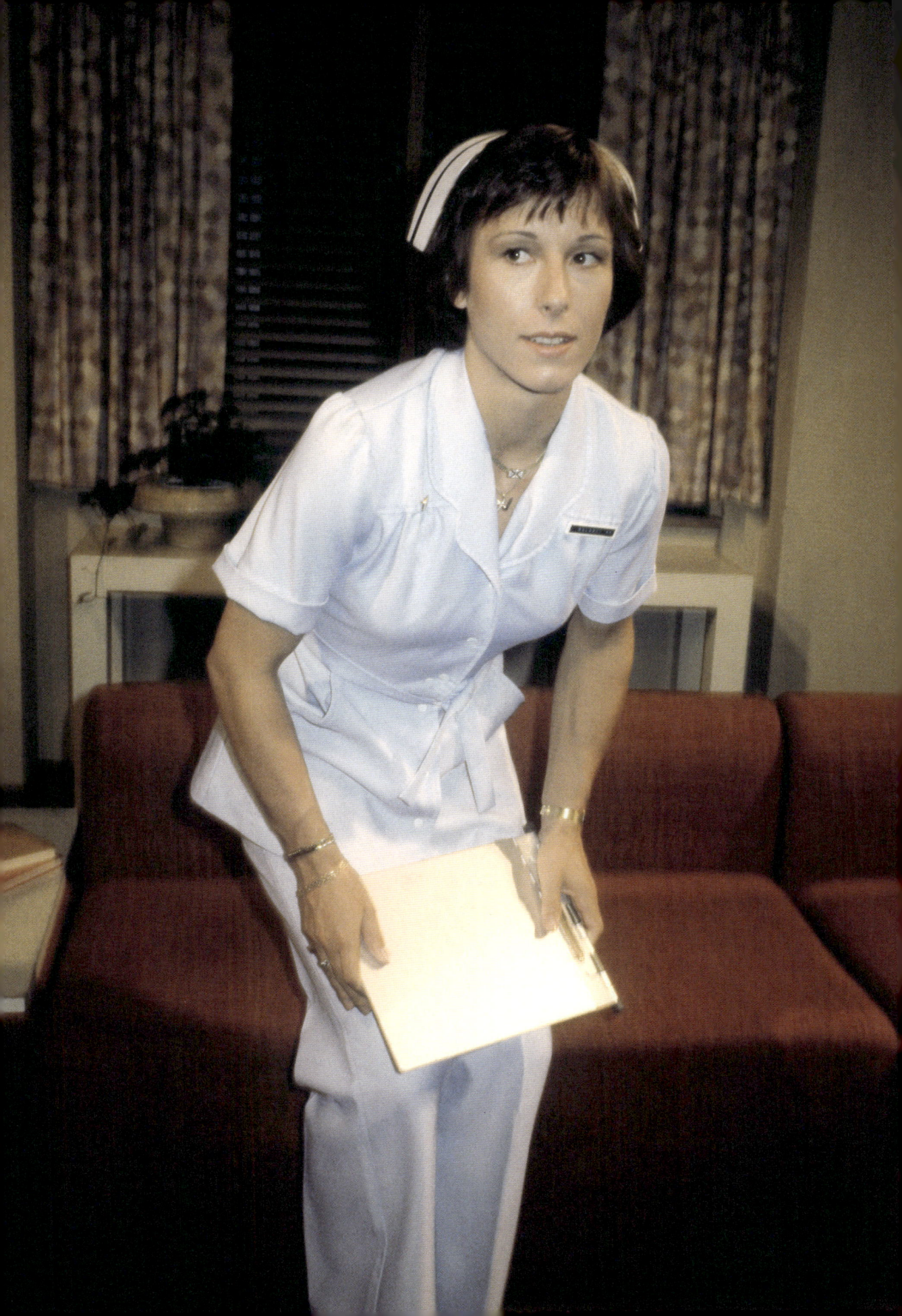

Megan Gallagher
New York City, ca. 1980

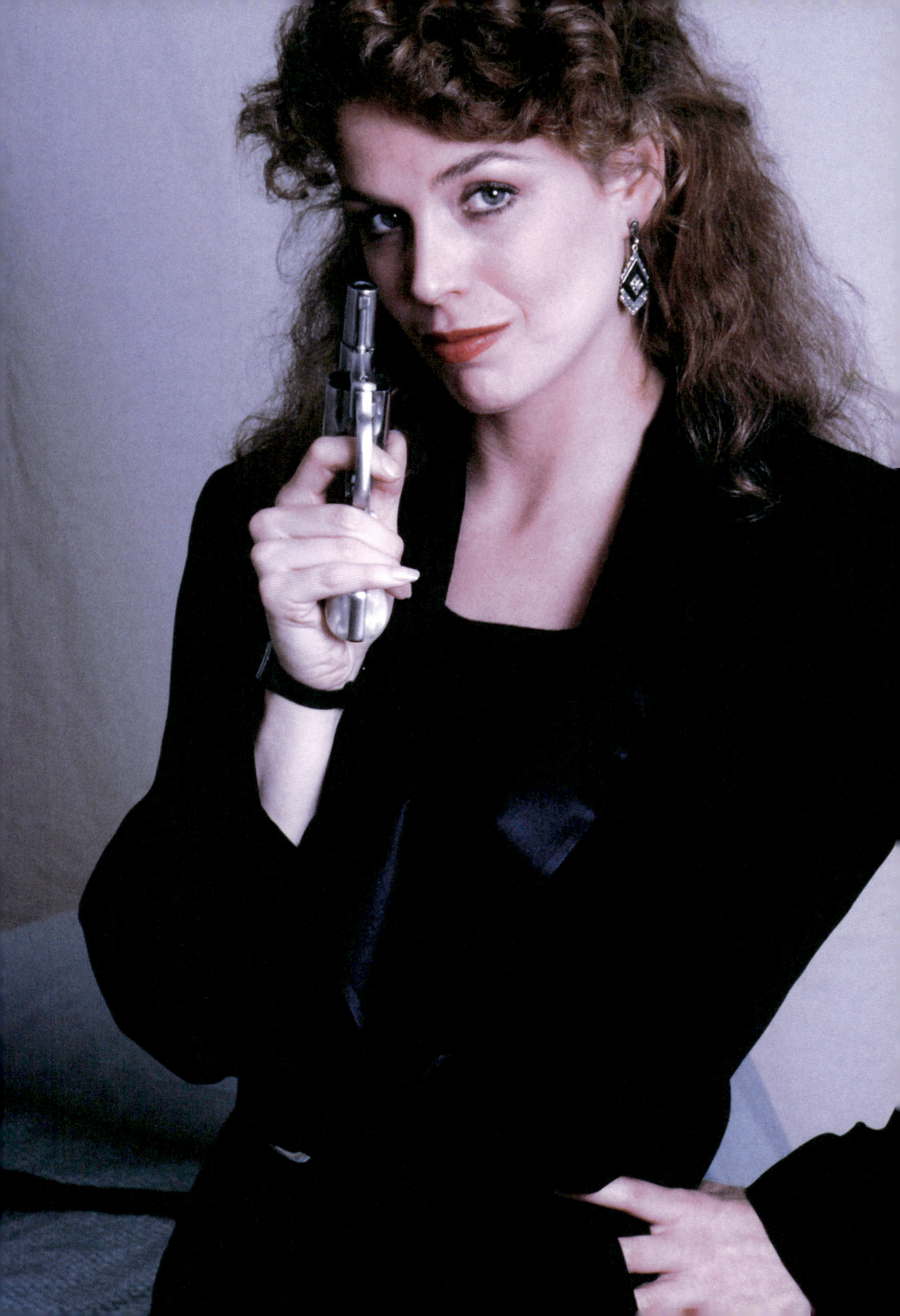

"Normally, I stay away from politics —
unless I'm going to run for president."

Grace Jones
New York City, 1985

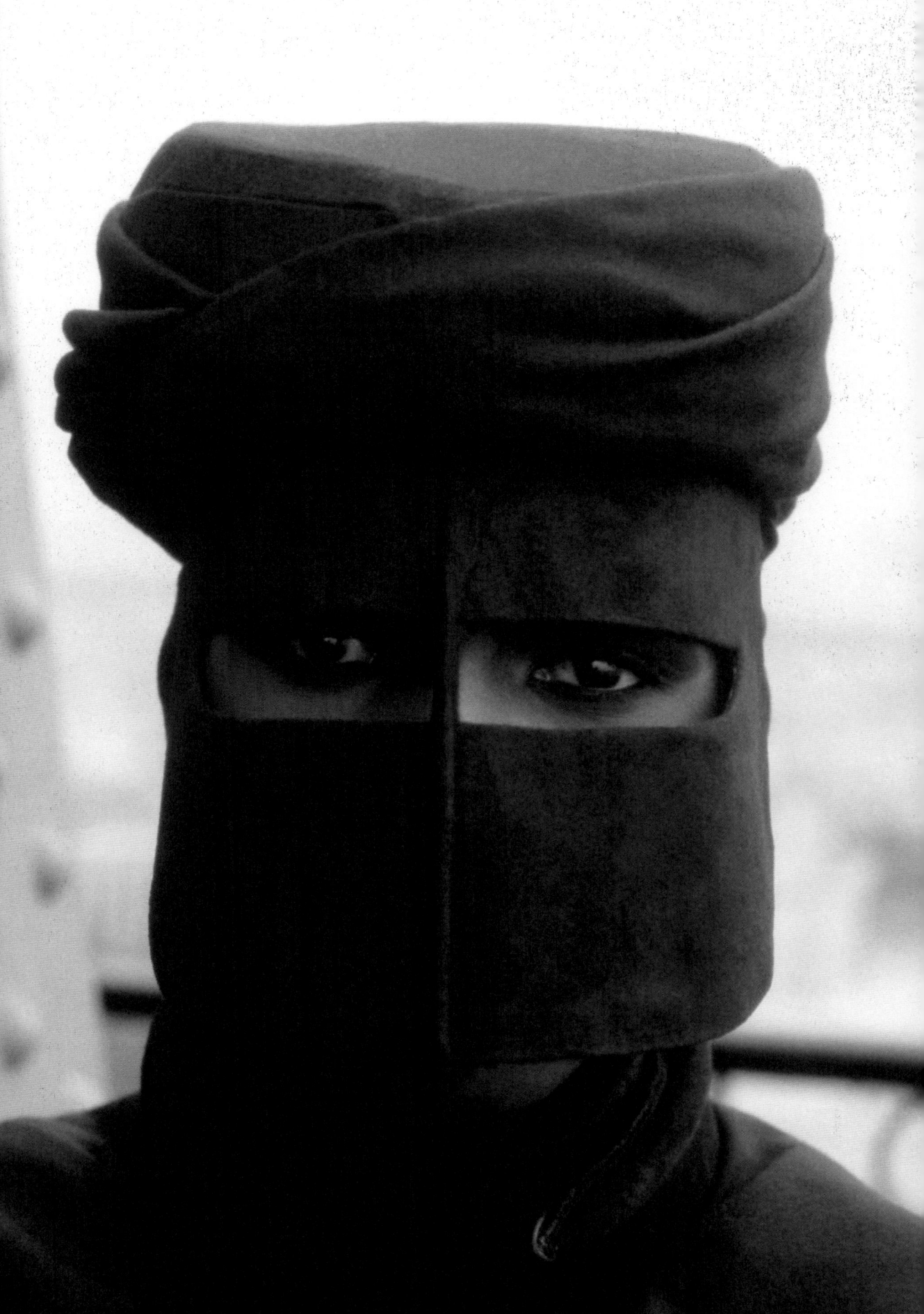

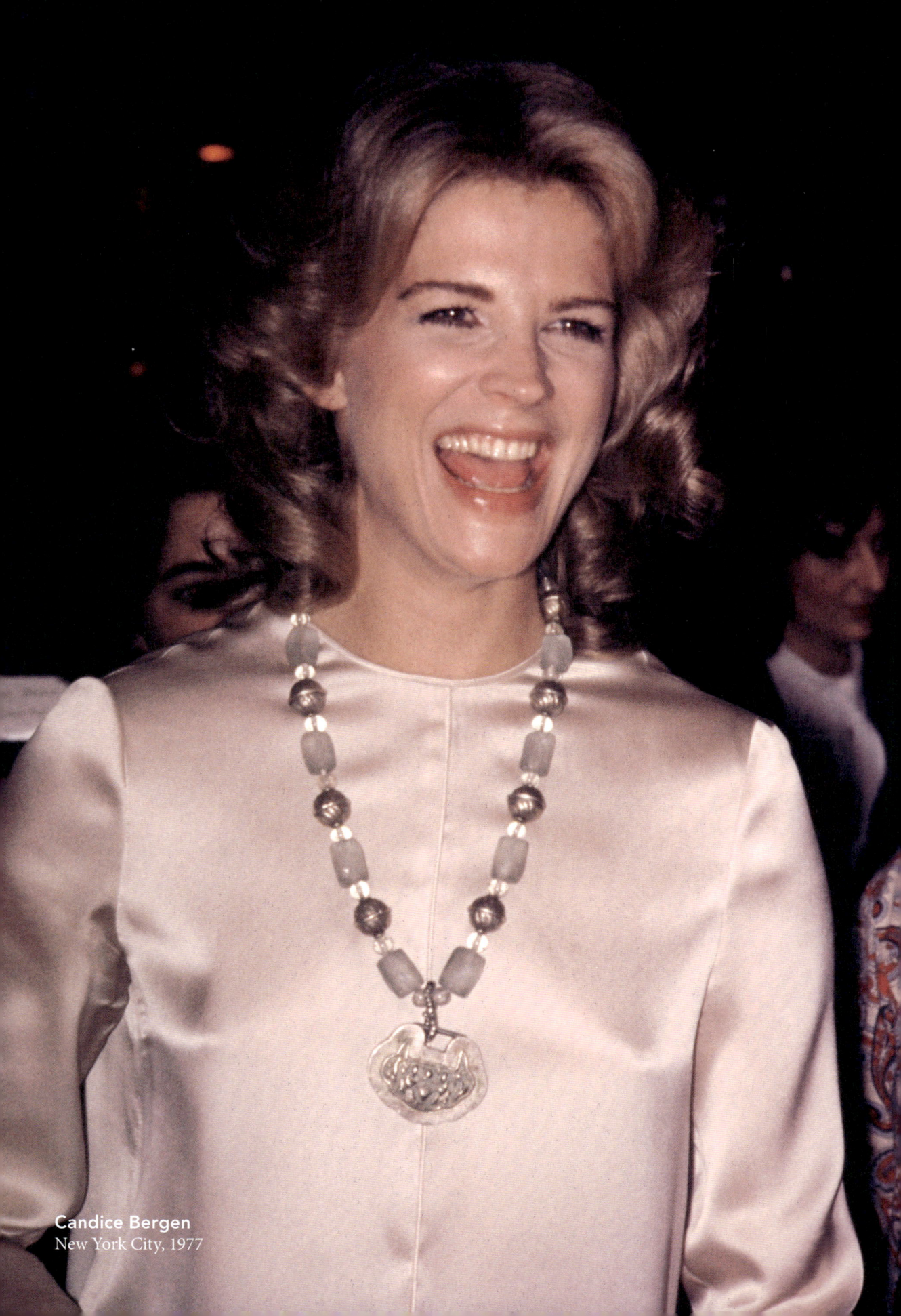

Candice Bergen
New York City, 1977

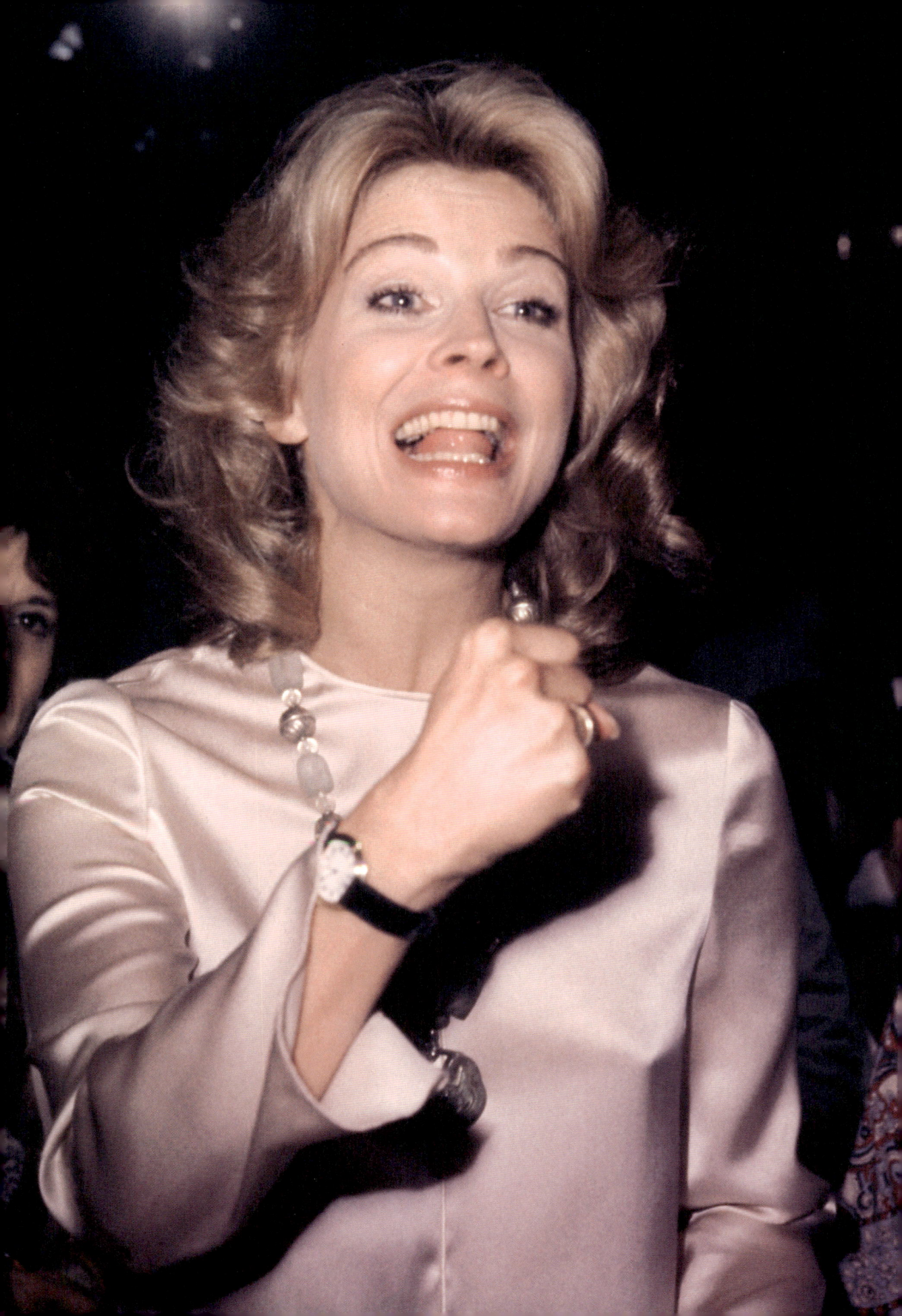

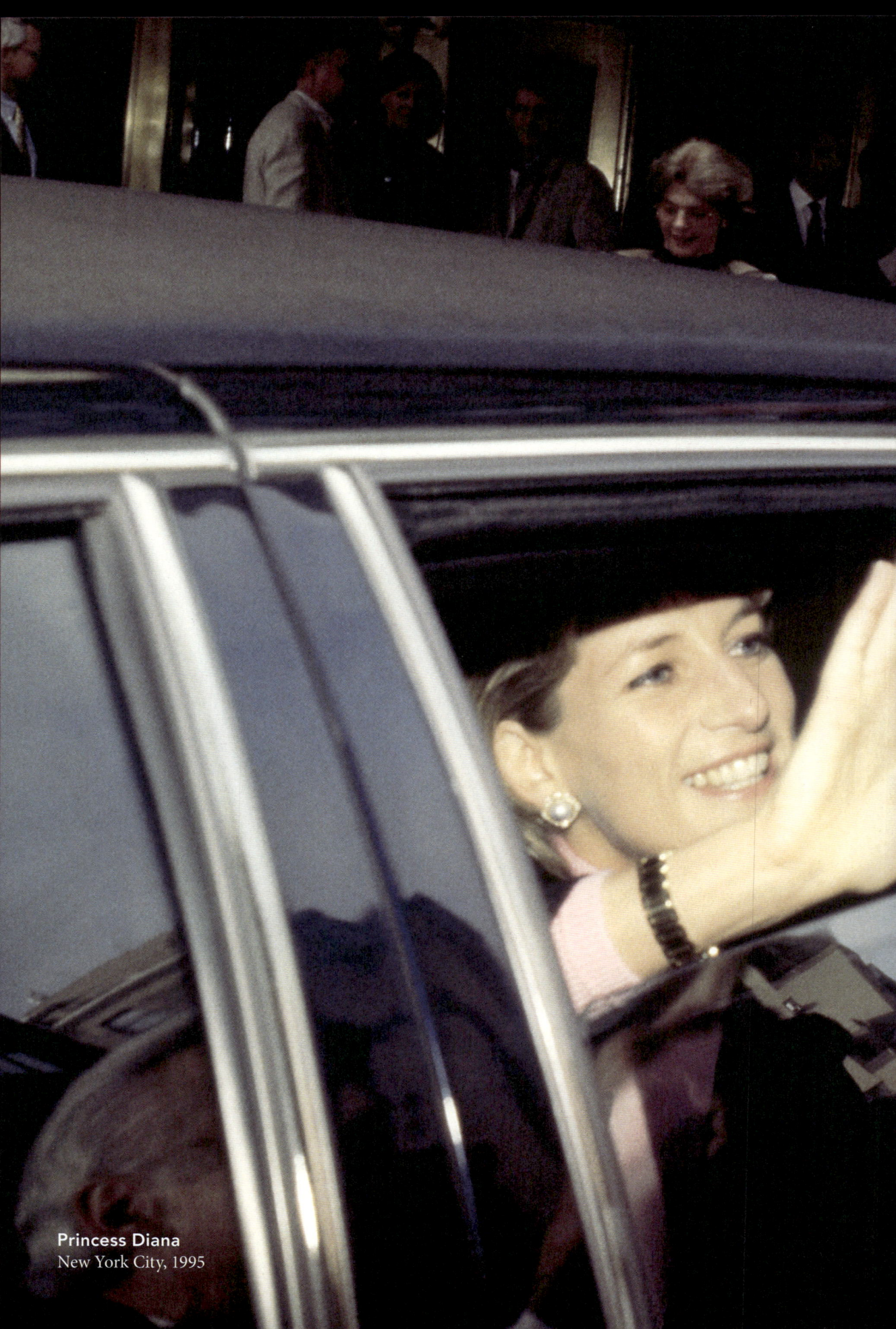

Princess Diana
New York City, 1995

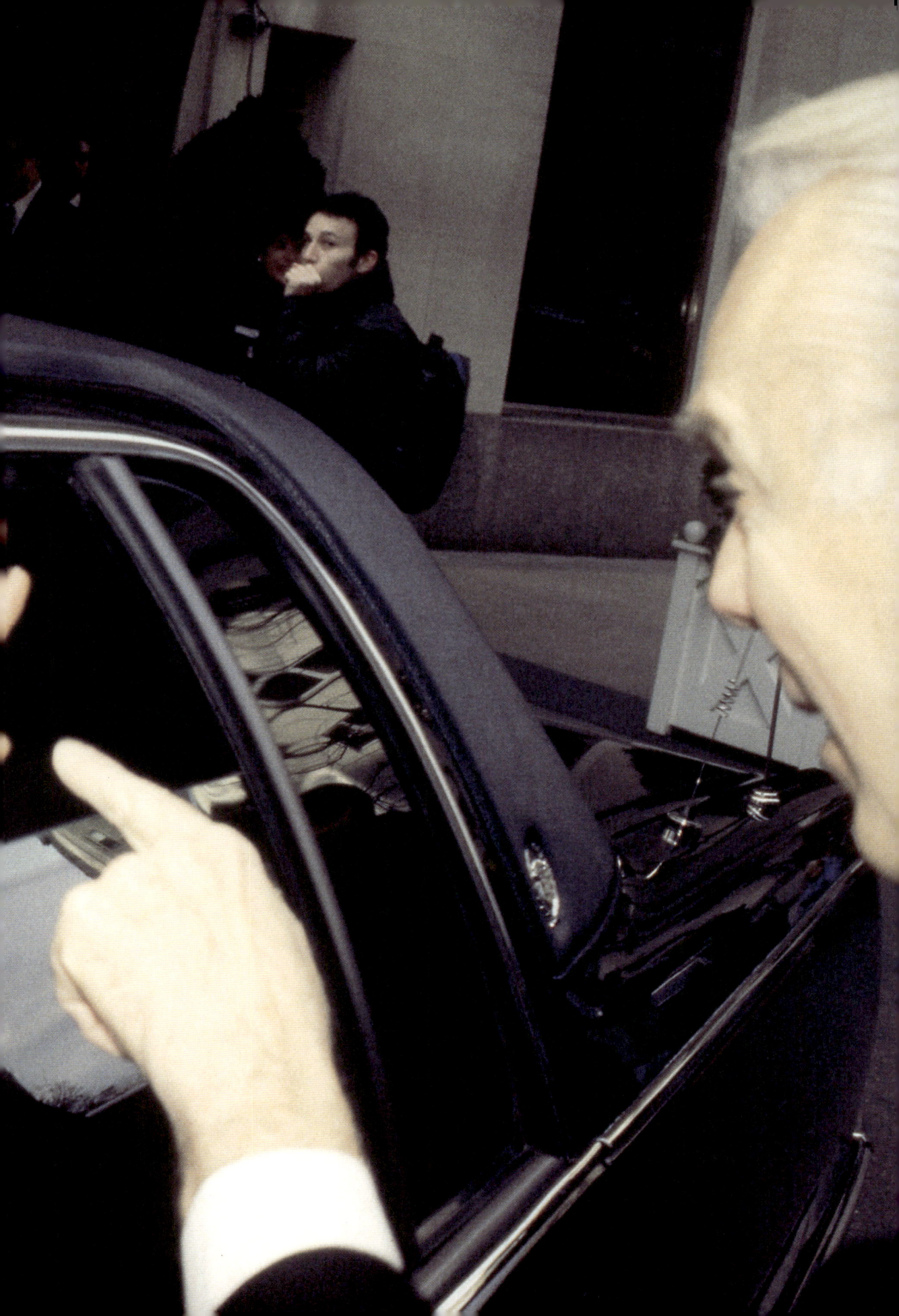

Meryl Streep
Baltimore, 1978

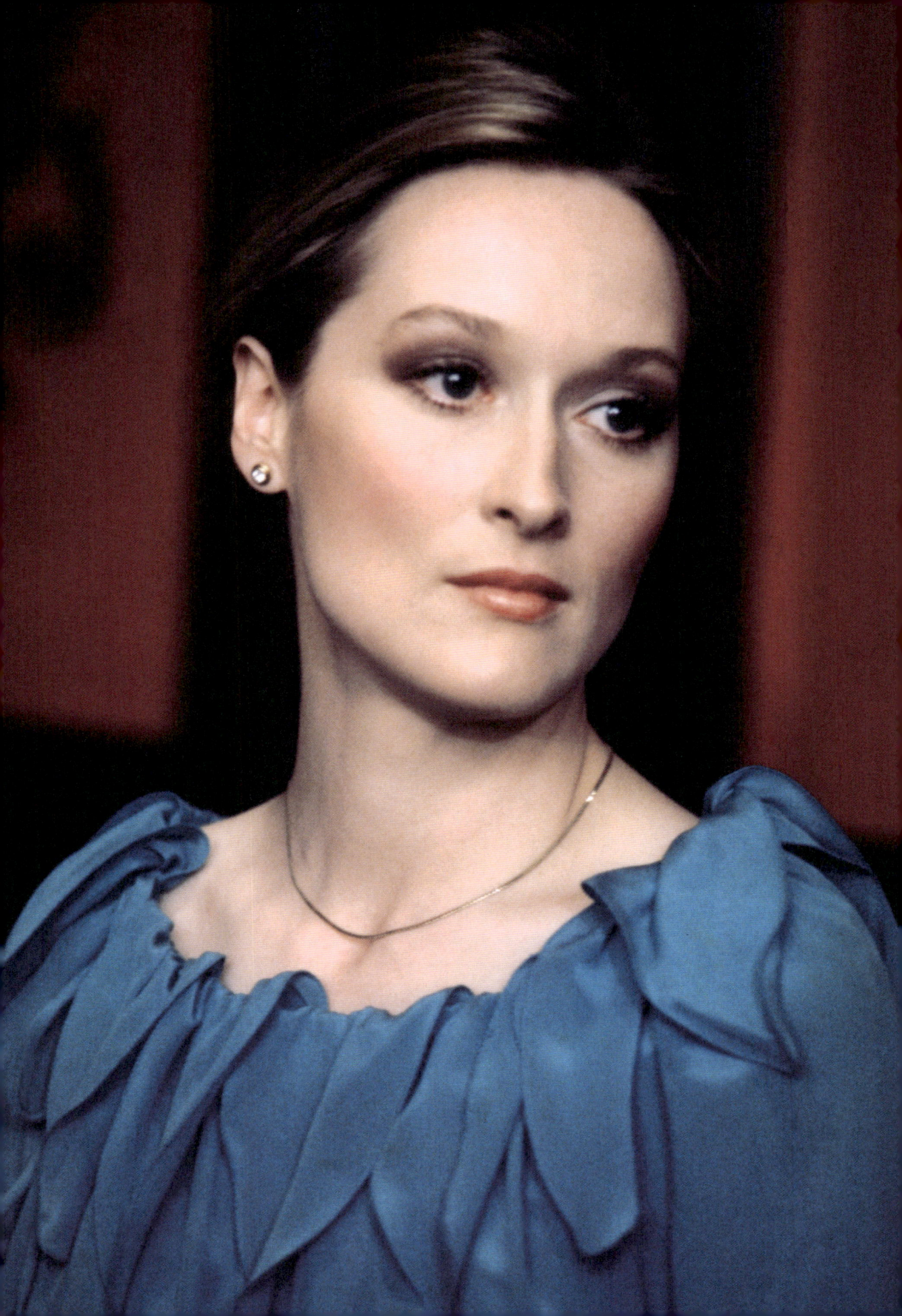

Betty Ford
New York City, ca. 1980

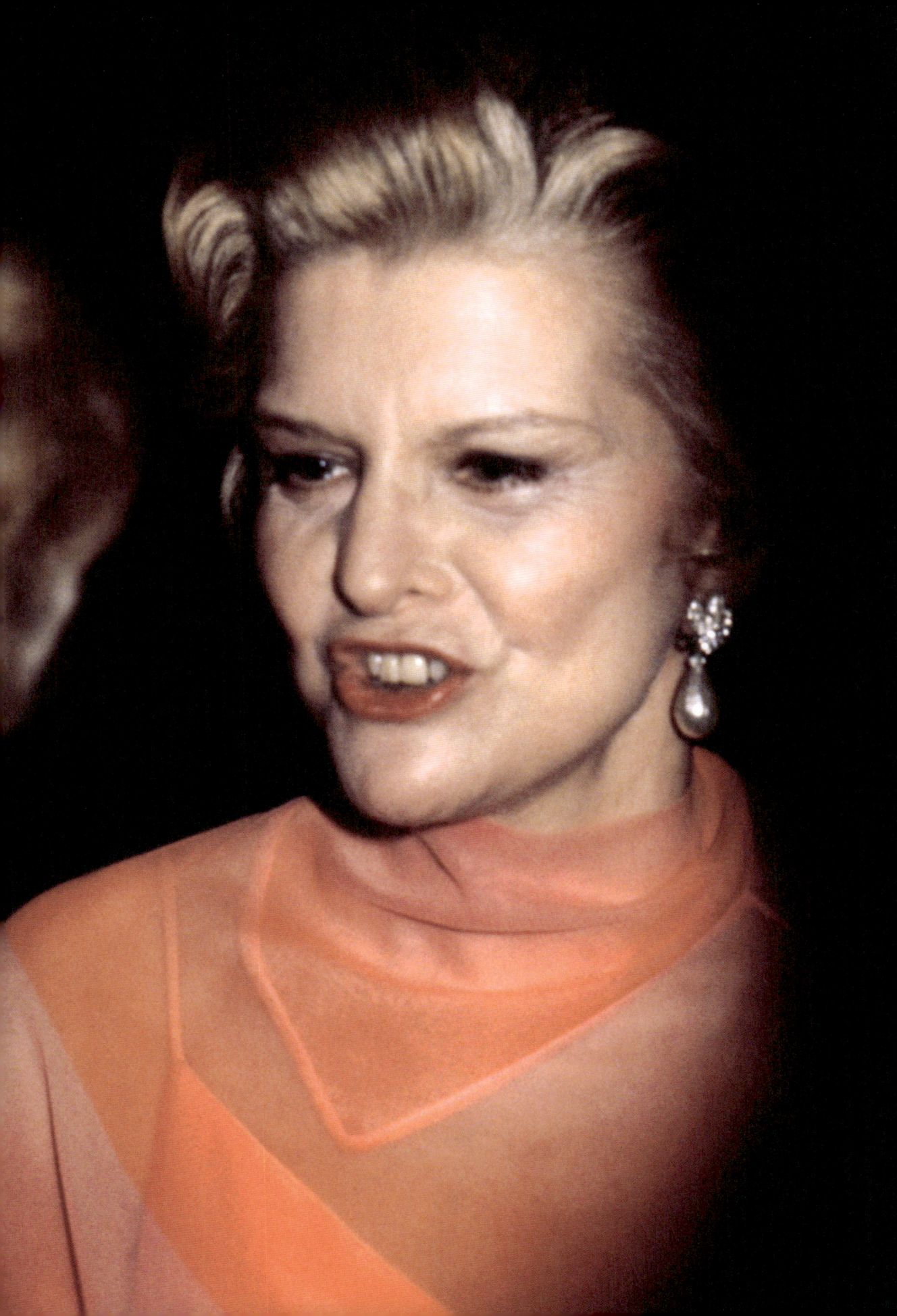

Michelle Pfeiffer
New York City, 1982

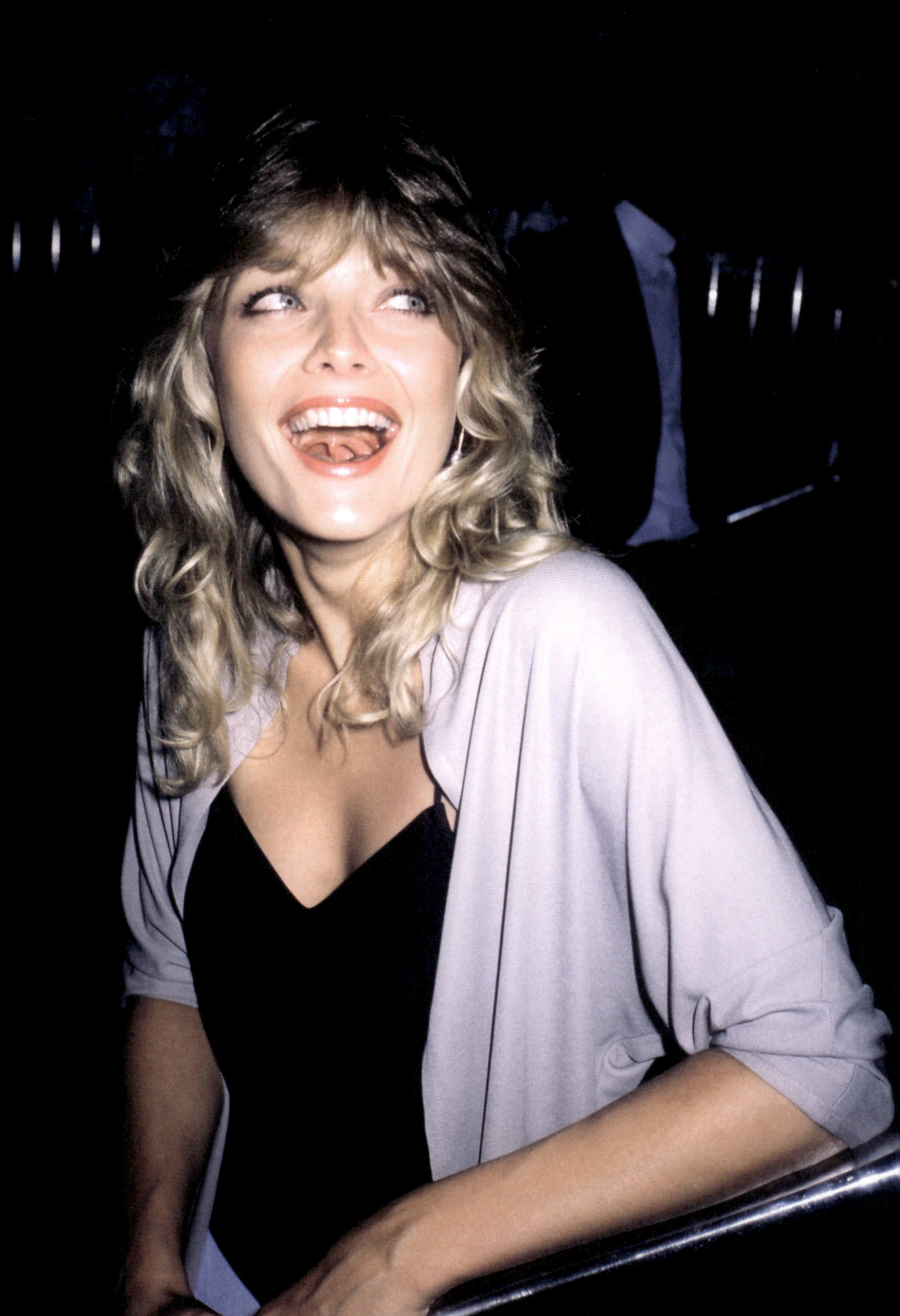

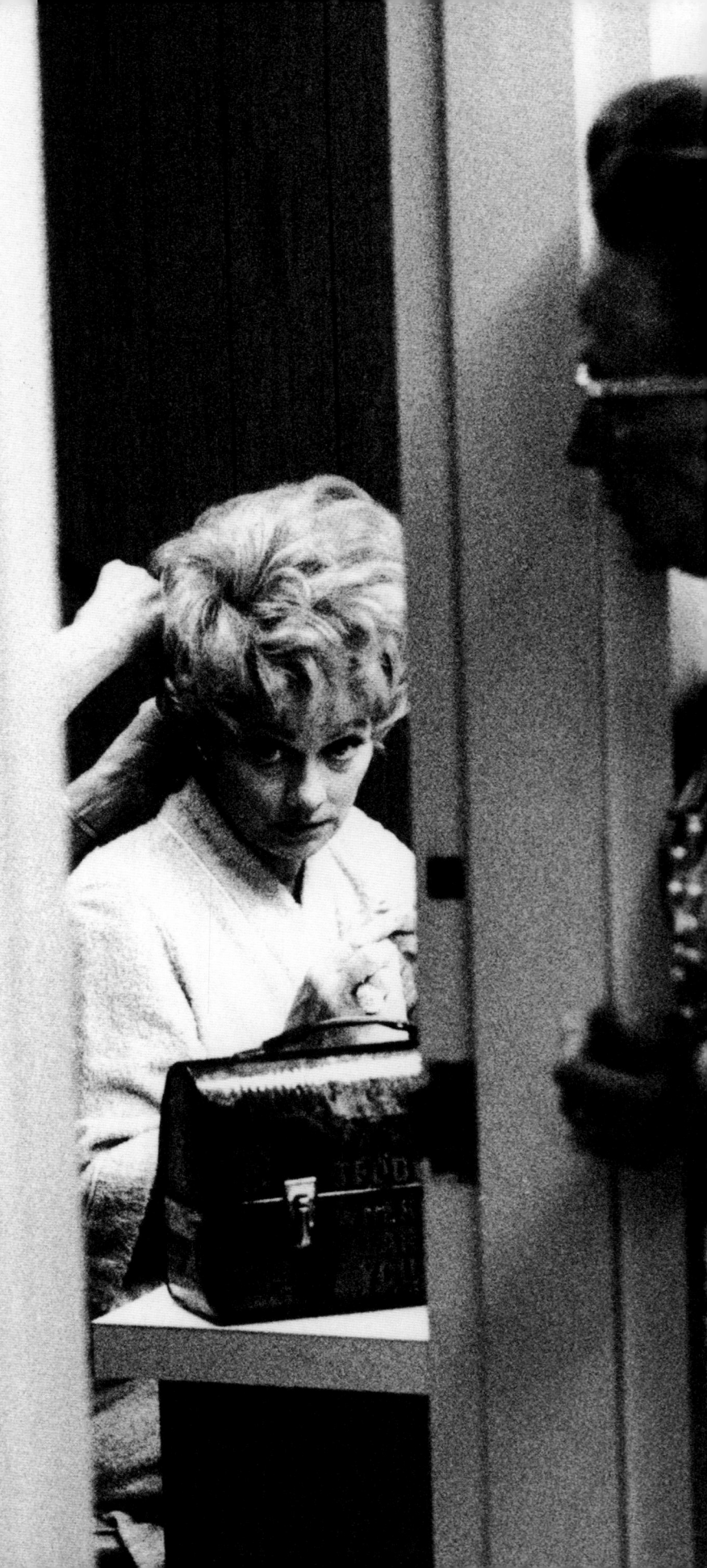

Lucille Ball
Los Angeles, 1968

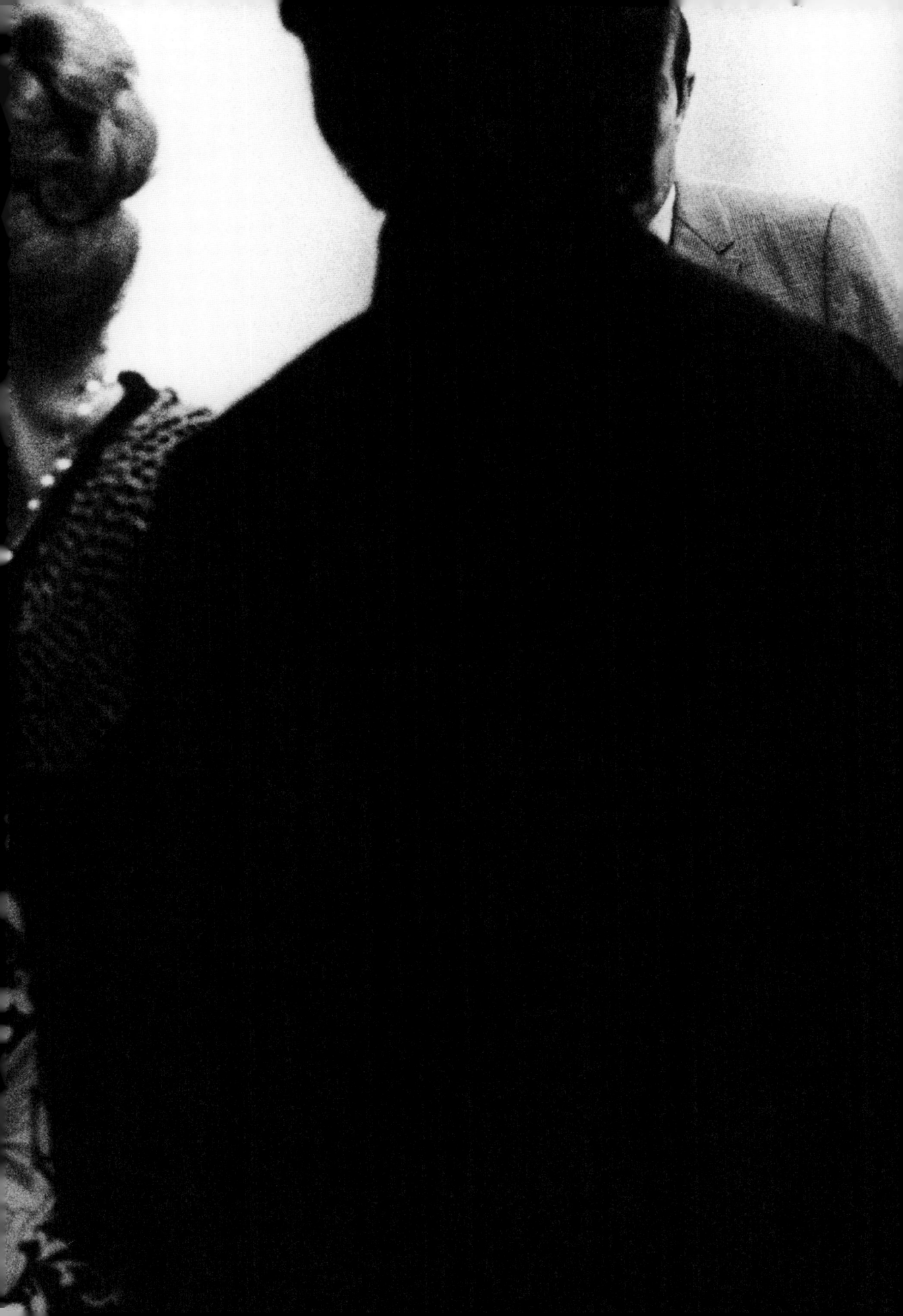

Françoise Gayat
New York City, 1979

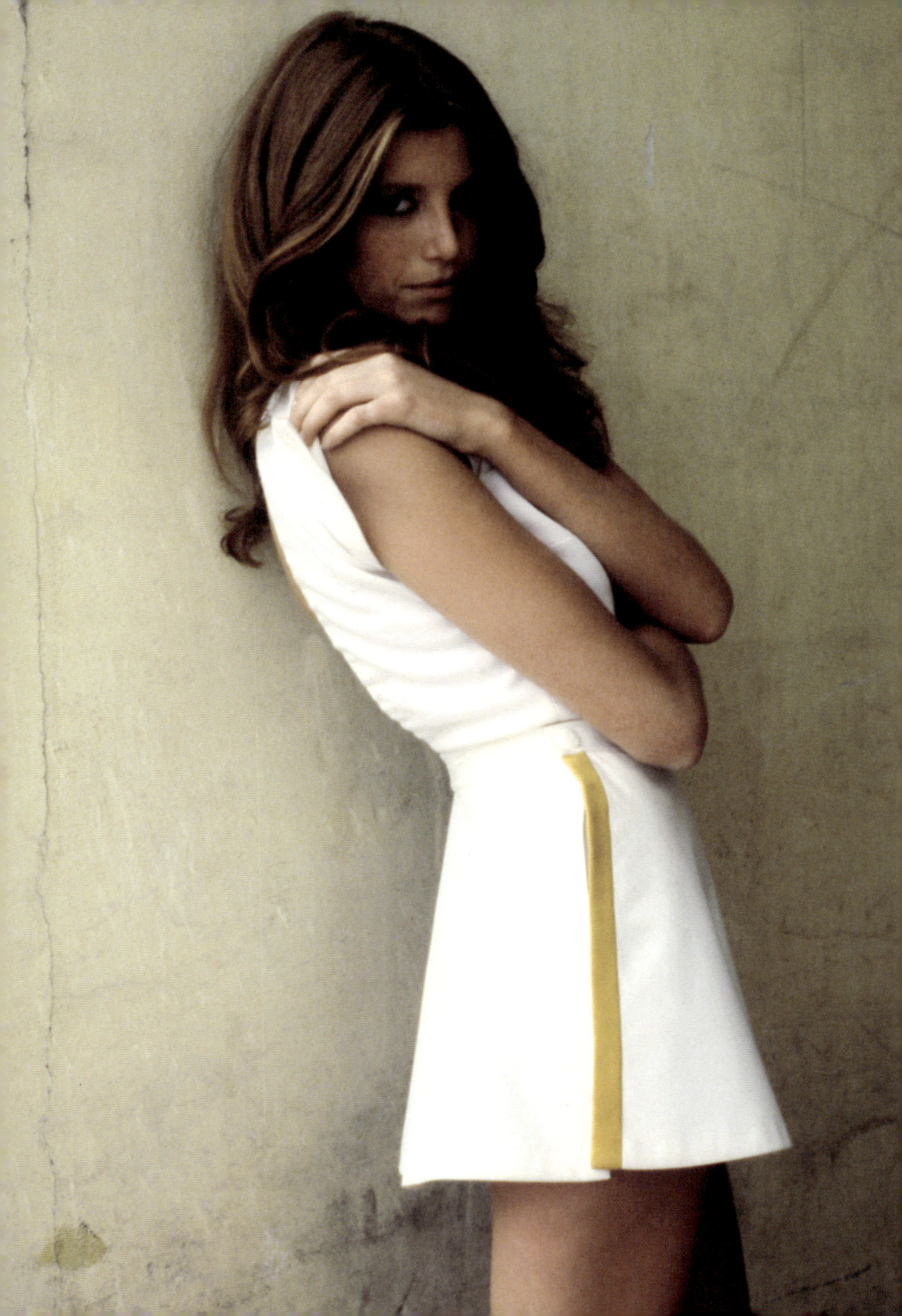

Bette Midler
New York City, 1973

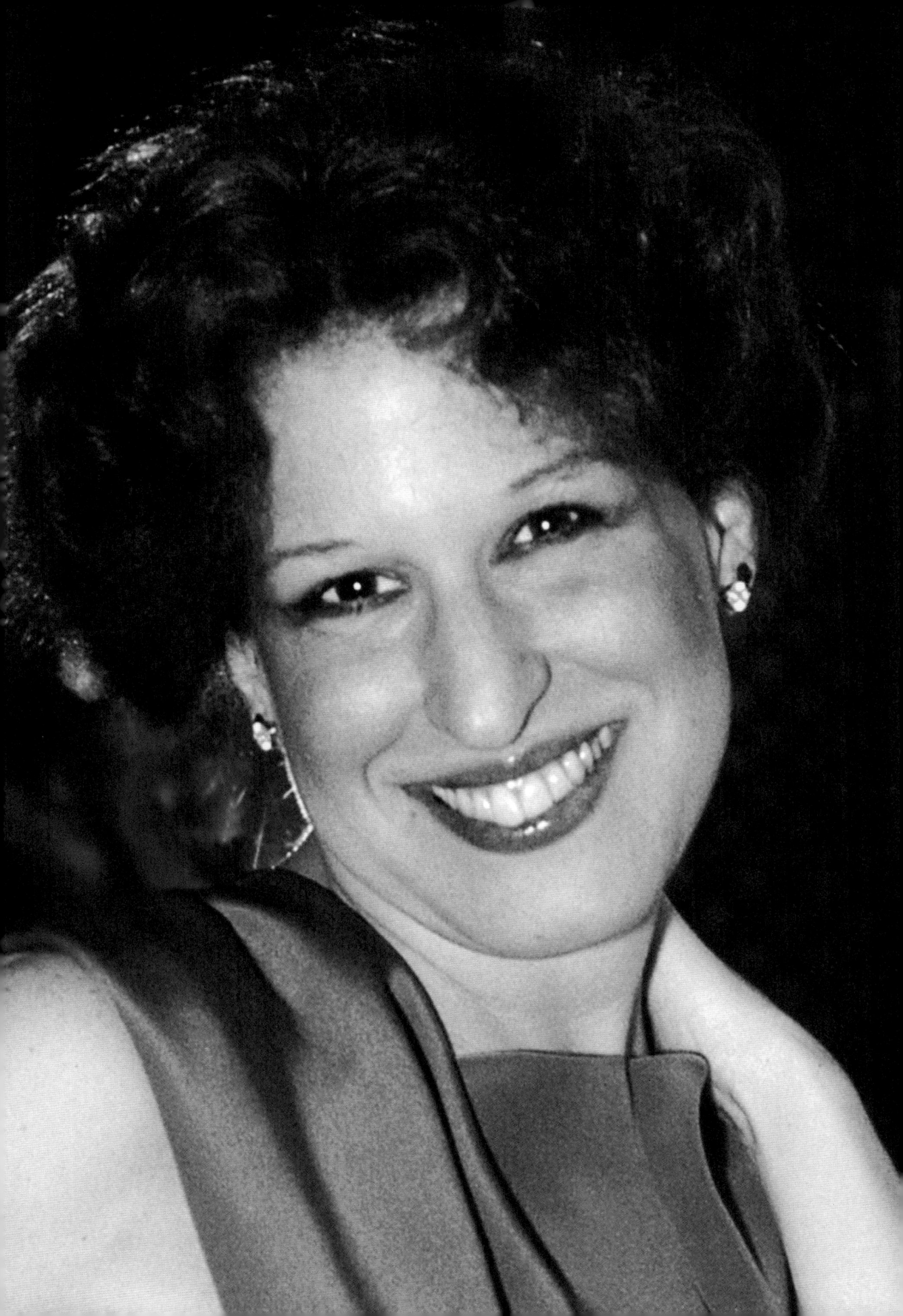

"Don't listen to anyone who doesn't know how to dream."

**Liza Minnelli and
Desi Arnaz Jr.**
New York City, 1973

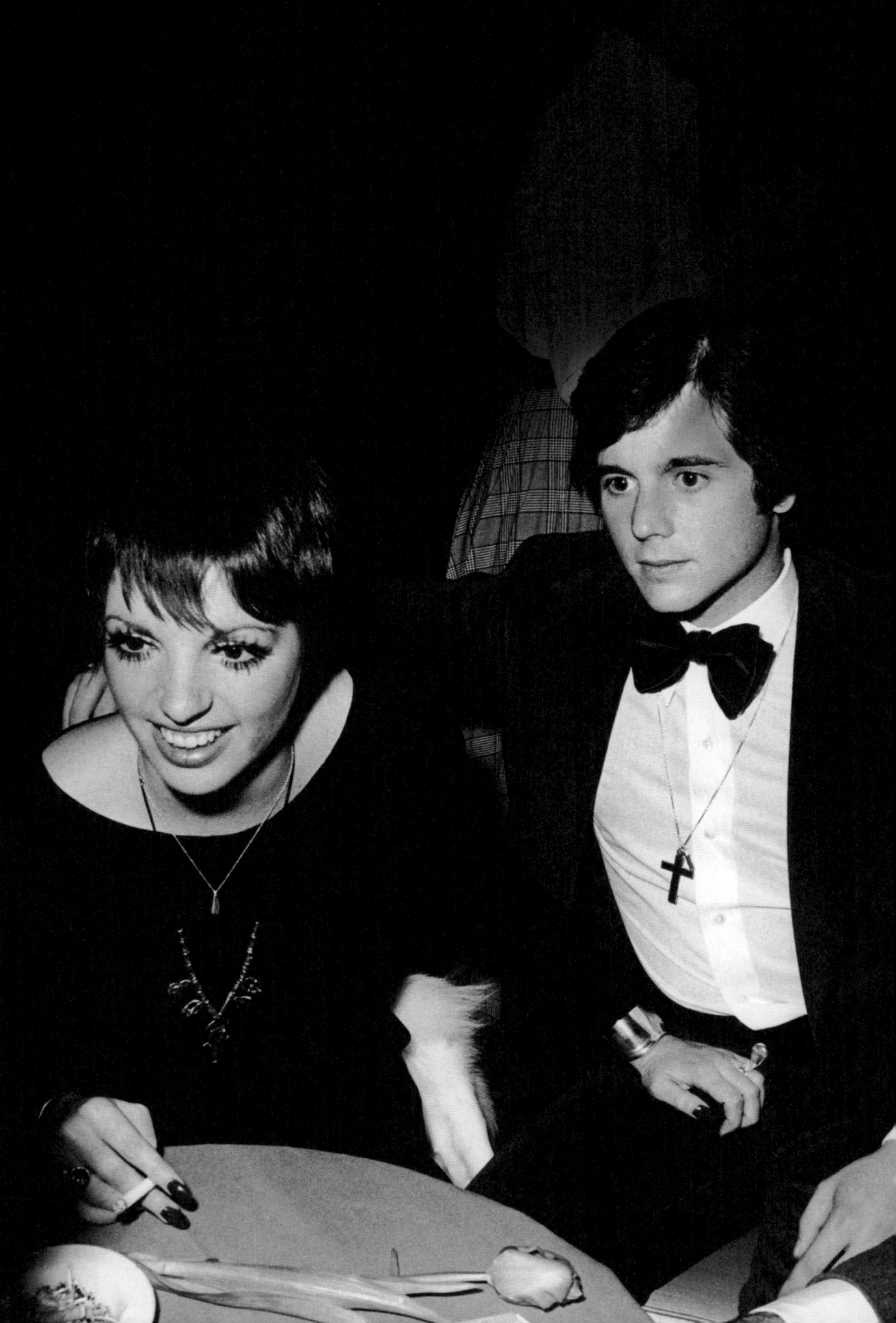

Mary Tyler Moore
New York City, ca. 1970

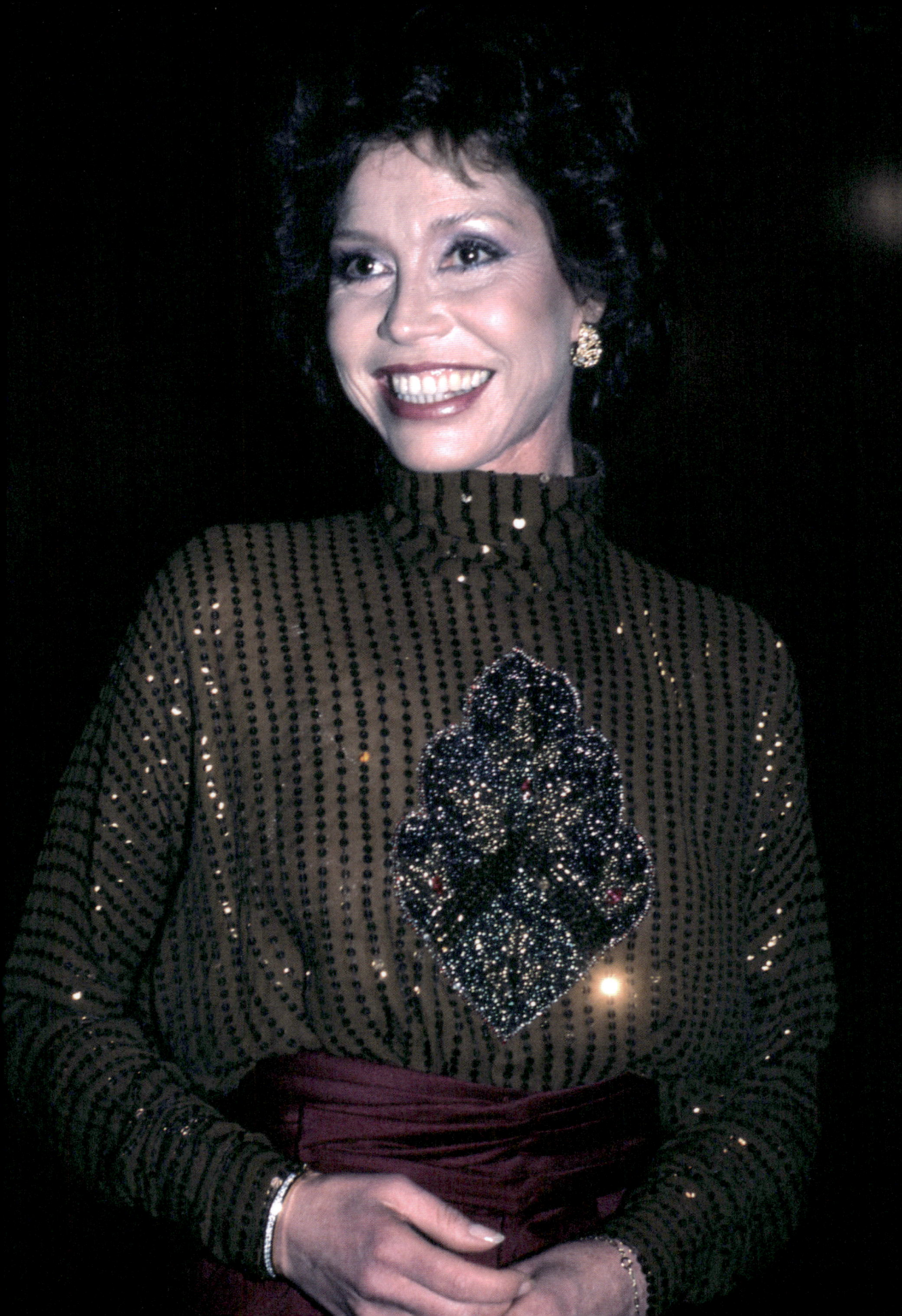

Joan Crawford
New York City, ca. 1970

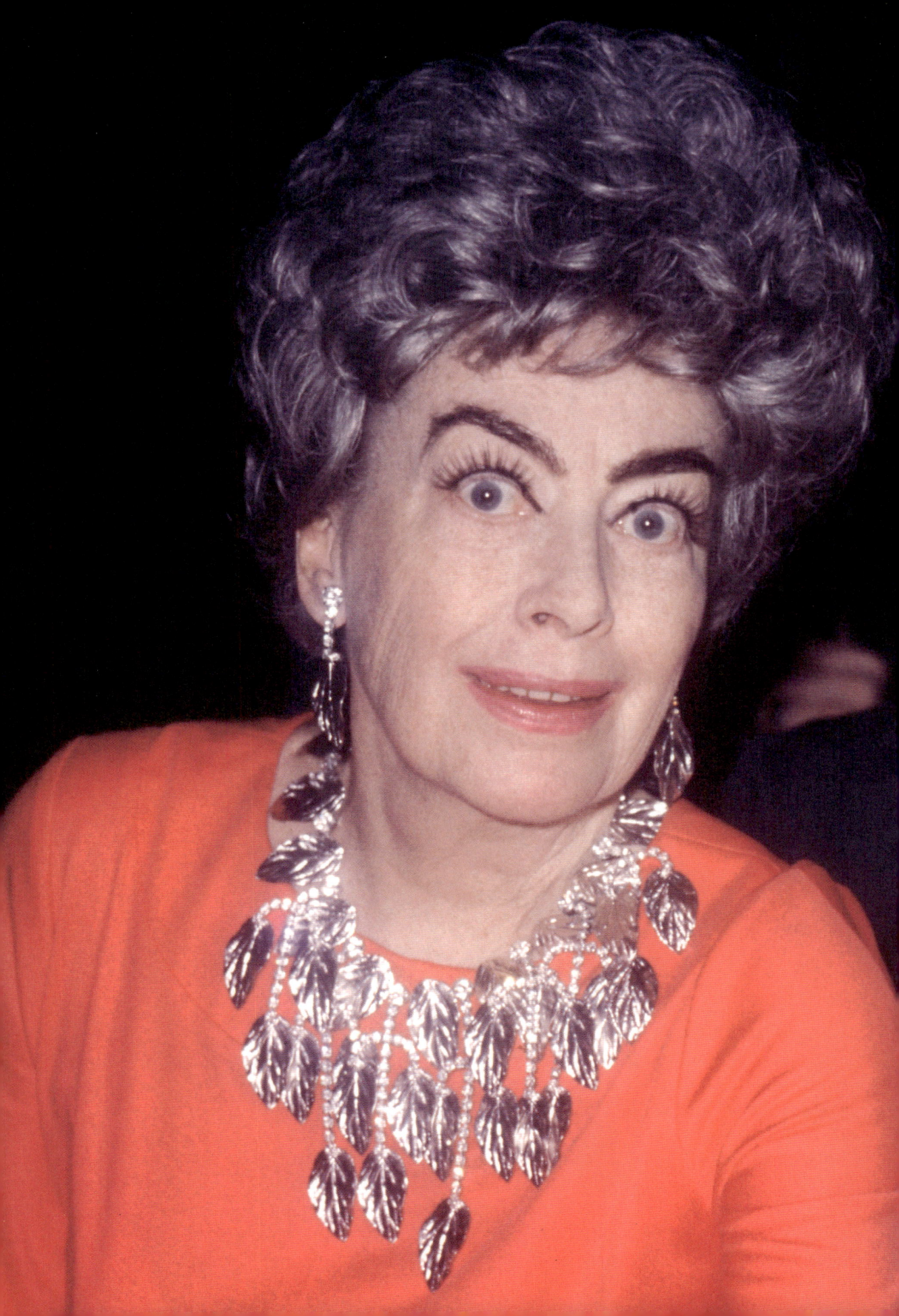

Tina Hudson
United Kingdom, 1983

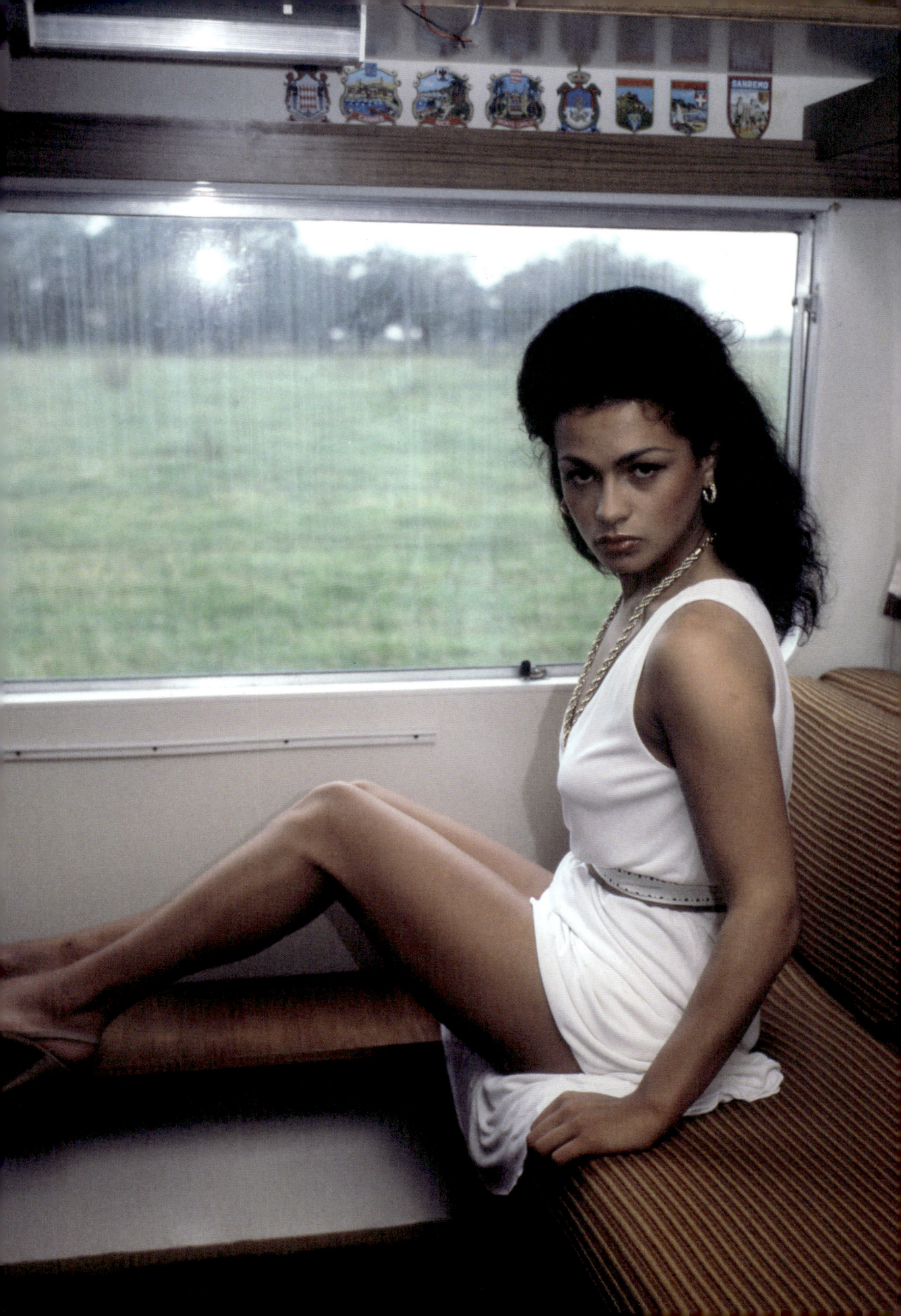

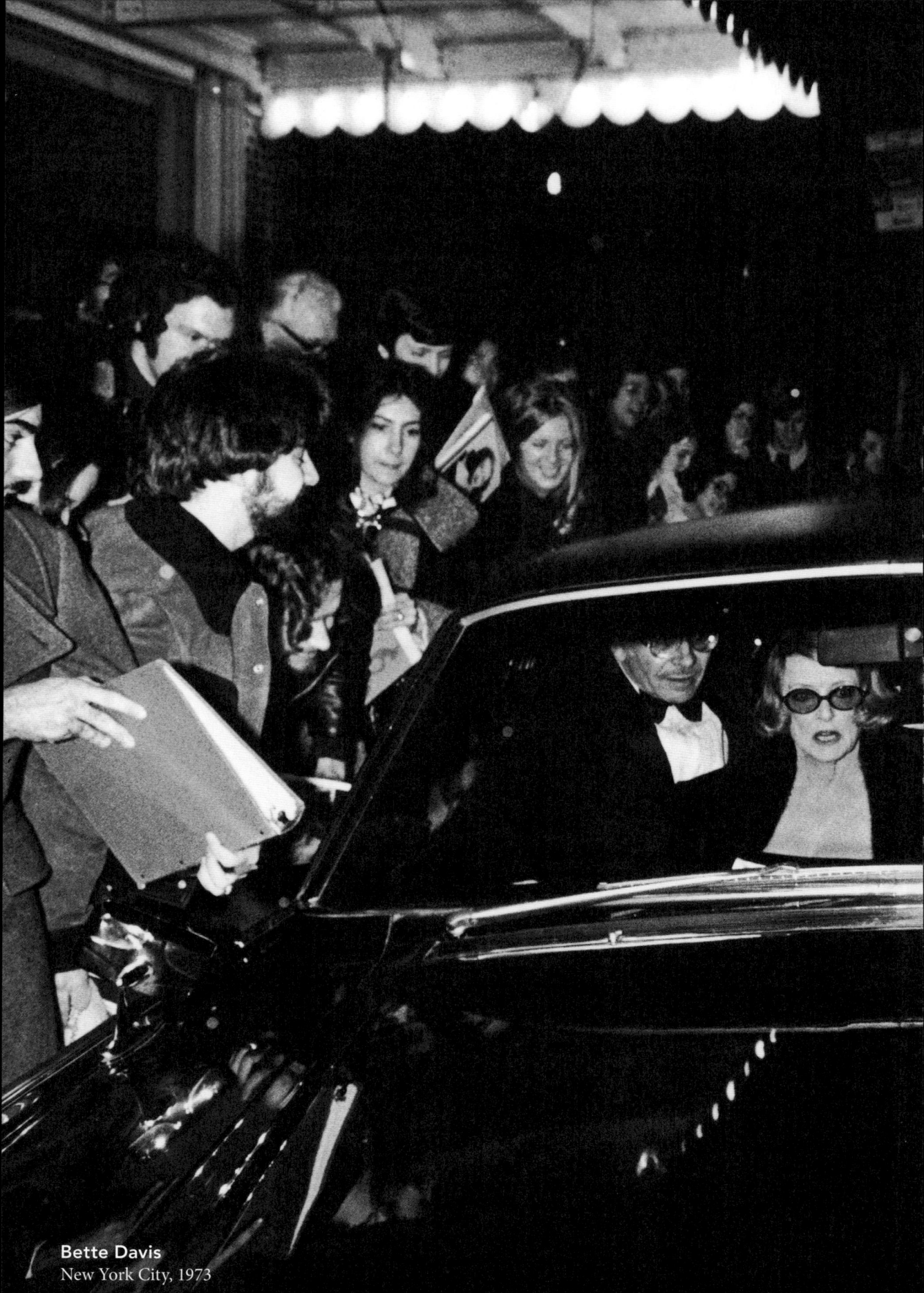

Bette Davis
New York City, 1973

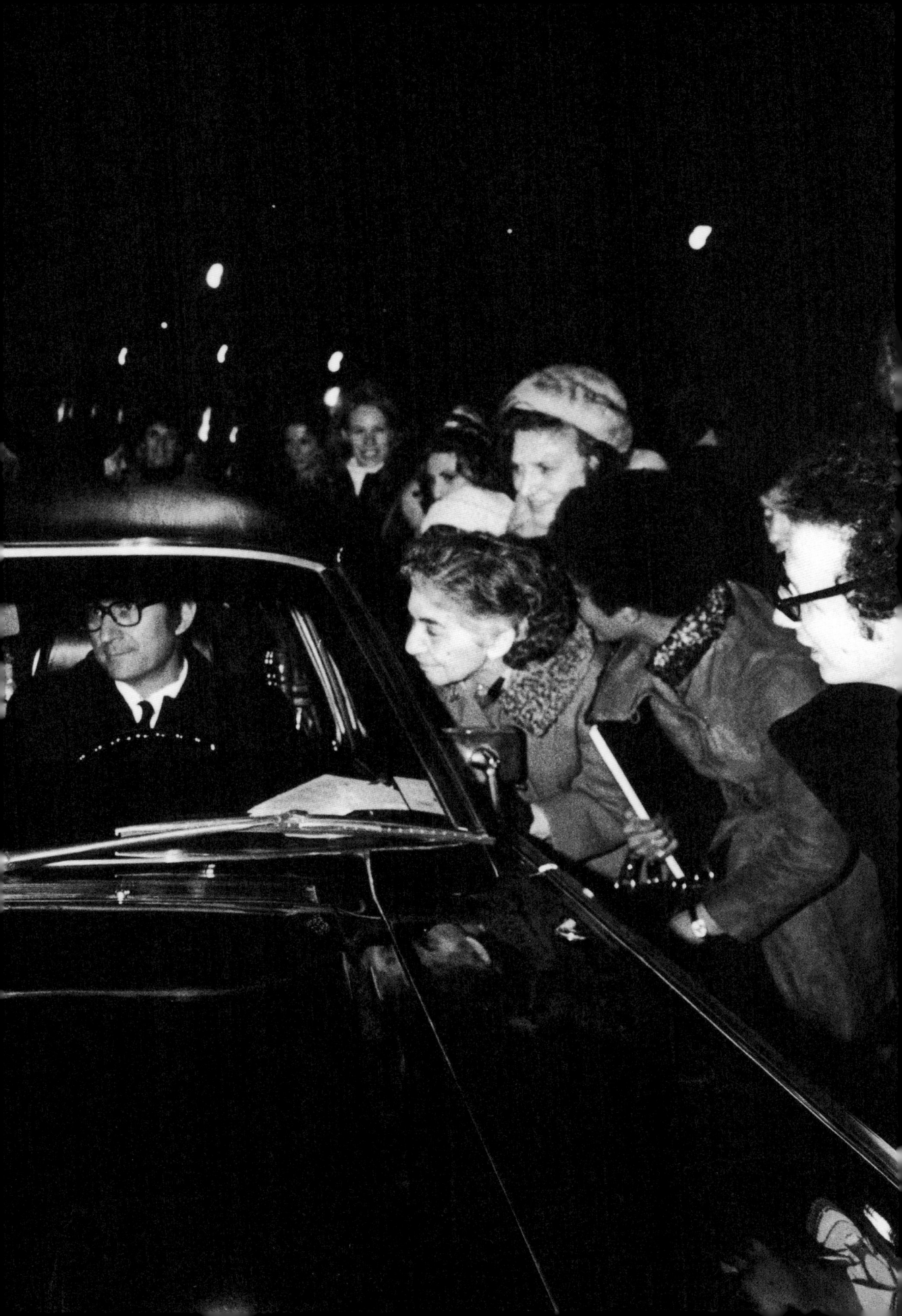

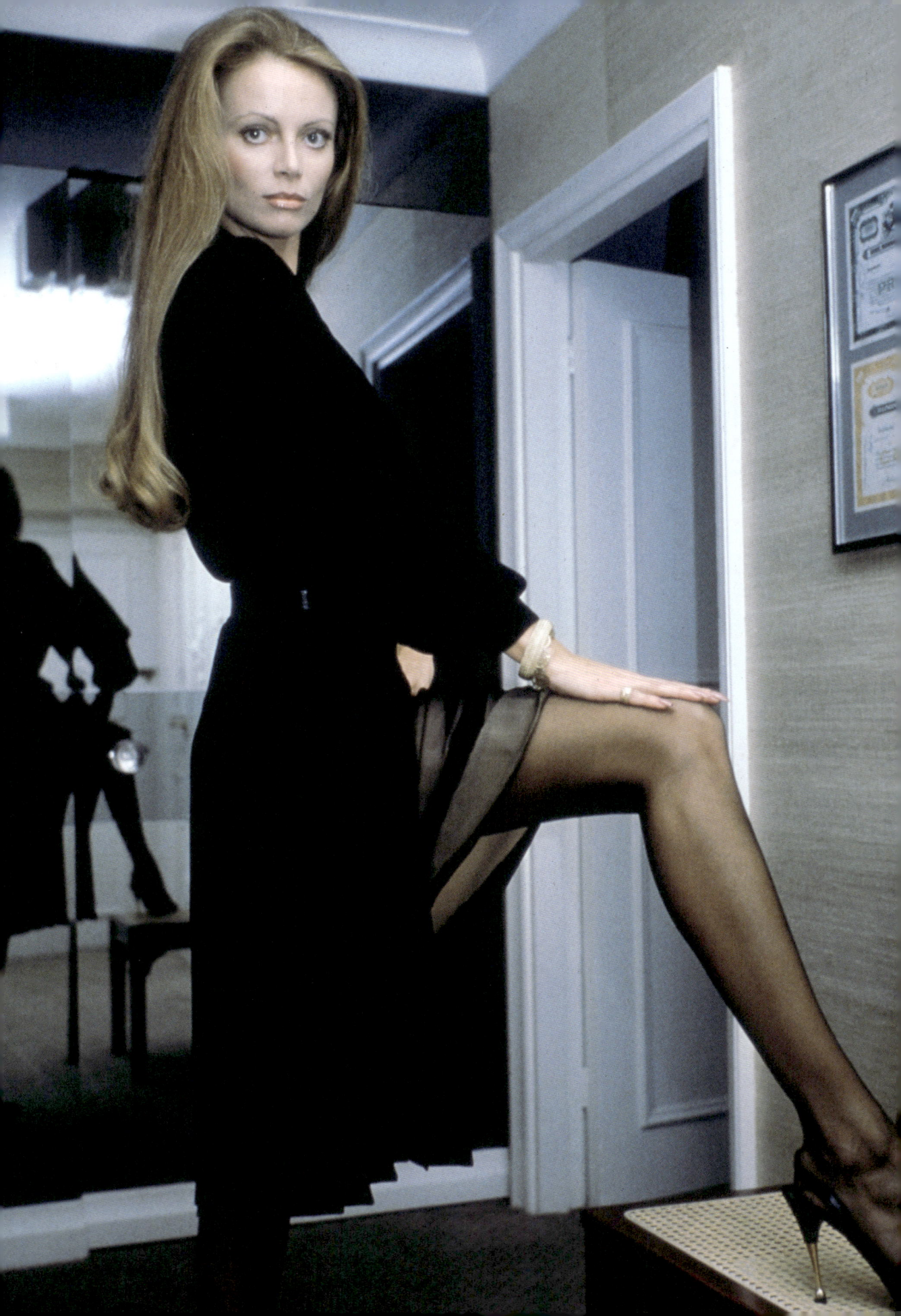

Cherry Gillespie
United Kingdom, 1983

Margaret Trudeau
Cannes, 1977

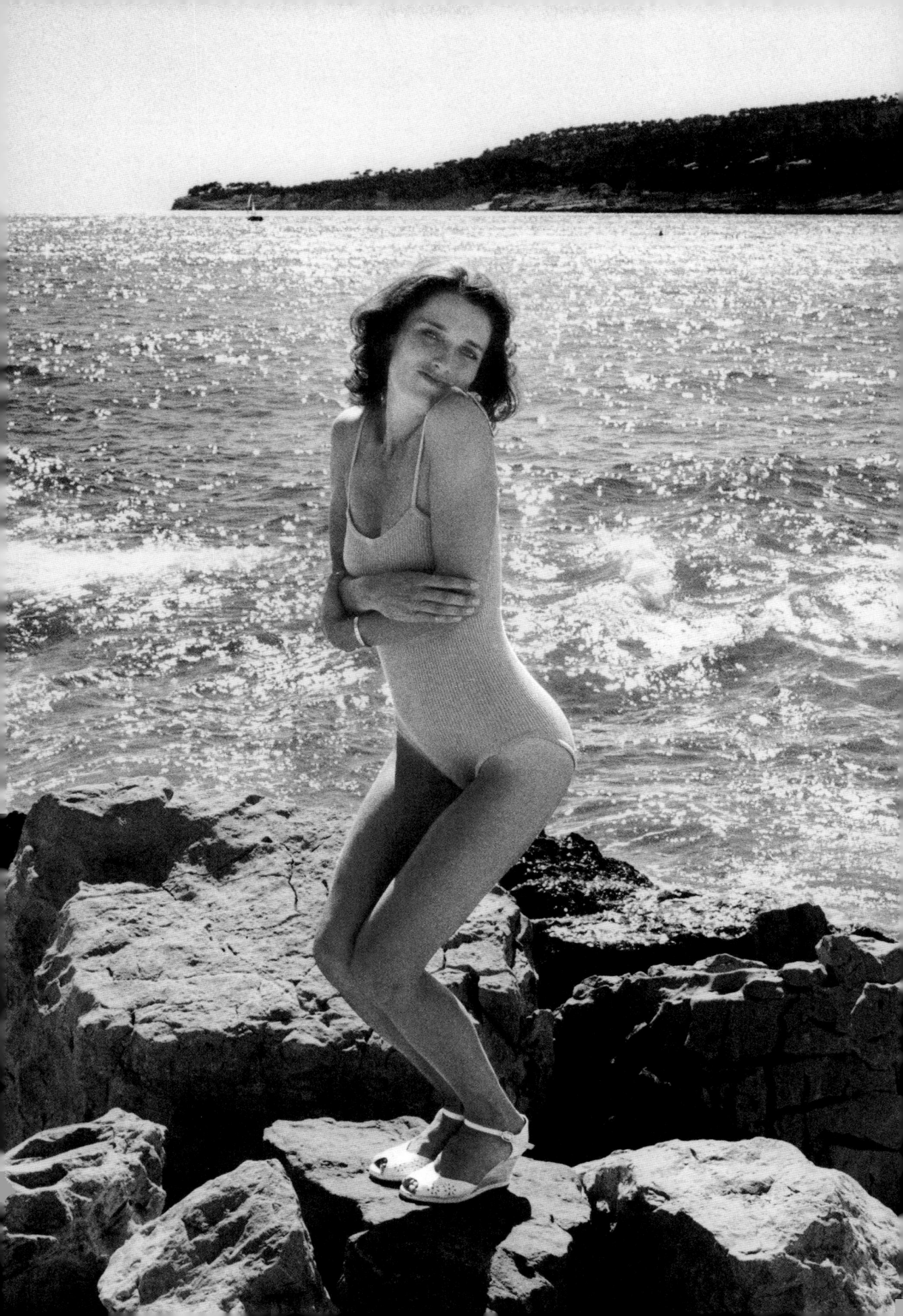

Twiggy
New York City, 1967

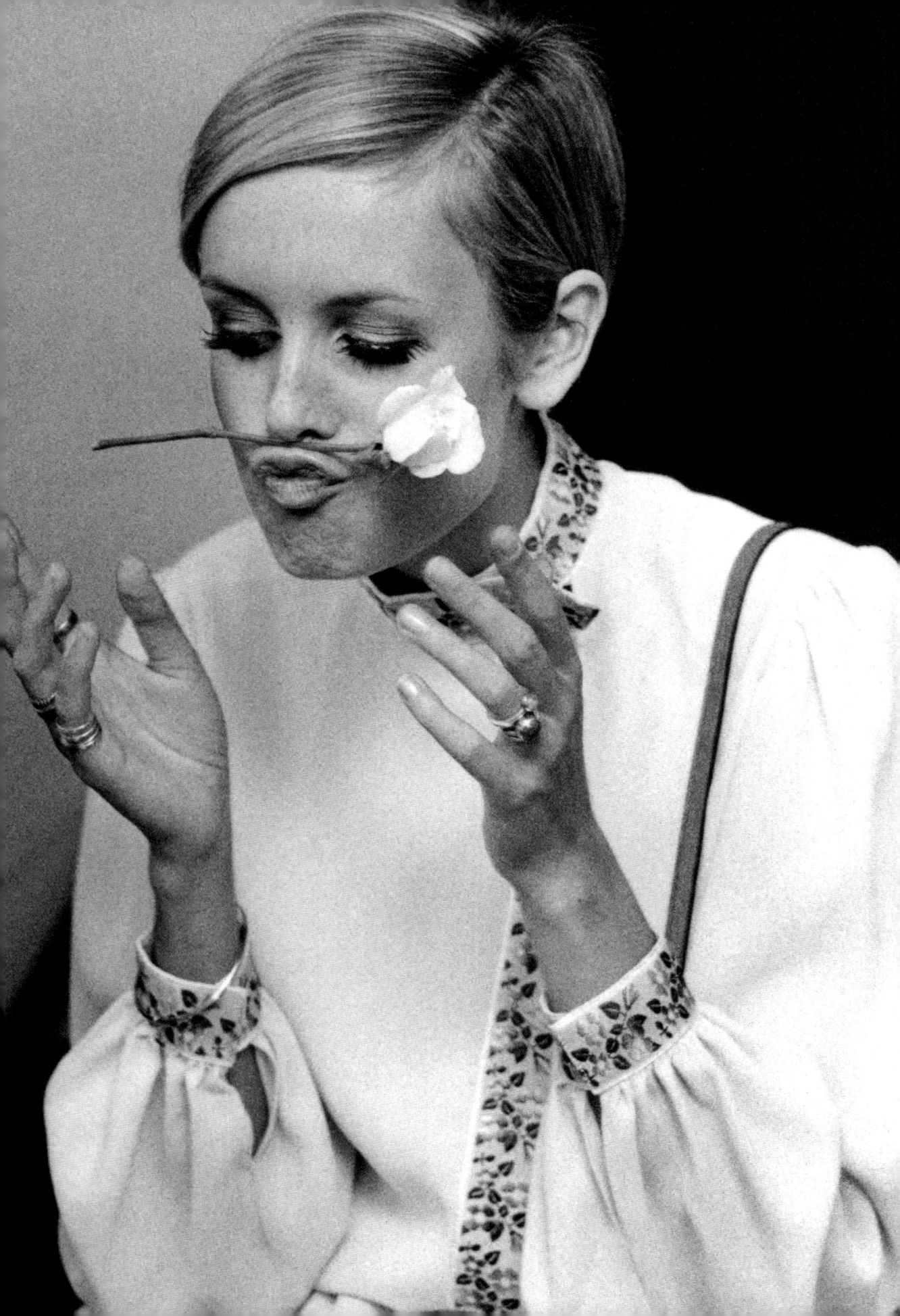

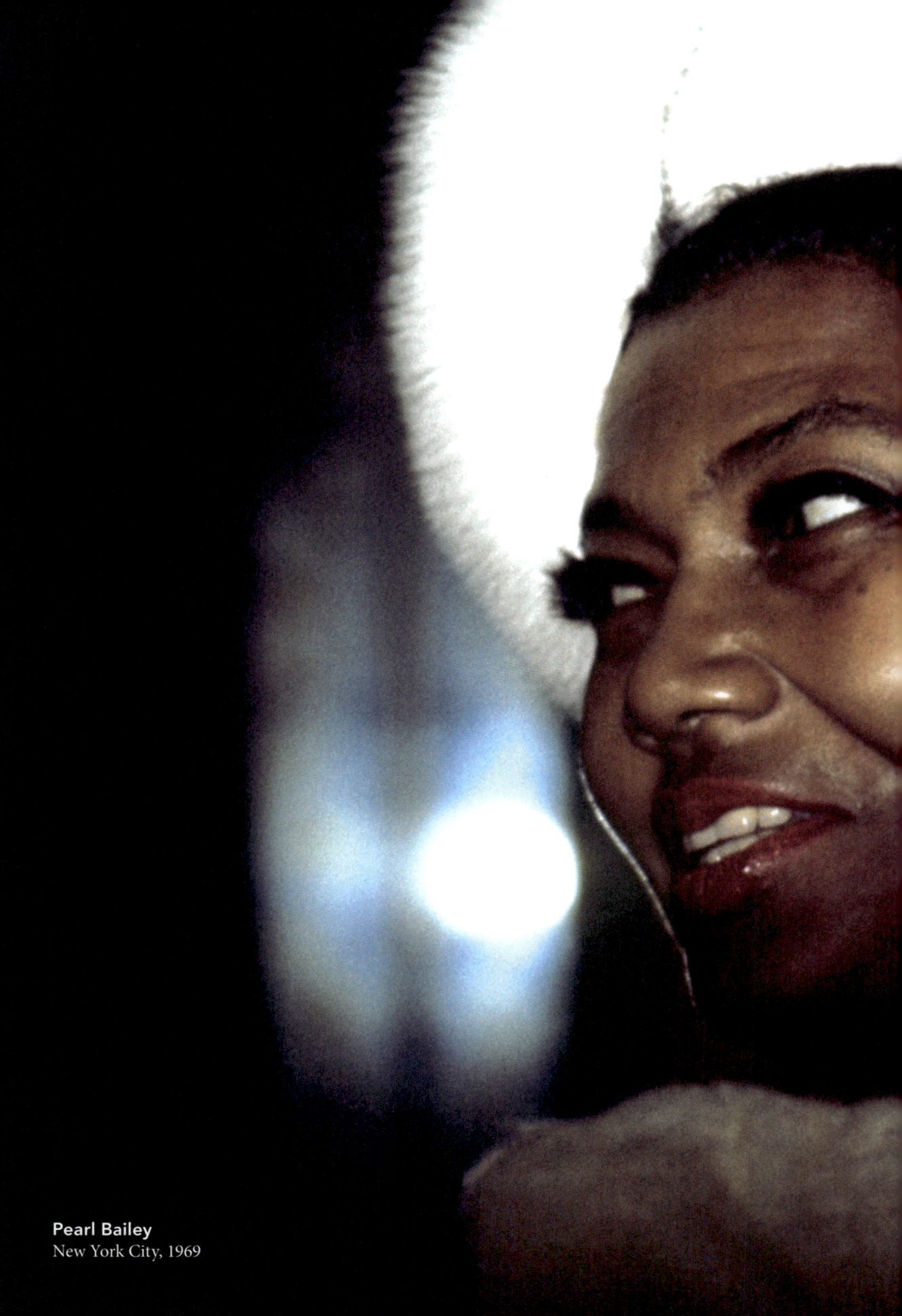

Pearl Bailey
New York City, 1969

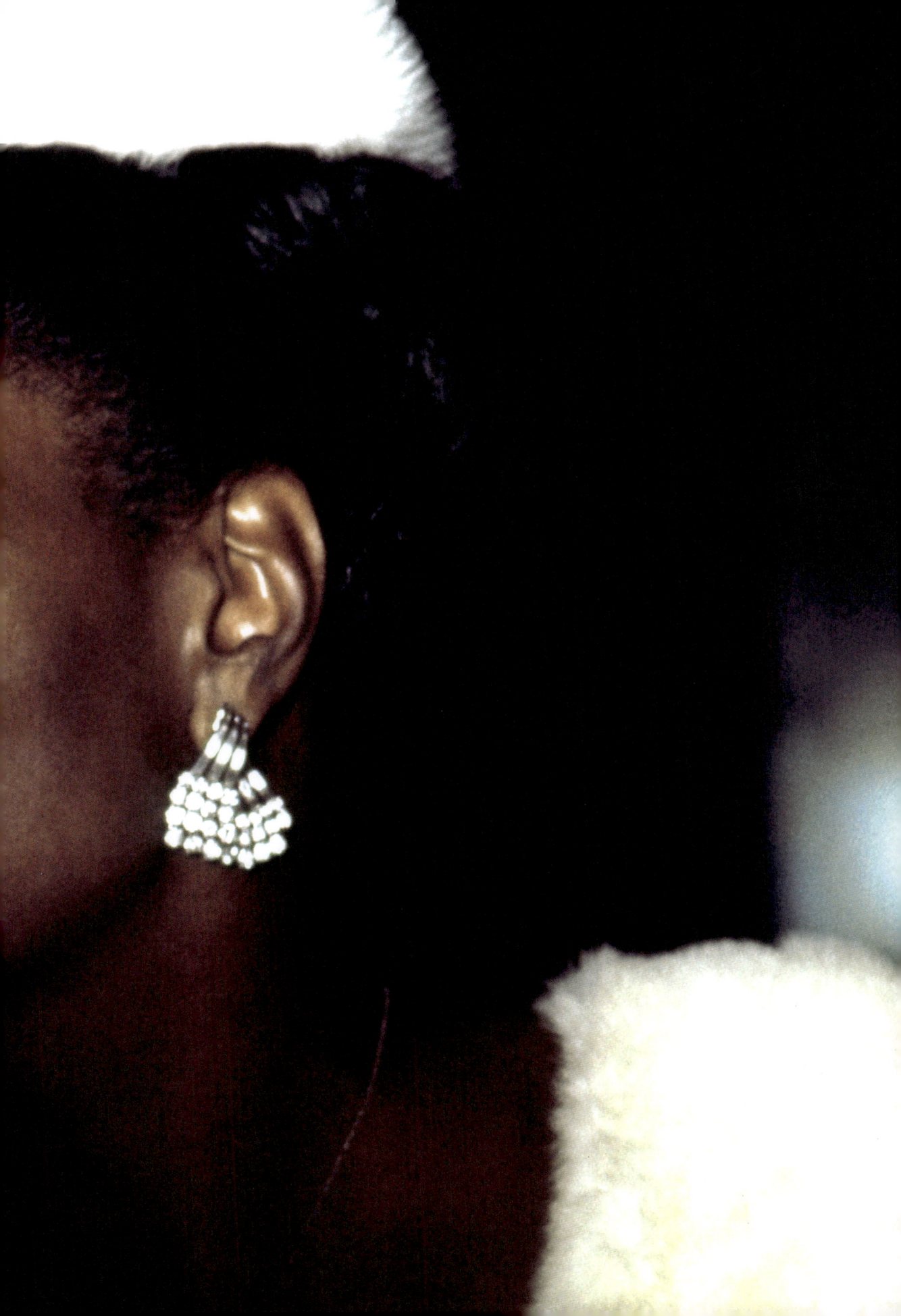

Rhinestones, rebellion, and a voice that defied the rules.

Some women shape their era. Cher built her own.

Oscar didn't pose her. He barely had to direct her. She moved like sculpture with attitude, a fashion editorial in motion. She drew power from vulnerability, made glamour untouchable, and turned reinvention into an art form.

With Cher, the image was never just about now. It hinted at what was to come — and she was already there waiting.

Cher
New York City, 1971

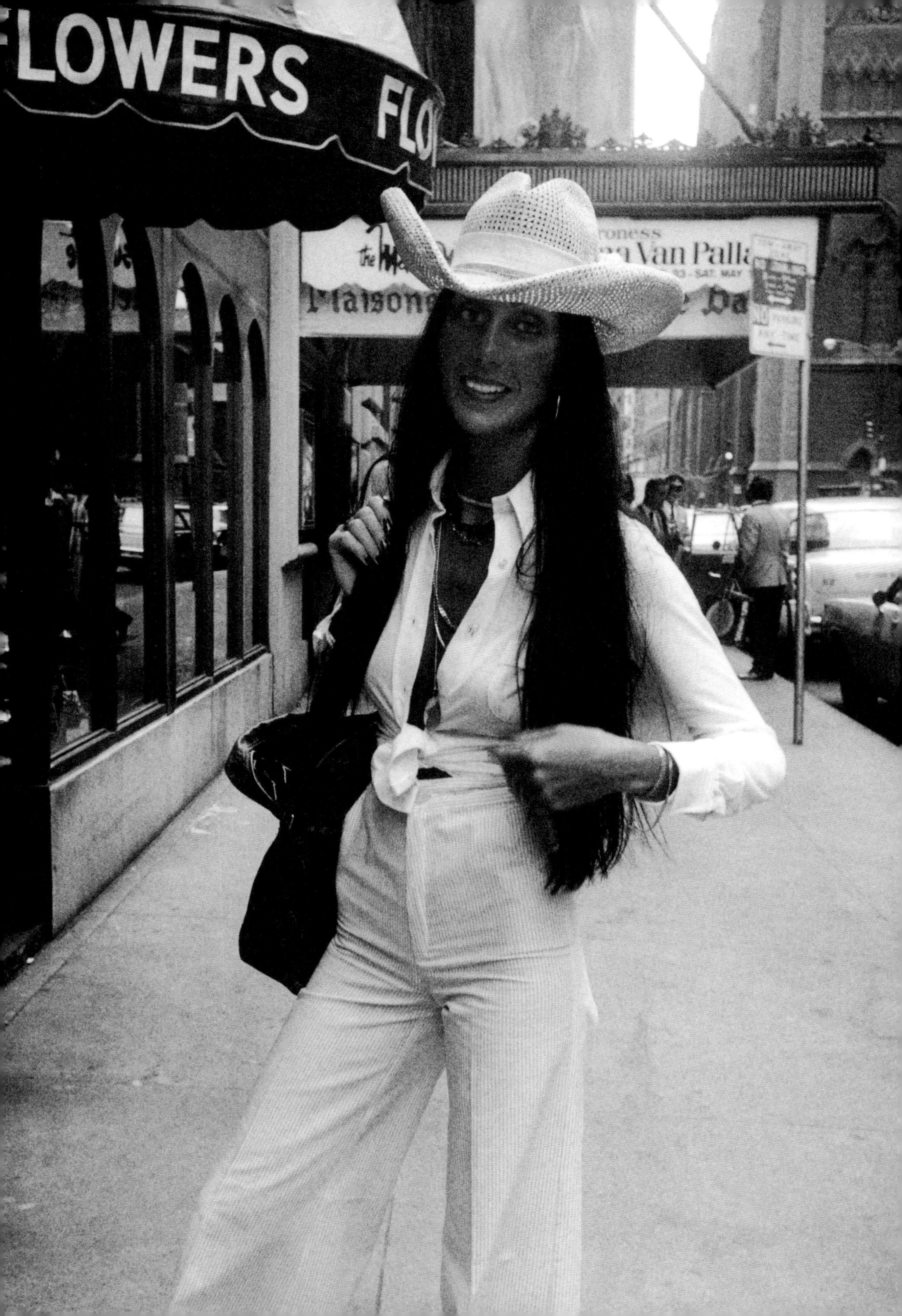
FLOWERS
FLO

Ann Wedgeworth
New York City, 1978

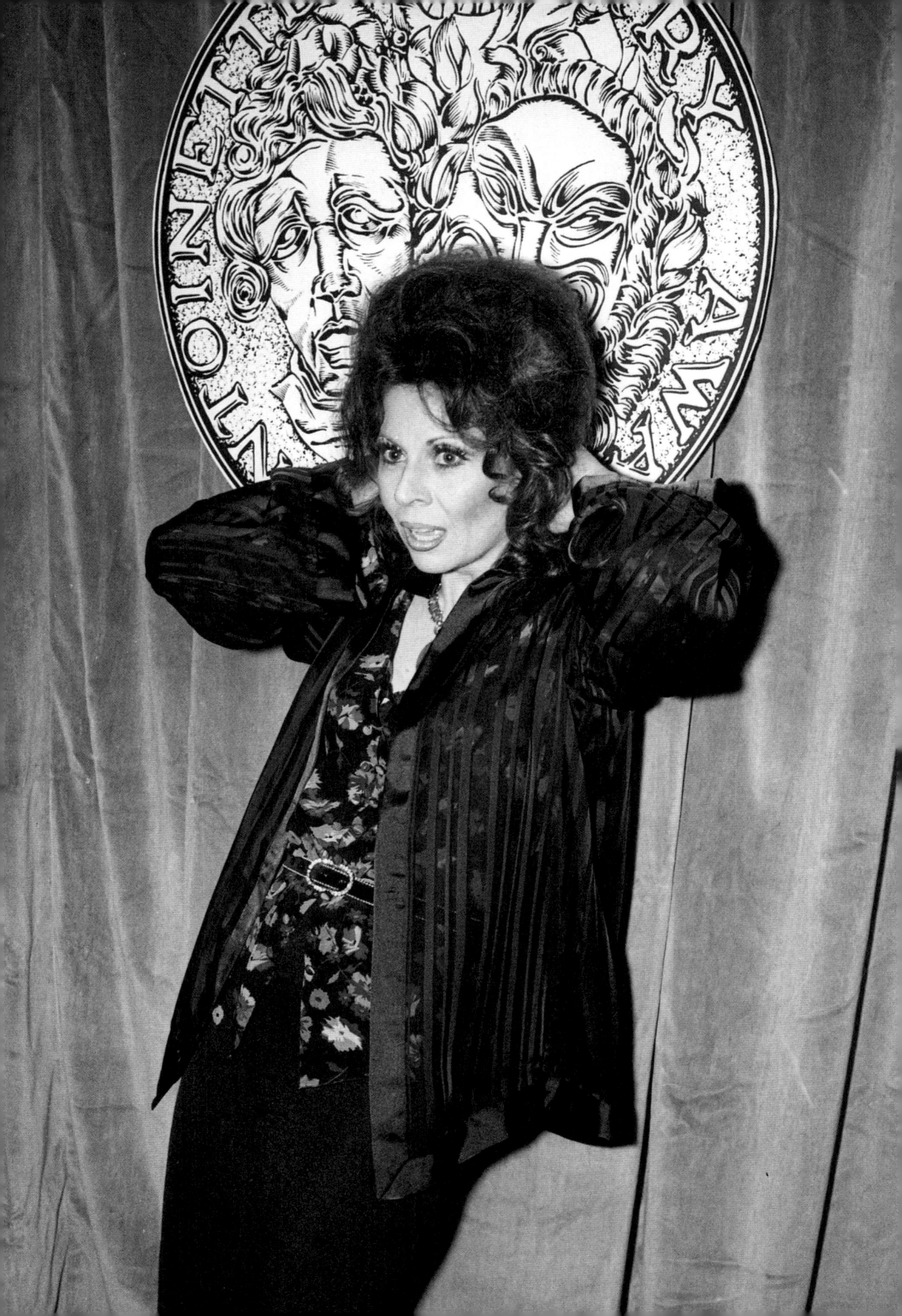

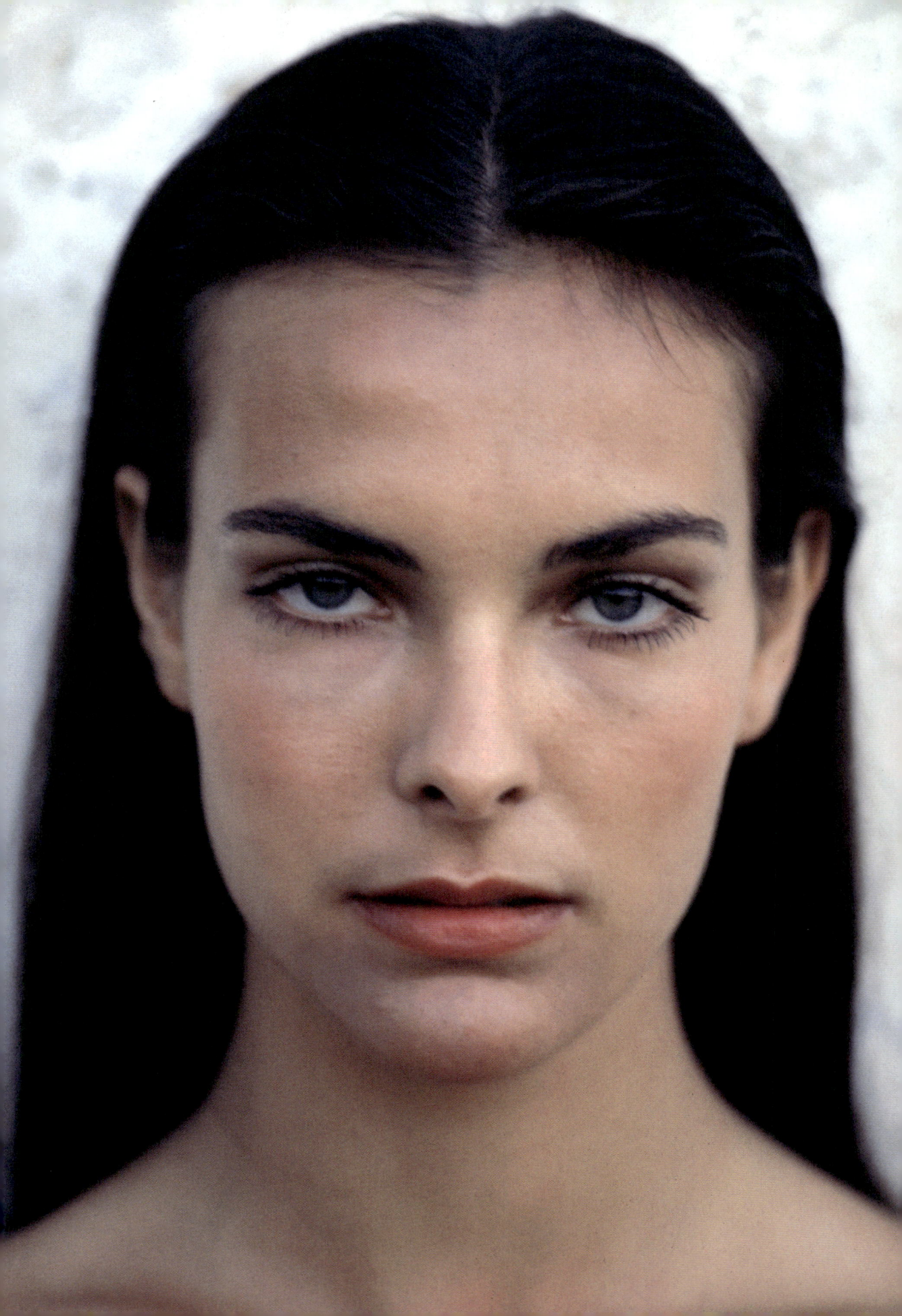

Carole Bouquet
Bahamas, 1980

"All anything takes, really,
is confidence."

Rachel Ward
Los Angeles, 1983

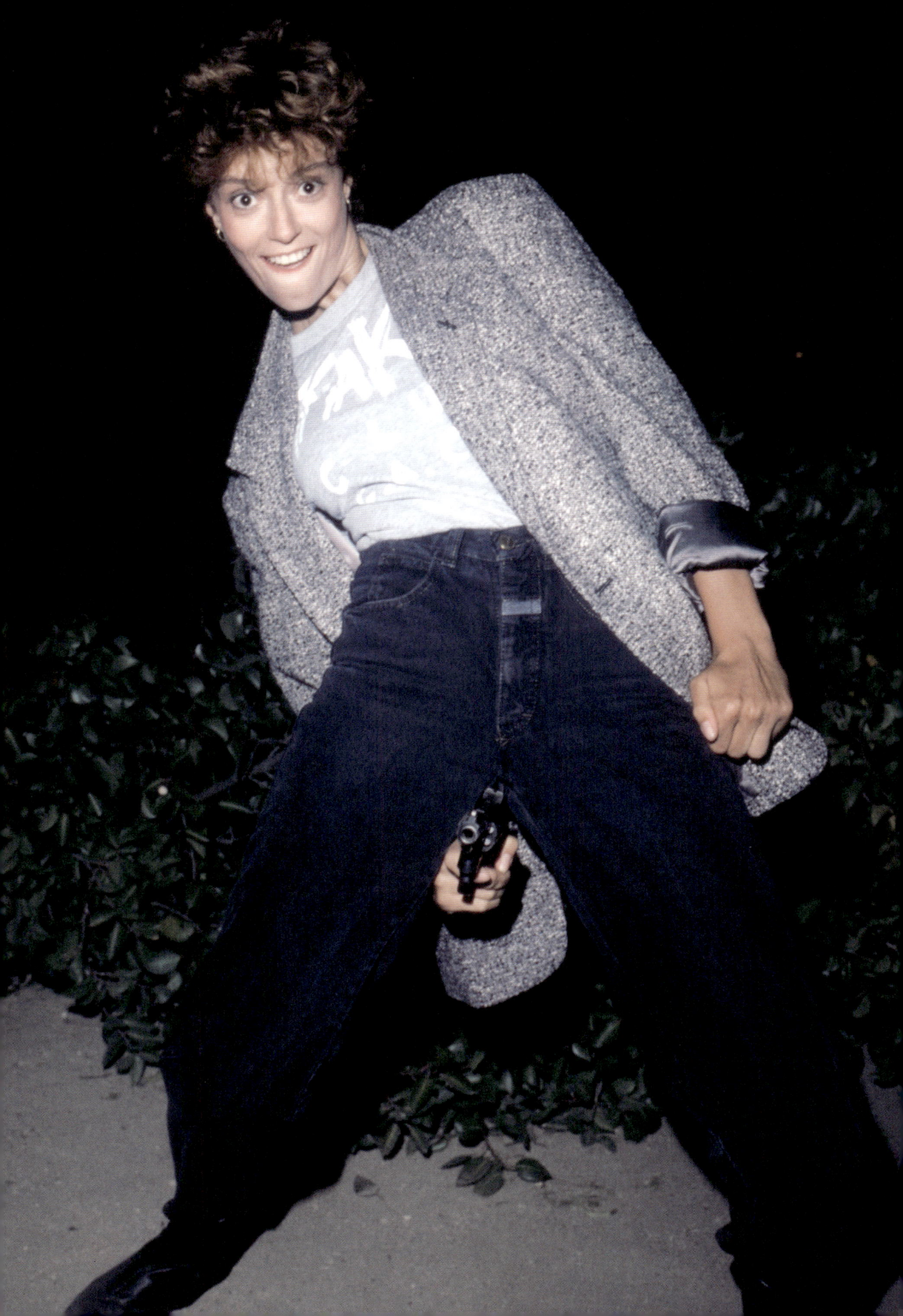

Dr. Ruth Westheimer
New York City, 1990

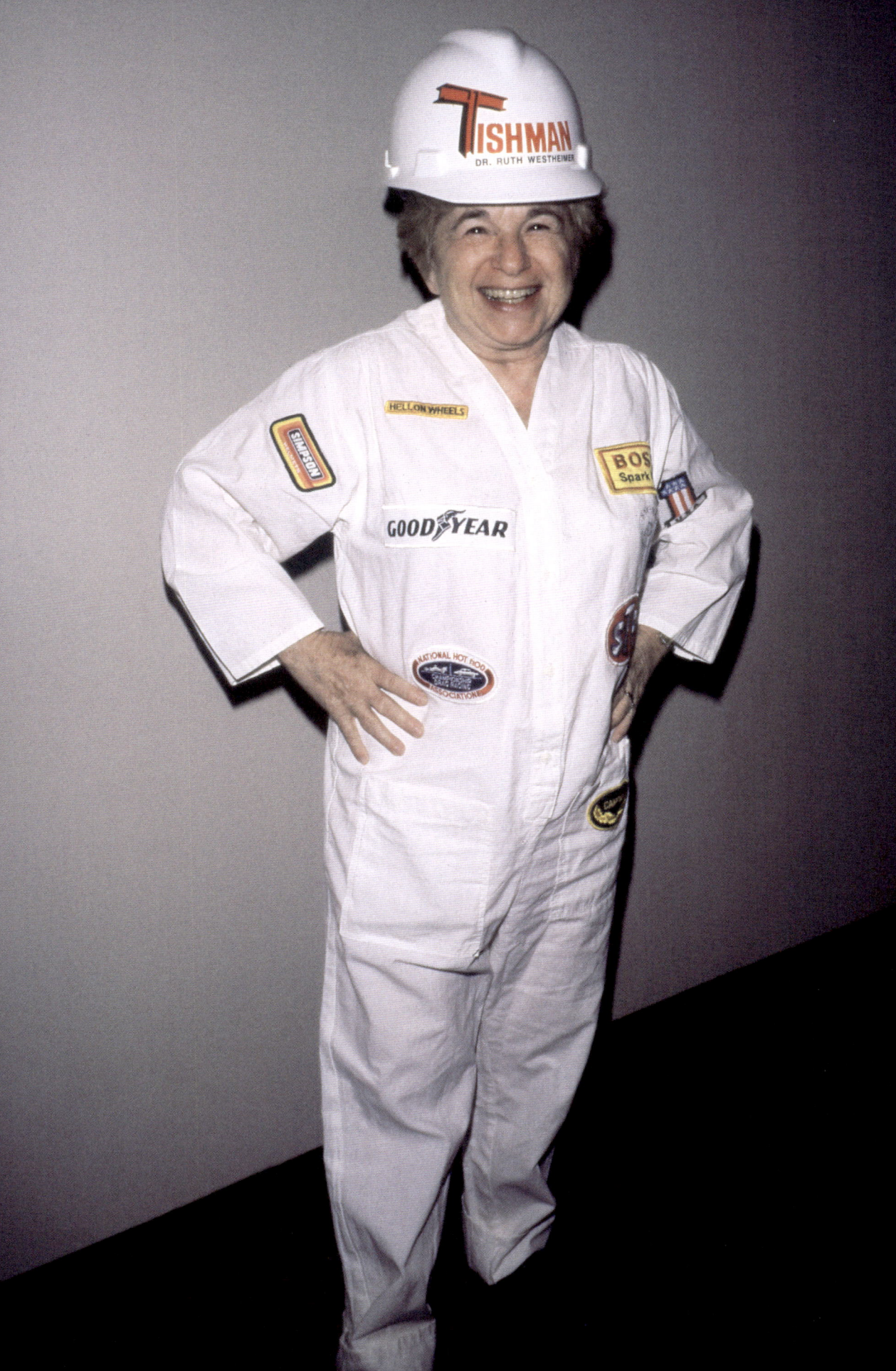

Sharon Tate
New York City, 1967

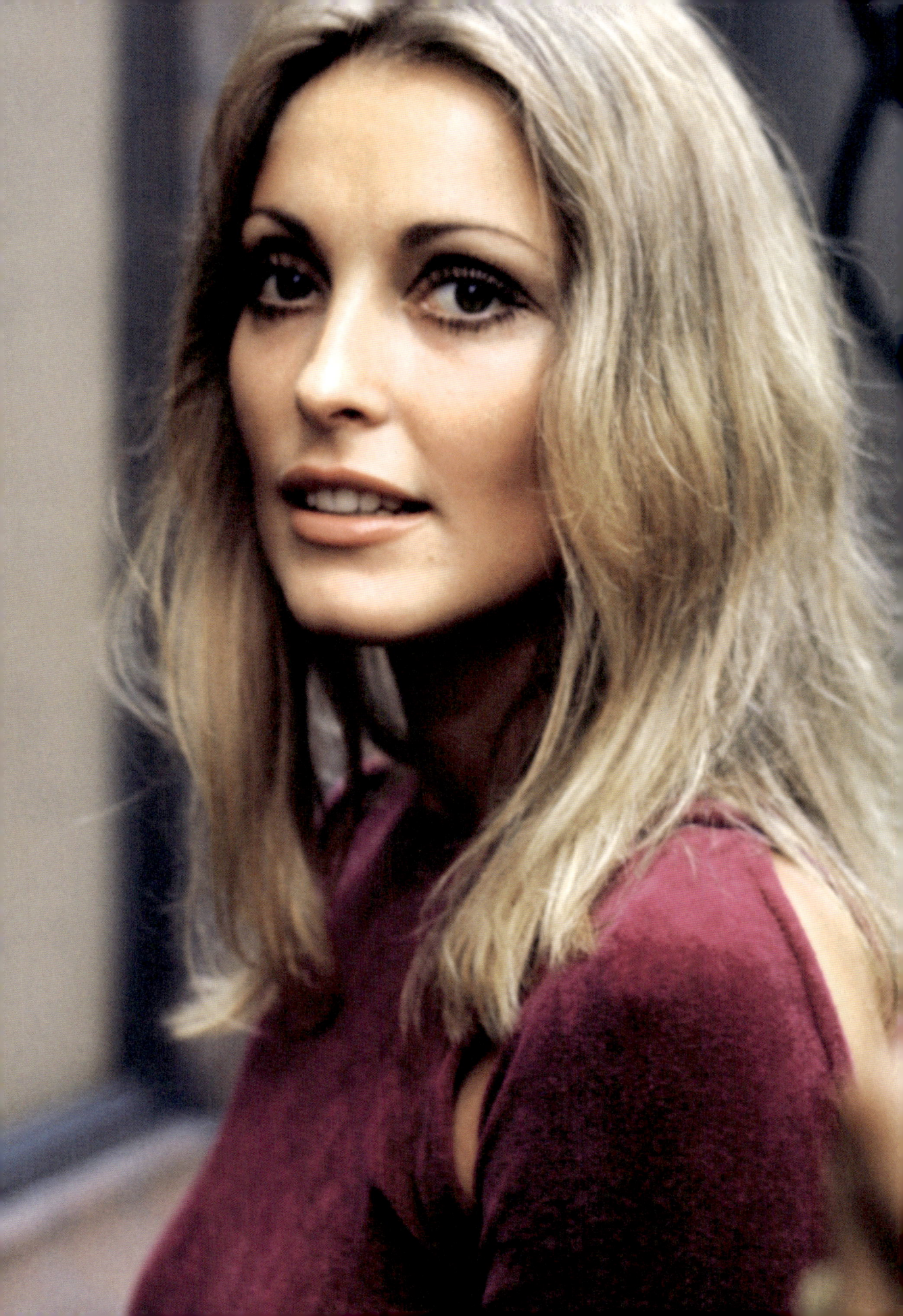

Shirley MacLaine
New York City, ca. 1980

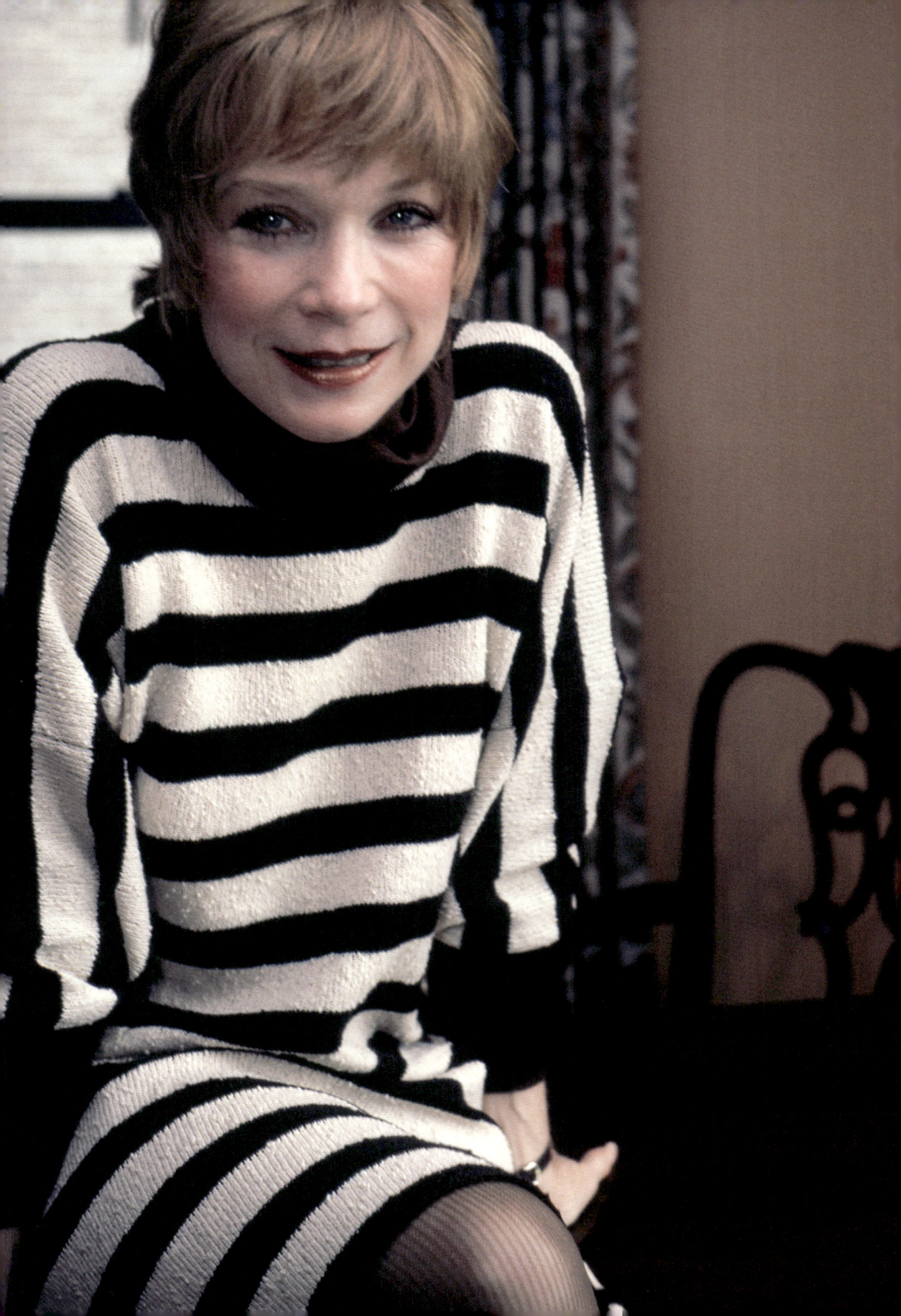

A presence like a force of nature — untamed and unforgettable.

There was no mistaking Diana Ross. Not on stage. Not on film. Not through a lens.

She moved like she was born in rhythm, dressed like the world might end tonight, and sang like she was going to save it.

Oscar didn't try to soften her. She wasn't soft. She was luminous, commanding, and absolutely self-possessed. She didn't need to be directed in front of the camera. She already knew how to own the frame.

Diana Ross
New York City, 1969

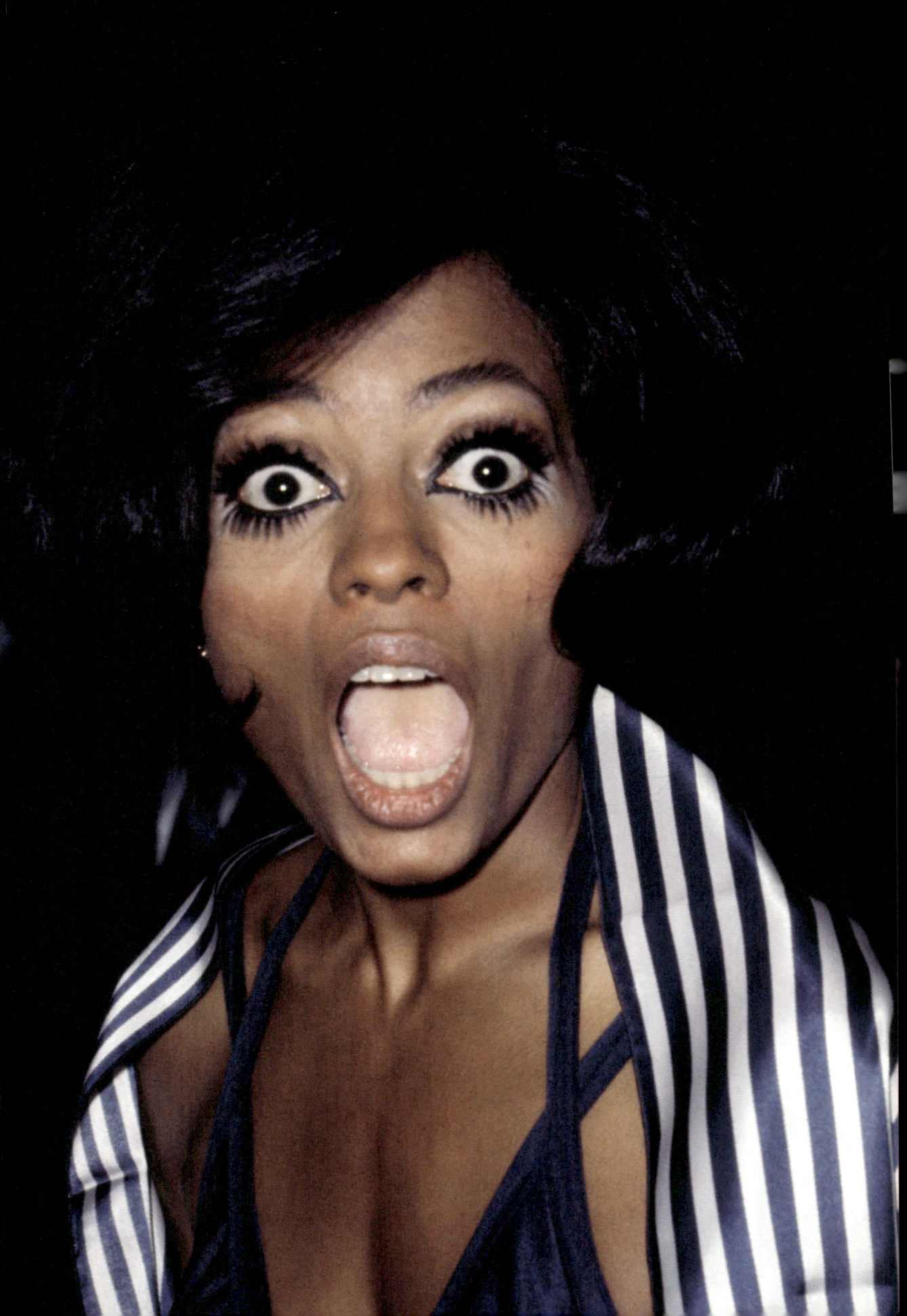

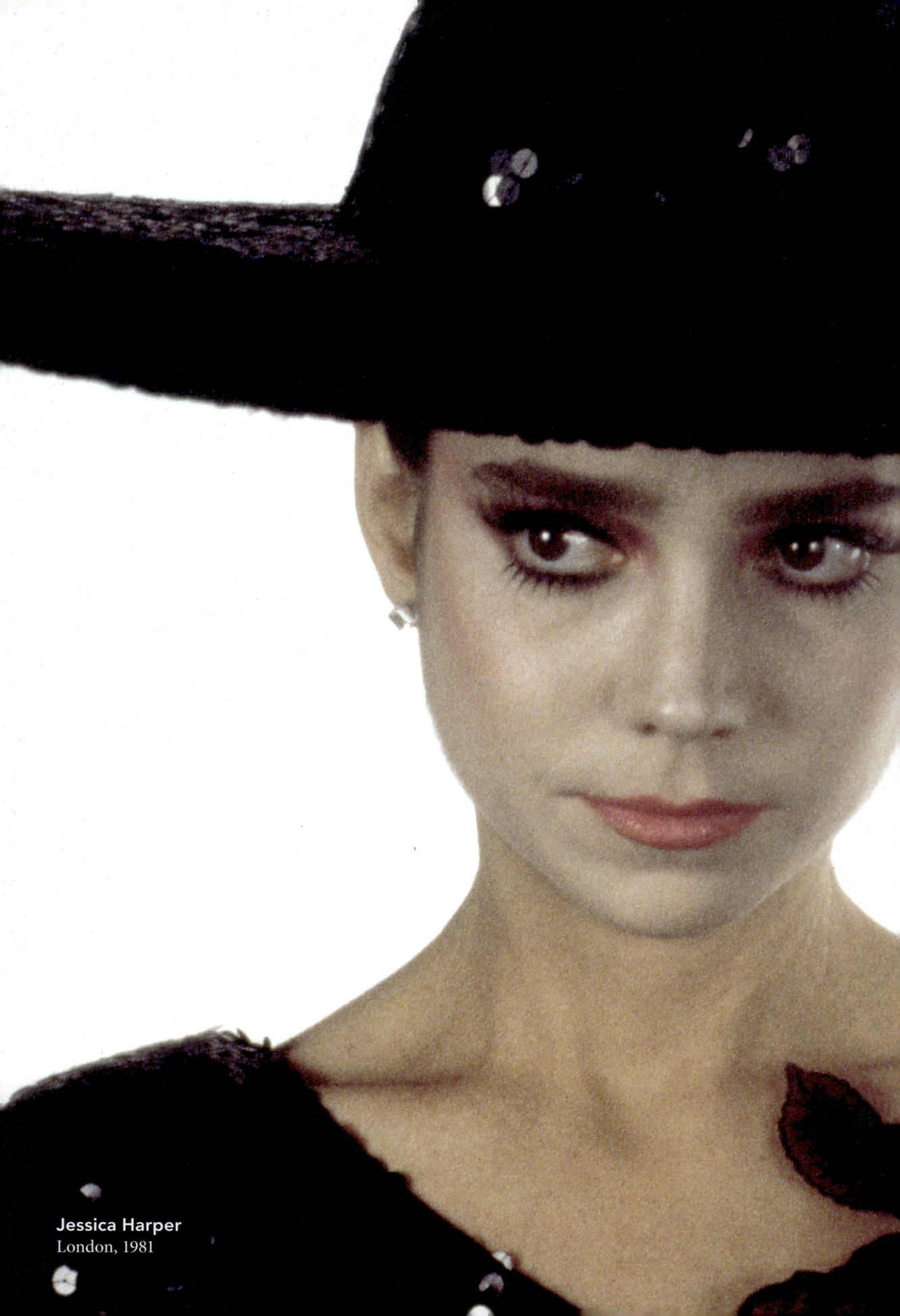

Jessica Harper
London, 1981

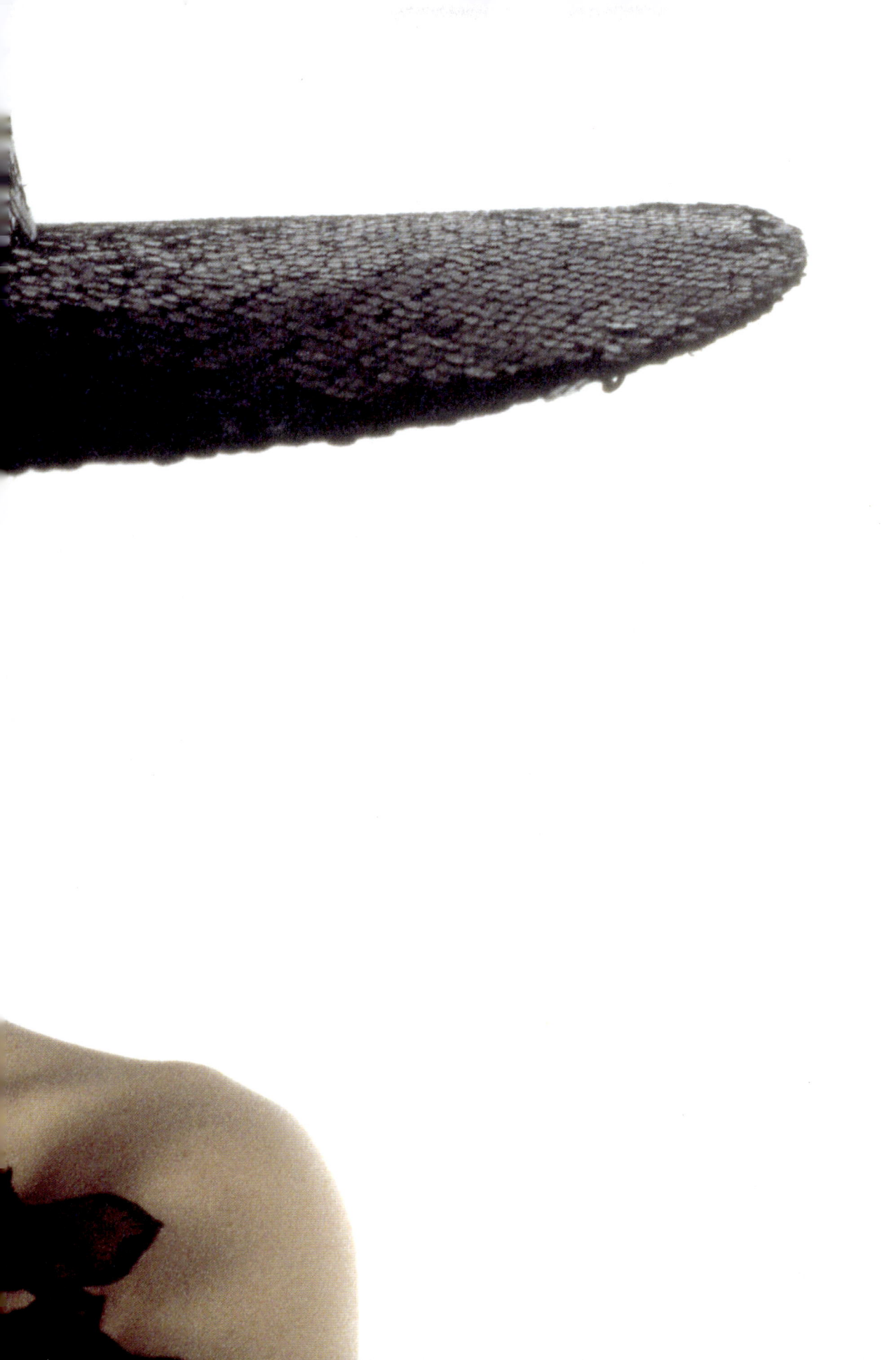

Sophia Loren
New York City, 1971

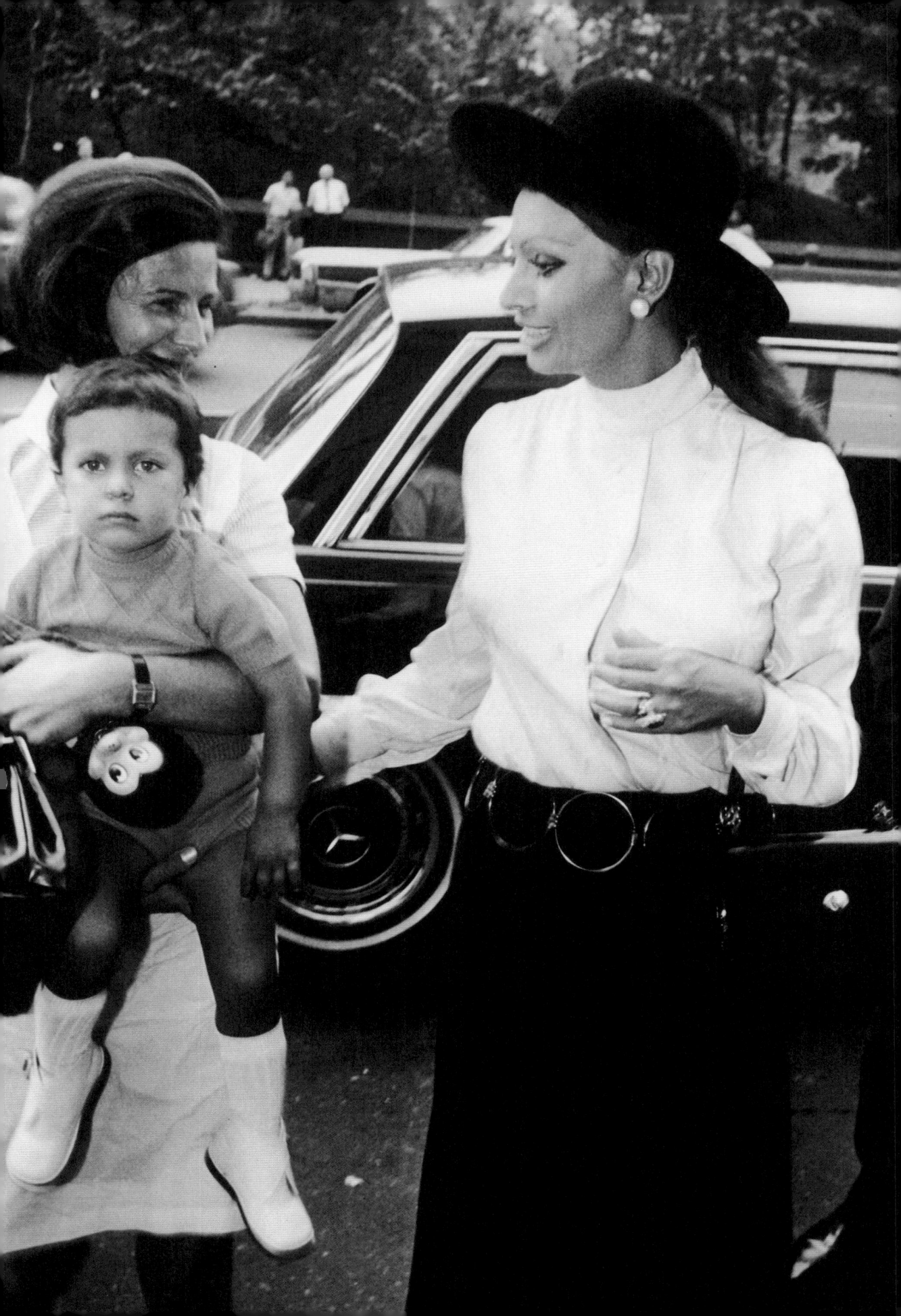

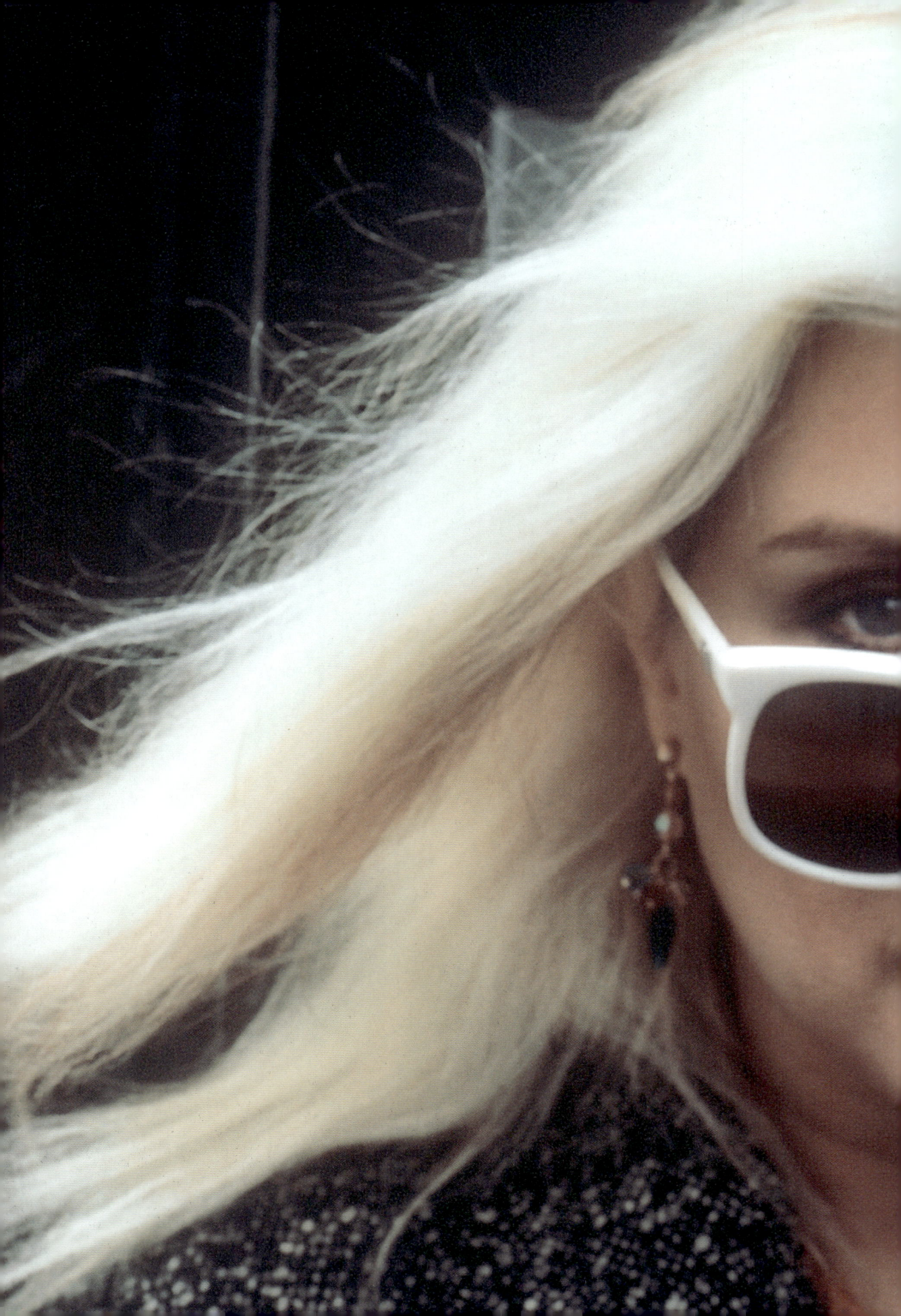

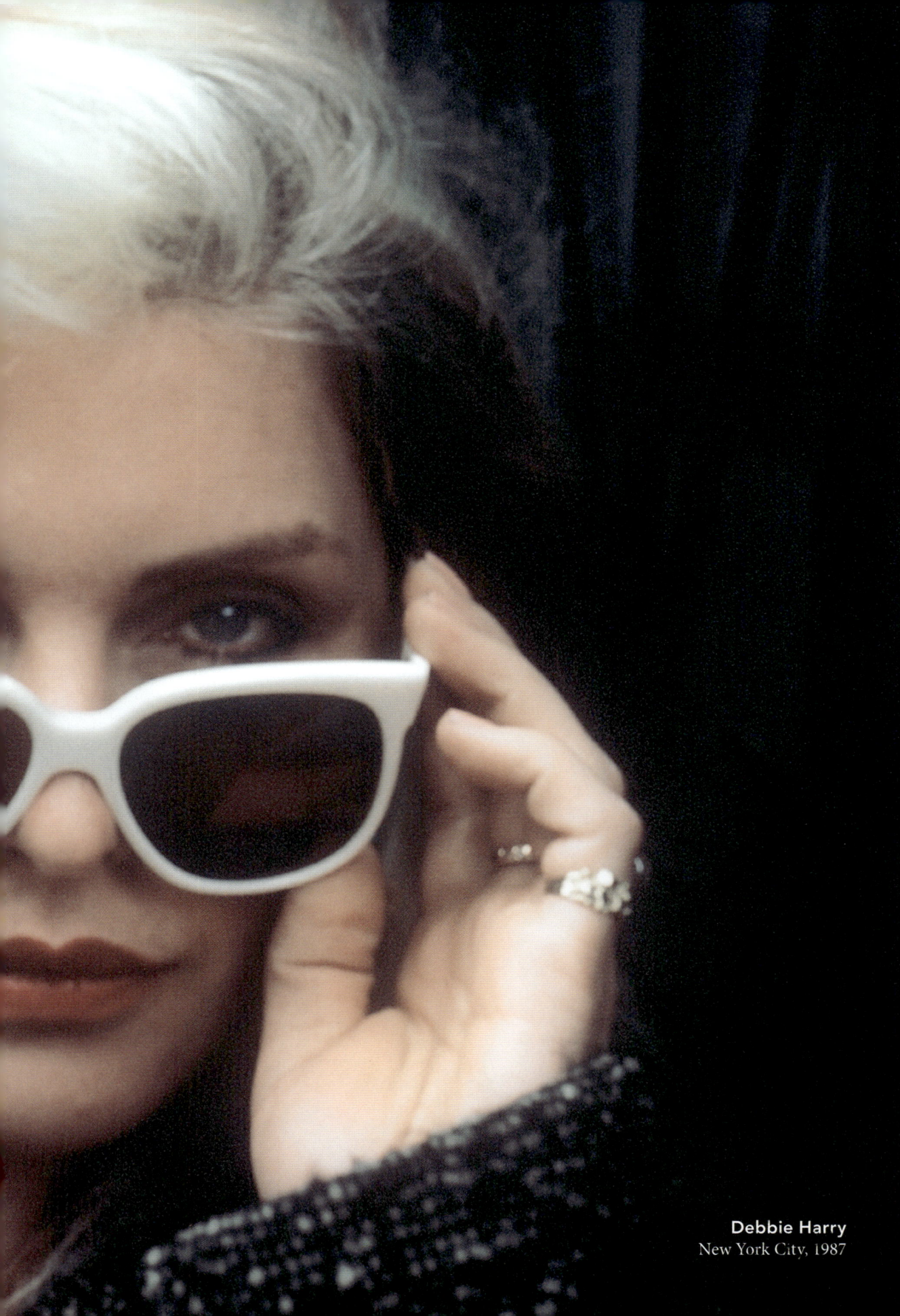

Debbie Harry
New York City, 1987

Kathy Silva
New York City, 1974

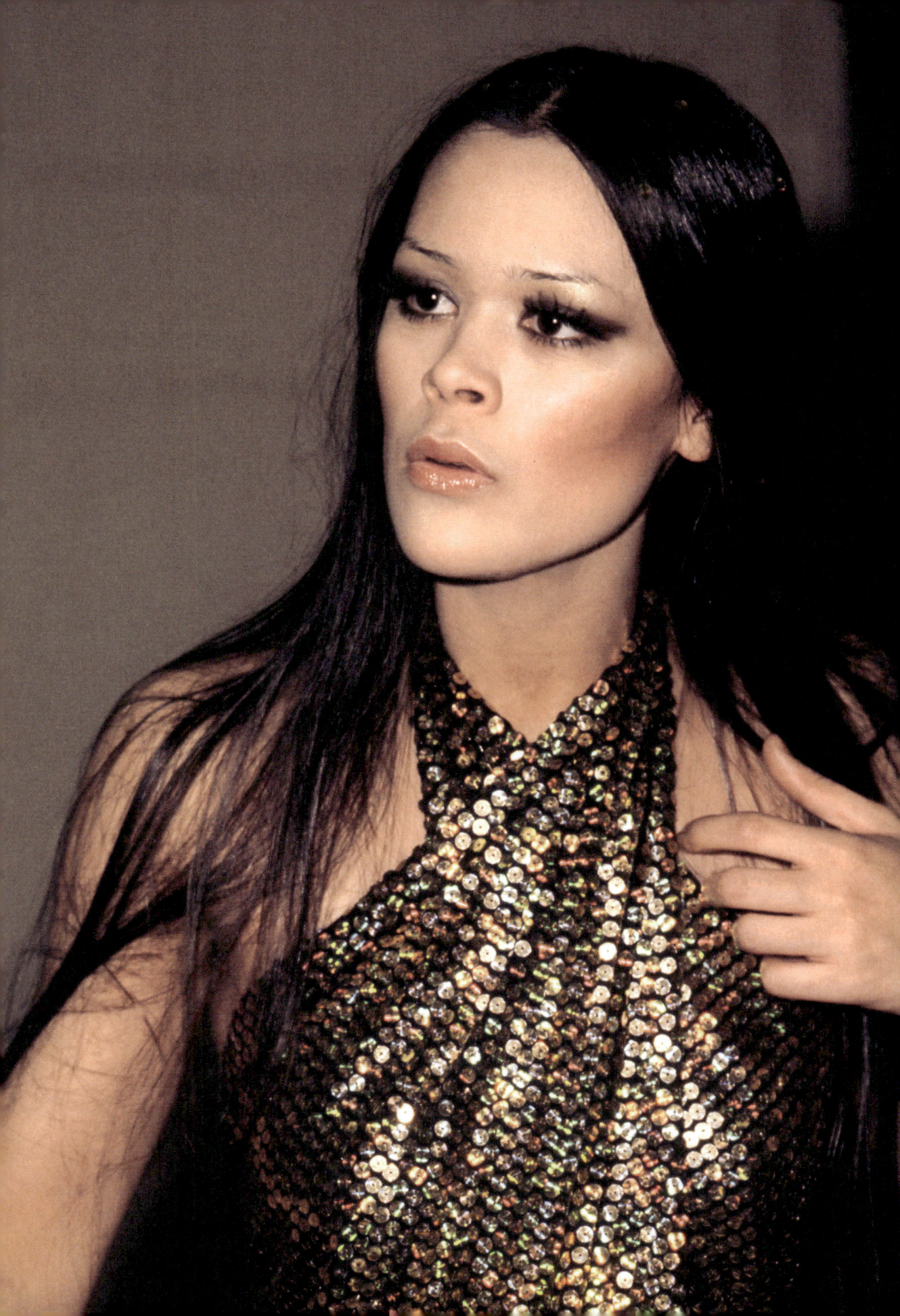

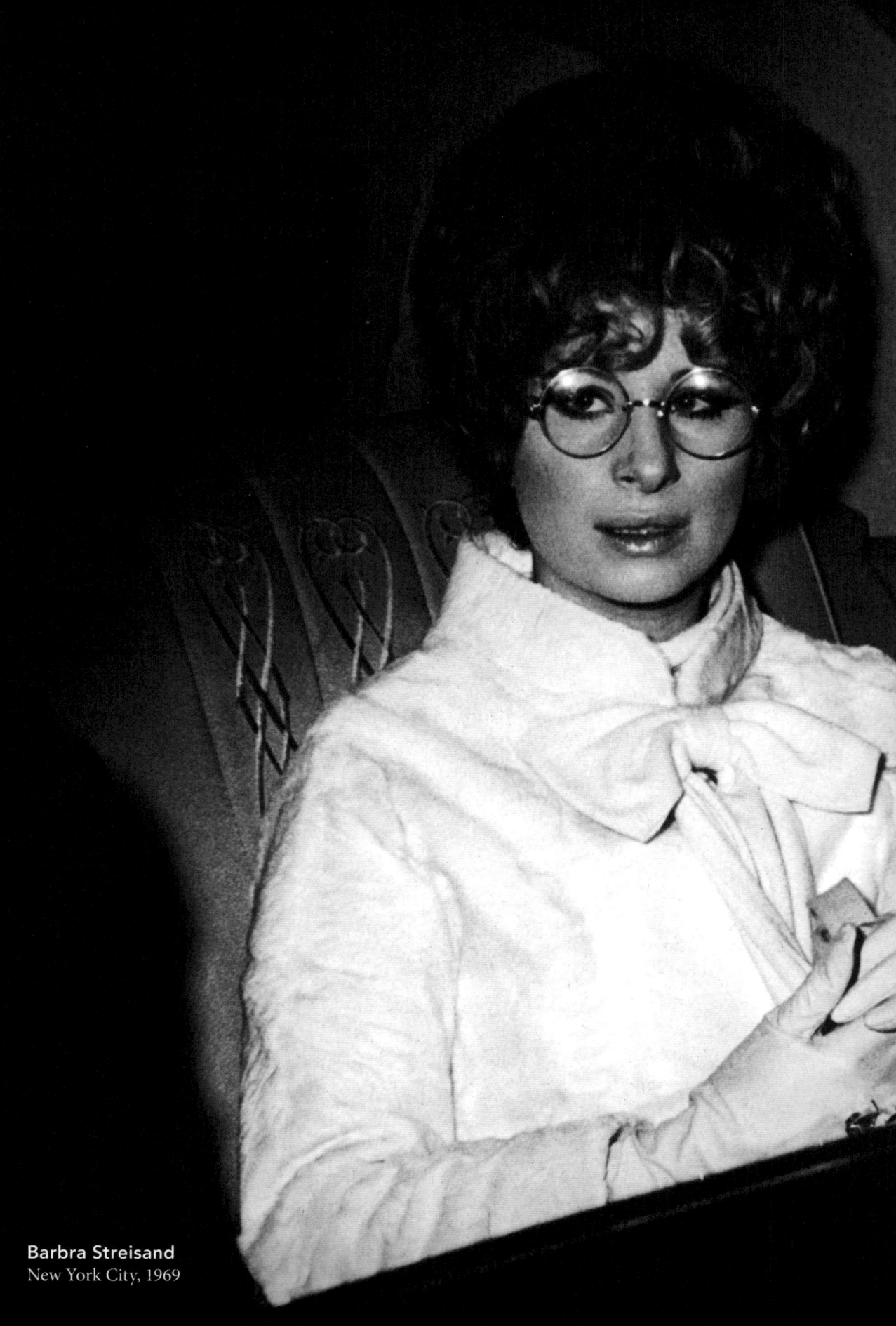

Barbra Streisand
New York City, 1969

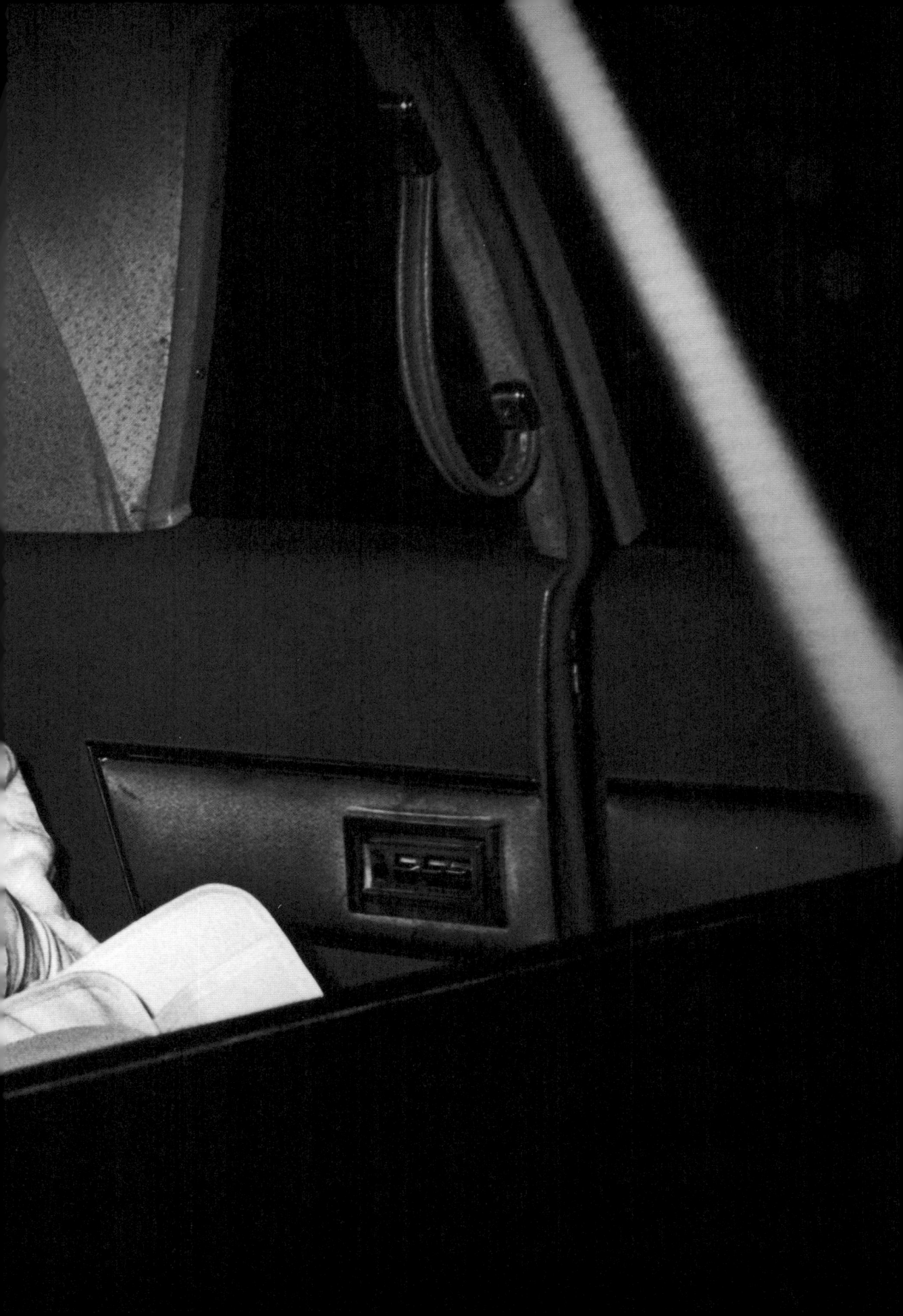

Bianca Jagger
New York City, 1975

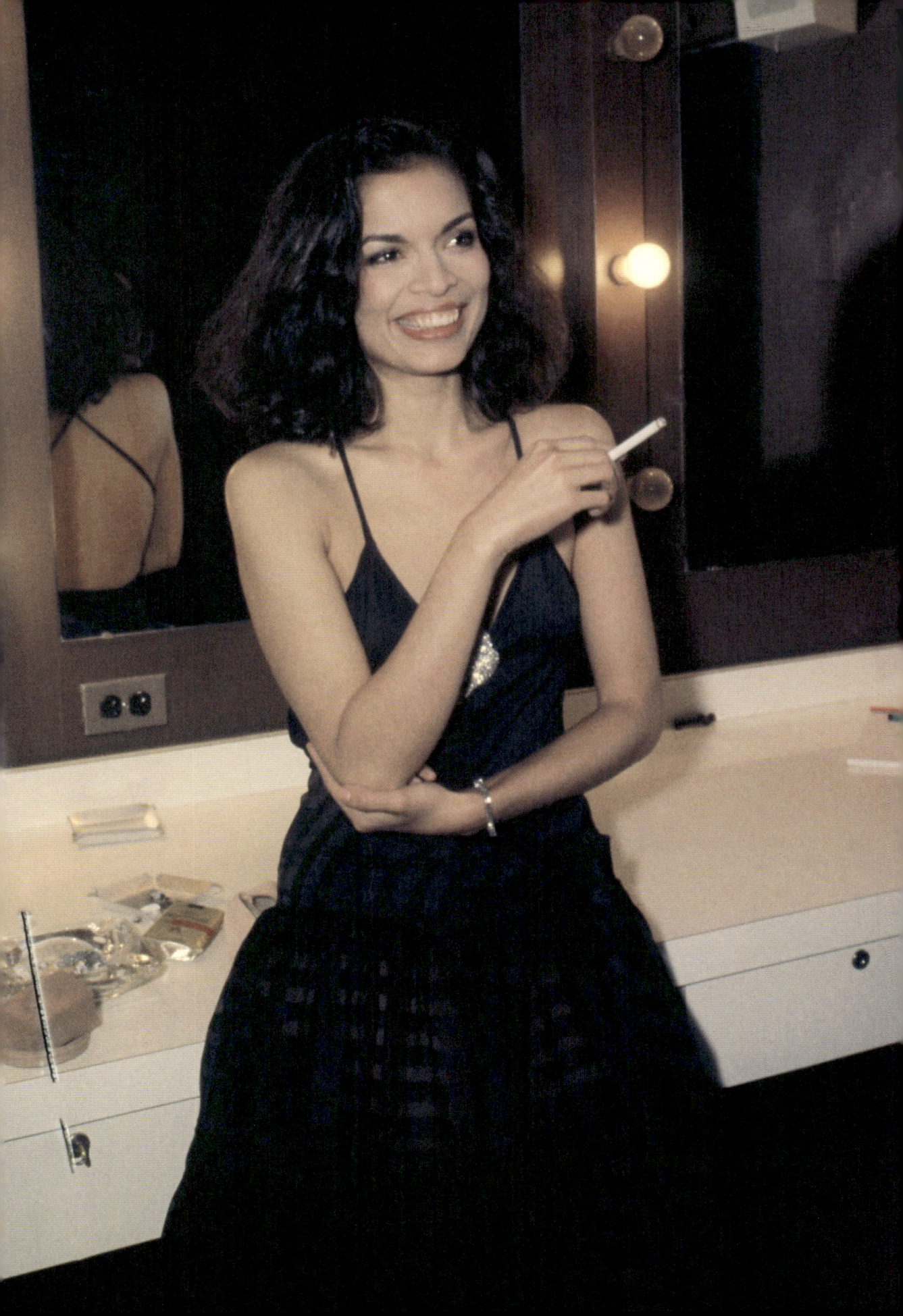

Never explain when you can entrance.

You couldn't read her — and she liked it that way.

Faye Dunaway didn't give away emotion. She hinted at it. With a glance, a tilt of the head, she could rewrite the entire tone of a photo. Oscar knew he wasn't photographing a person — he was catching a moment in a performance of spellbinding mystery.

She didn't need to speak. She let the light and the silence do it for her.

Faye Dunaway
New York City, 1967

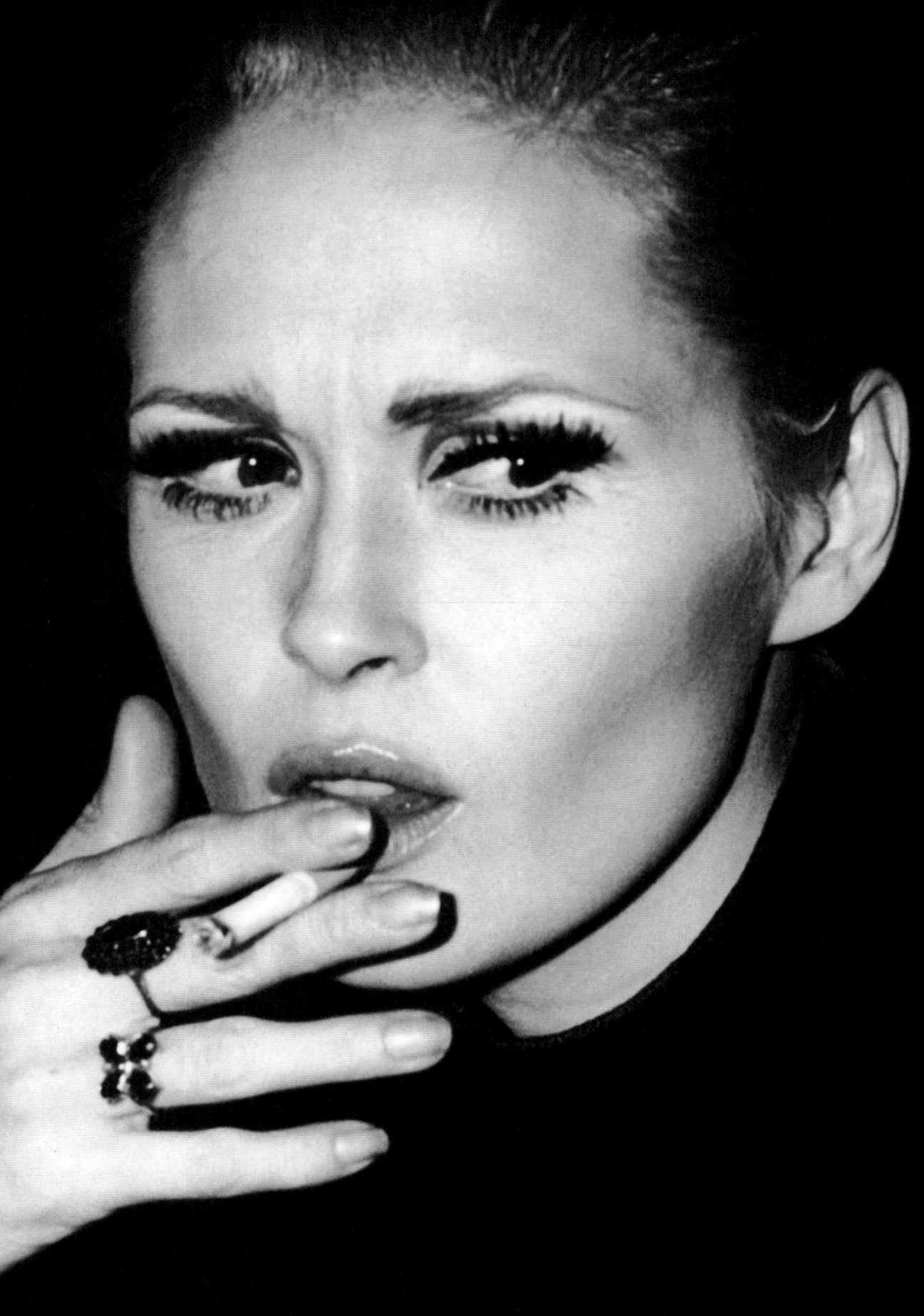

Ingrid Bergman
New York City, 1969

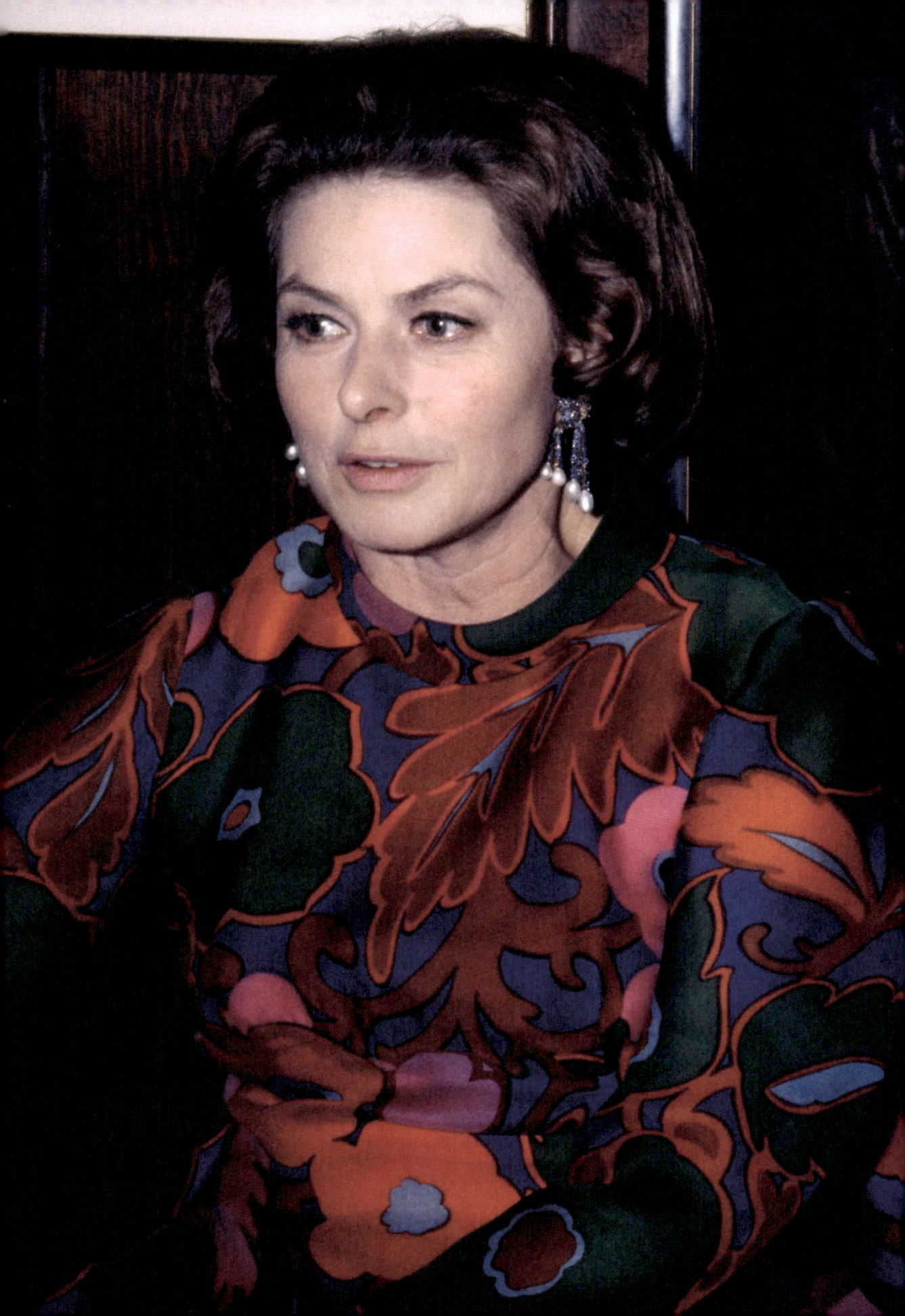

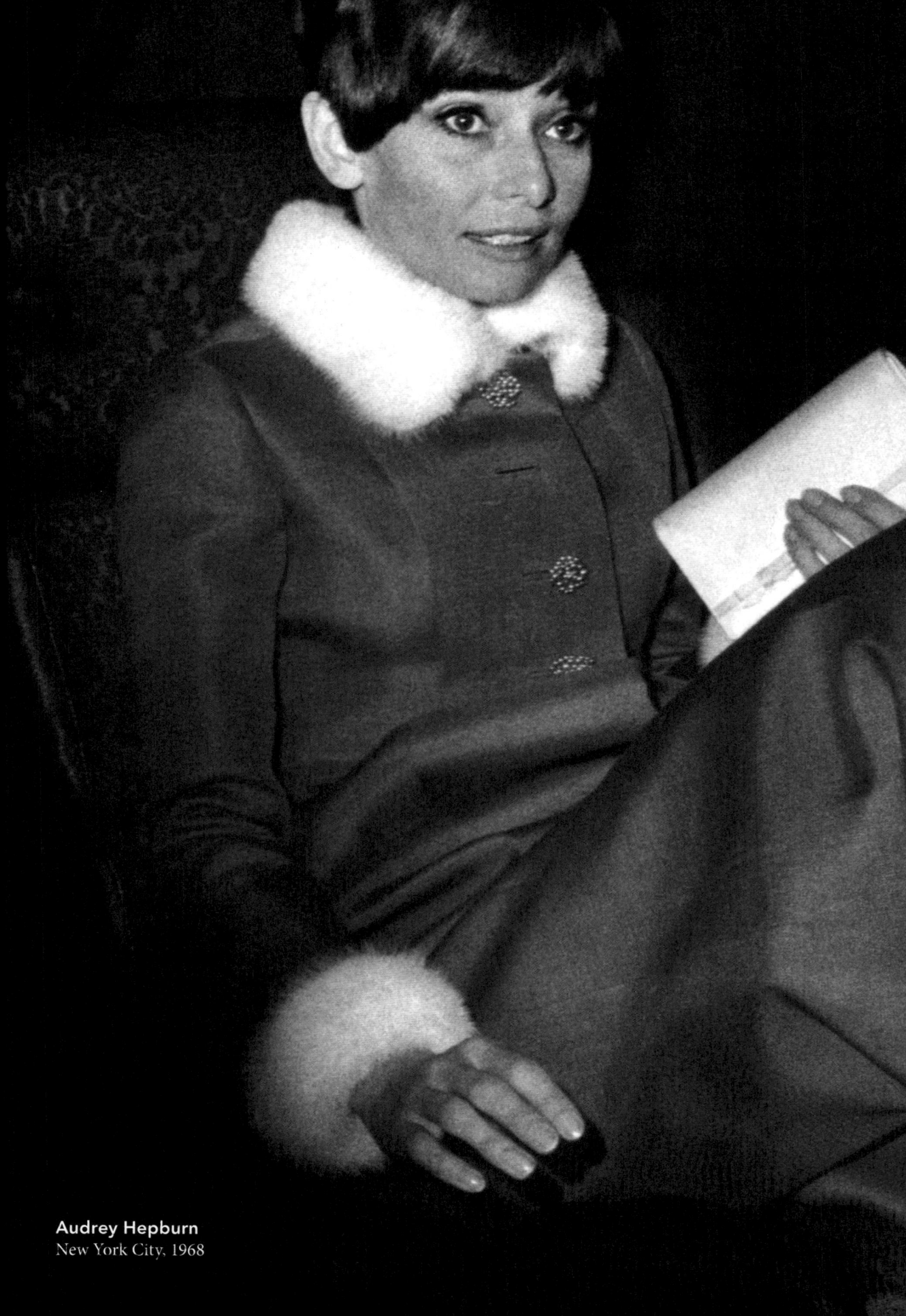

Audrey Hepburn
New York City, 1968

Diane von Fürstenberg
New York City, ca. 1978

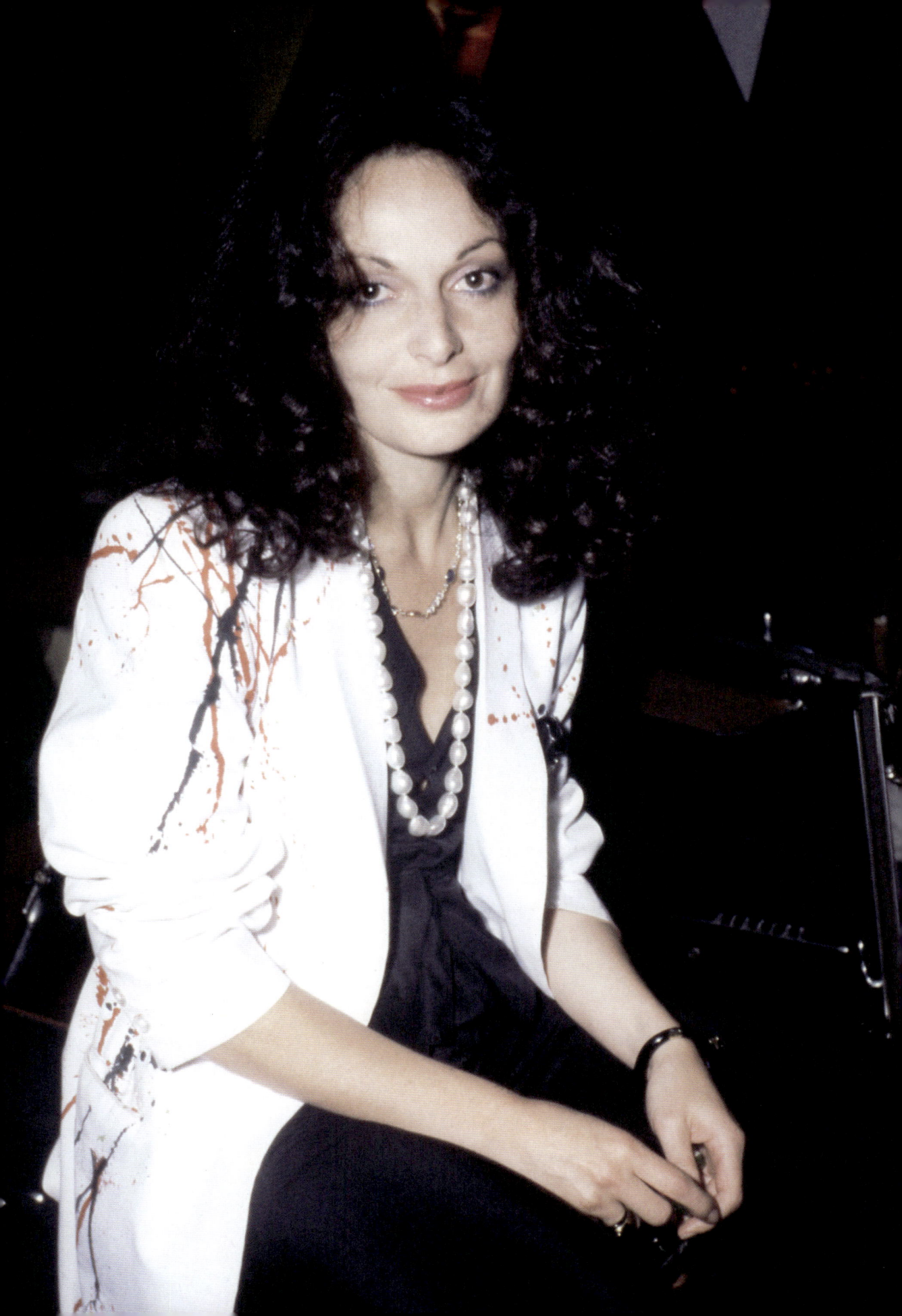

The voice that refused to be shaped — and shaped the world instead.

She didn't look the way Hollywood thought she should. So she changed what Hollywood looked like.

Barbra Streisand never asked for permission — not to sing, not to direct, not to be seen exactly as she was. Oscar approached her with reverence. He knew she wasn't interested in flattery. She was interested in truth — and excellence.

This photo shows her at her most direct. A face full of story, defiance, genius. She wasn't asking to be captured. She was telling you to get it right.

Barbra Streisand
New York City, 1975

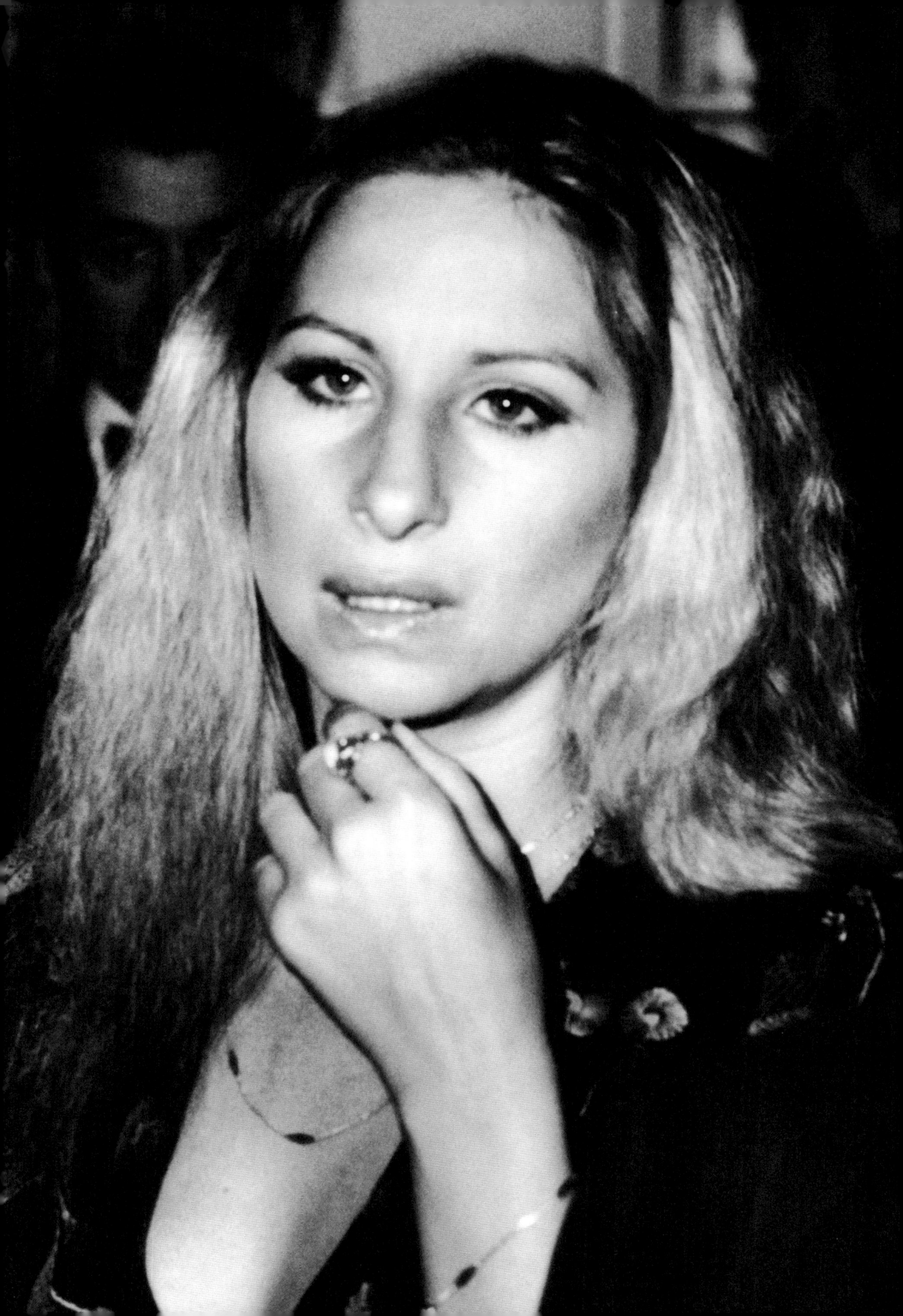

Margaret Trudeau
New York City, ca. 1977

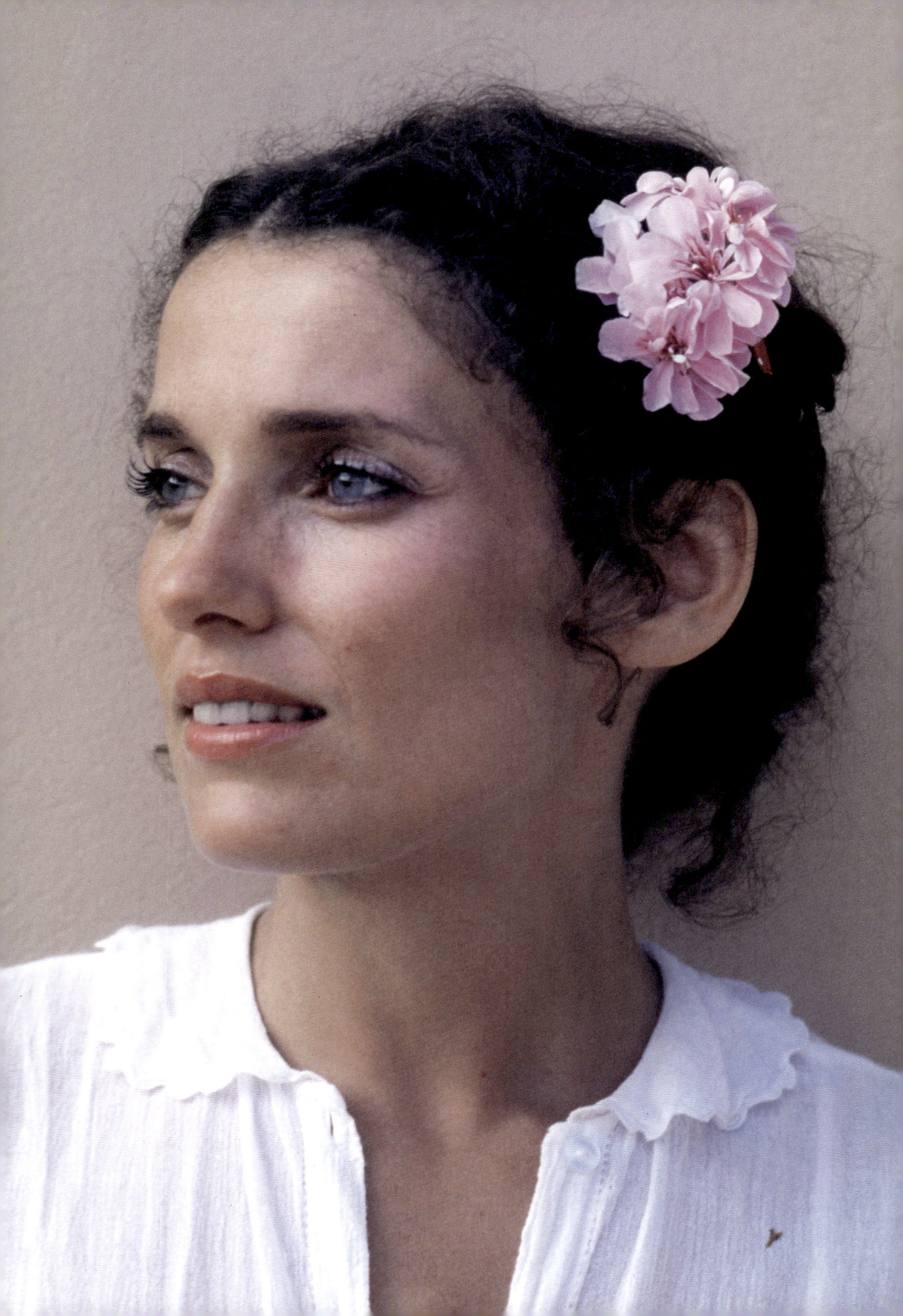

Laughter made her iconic — but silence gave her mystery.

She was the queen of timing — the face of comedy for a generation. But when the cameras weren't rolling, Lucille Ball carried a different energy. Quiet, deliberate, observant.

Oscar caught her in that stillness. No laughter, no punchlines. Just a woman who had built an empire out of being seen, and who — in rare moments — allowed herself to disappear behind her own gaze. There was a gravity to her that surprised him. She had nothing to prove. And maybe that's when the real performance began.

Lucille Ball
New York City, 1974

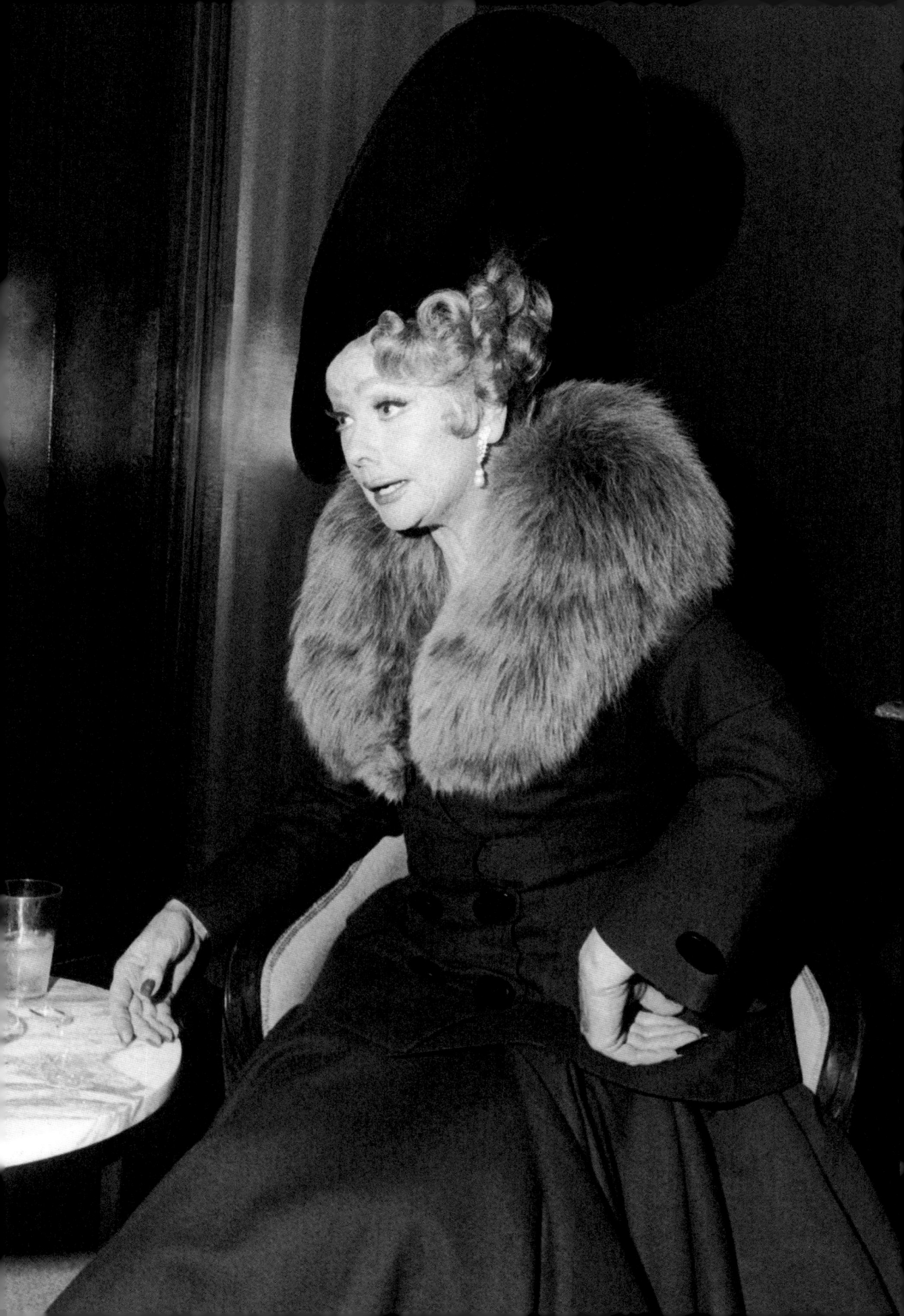

Julie Newmar
New York City, 1979

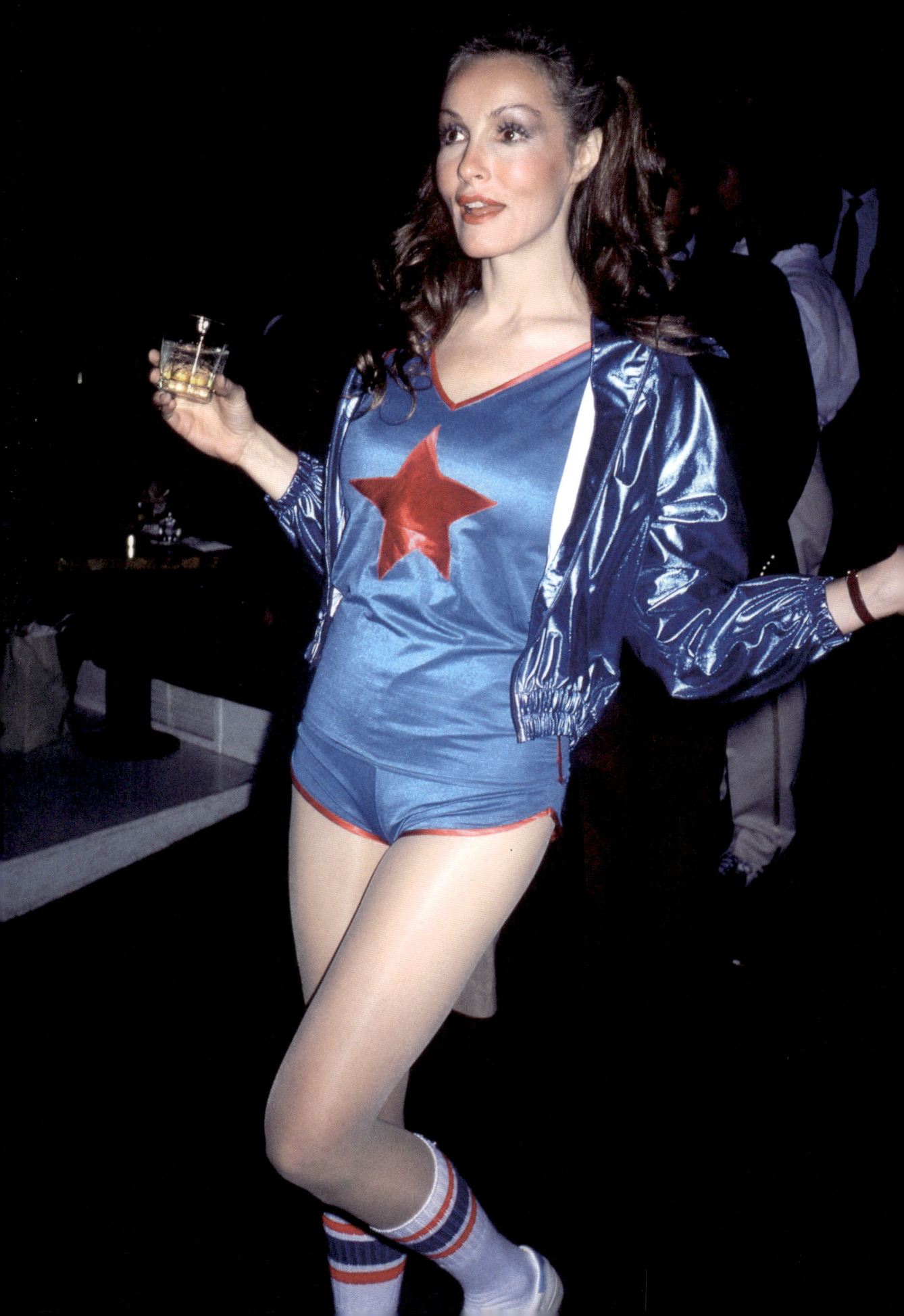

Yma Súmac
New York City, 1987

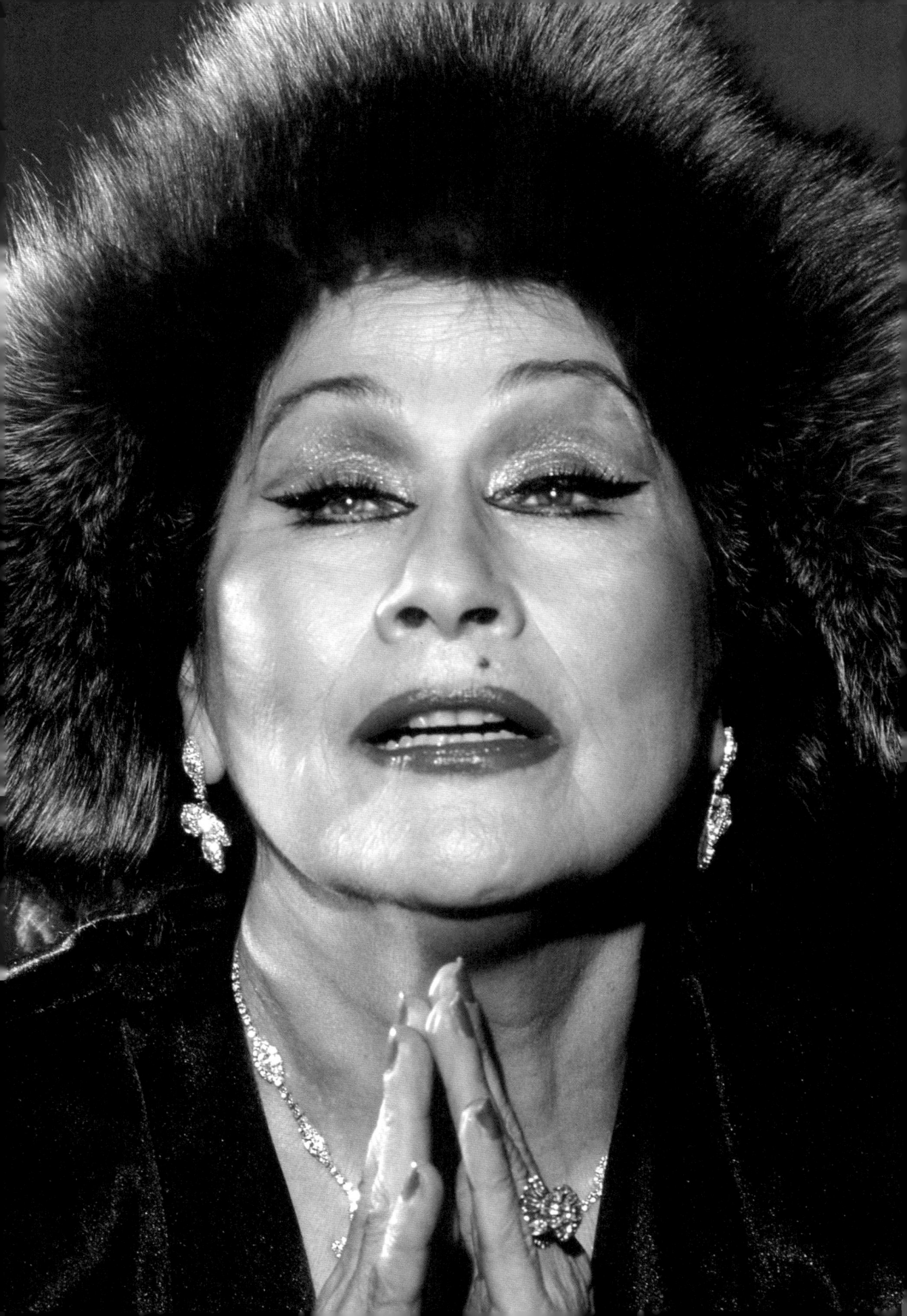

Mae West
New York City, 1970

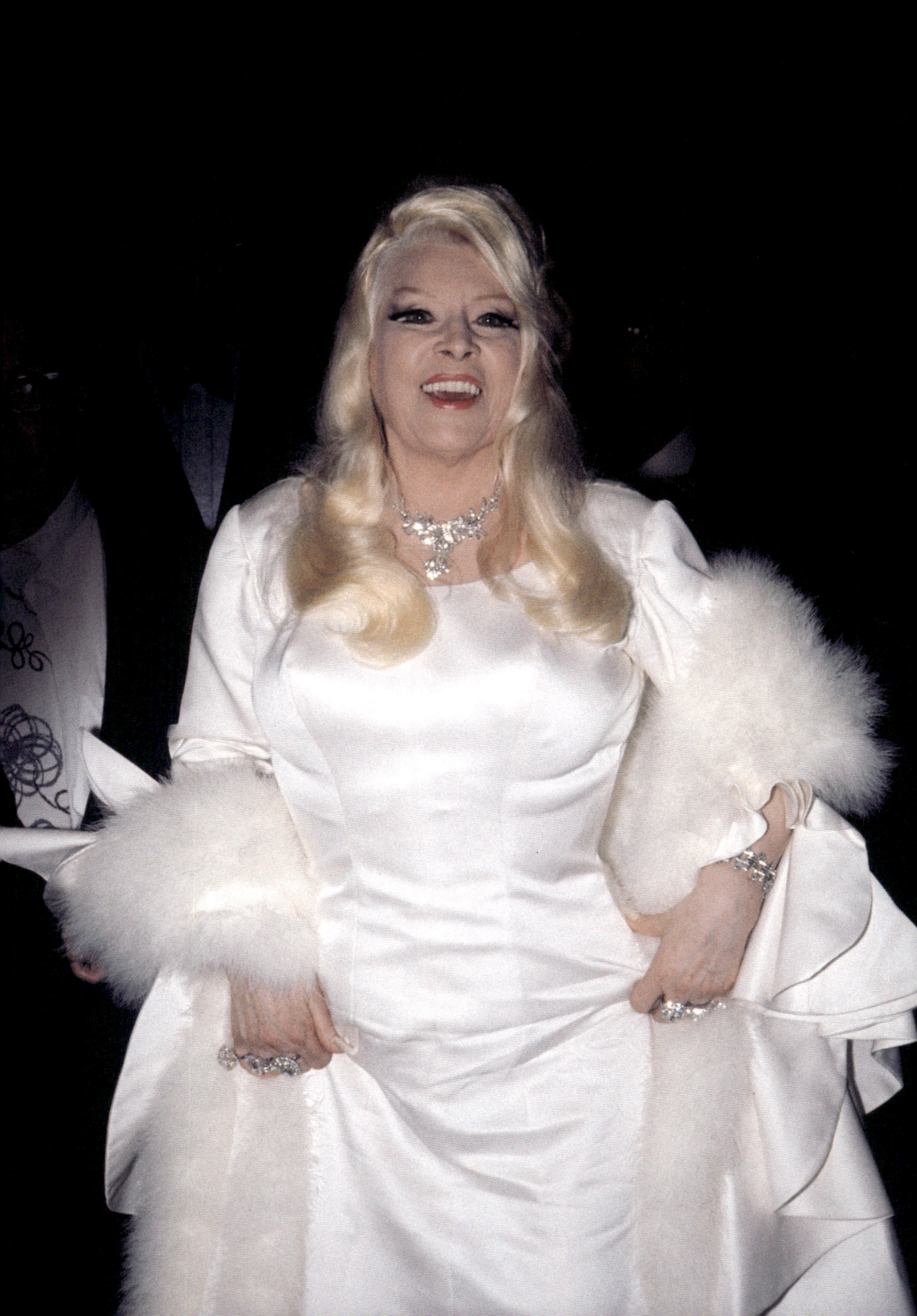

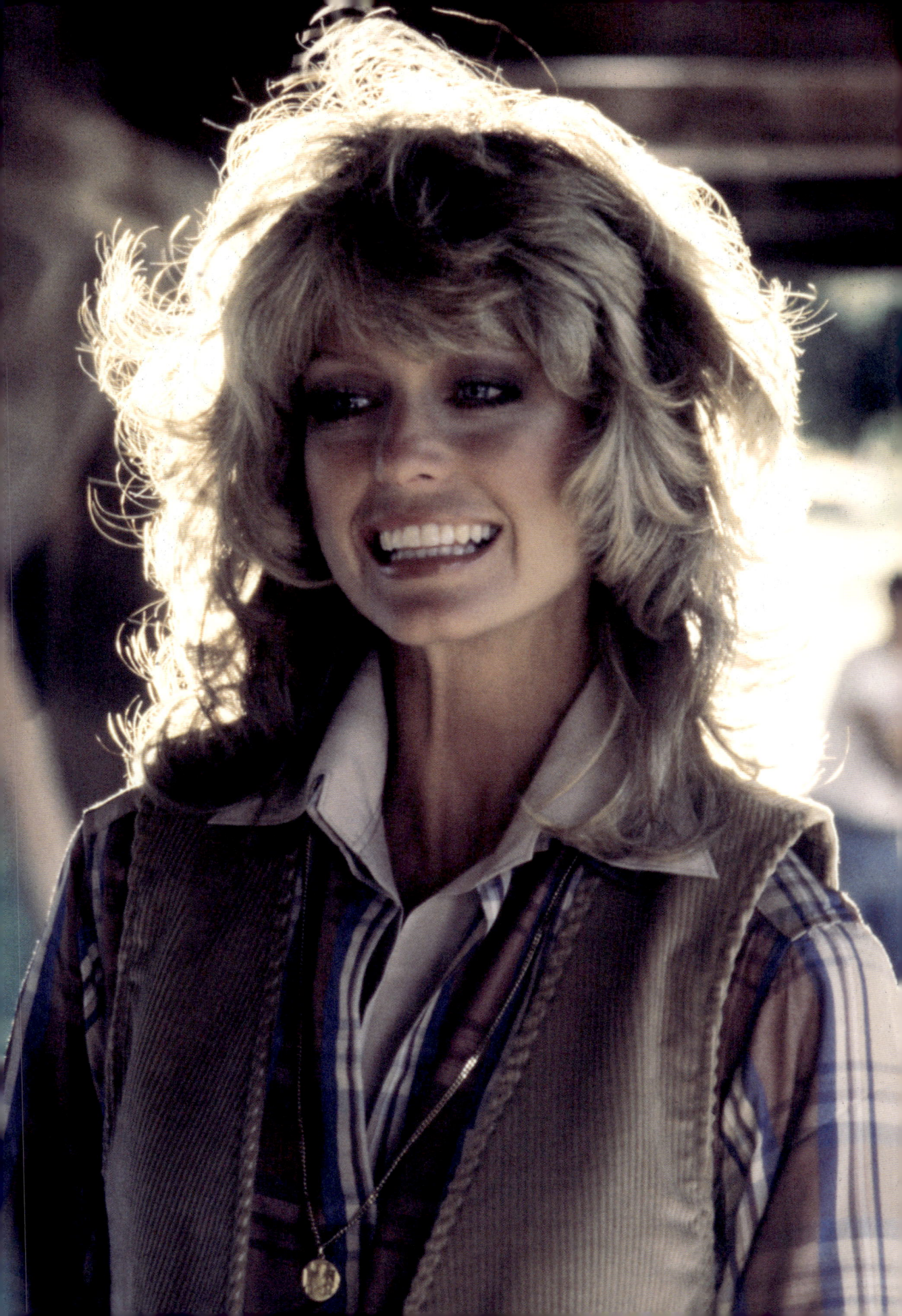

Farrah Fawcett
New York City, 1977

Jackie Kennedy Onassis
New York City, 1978

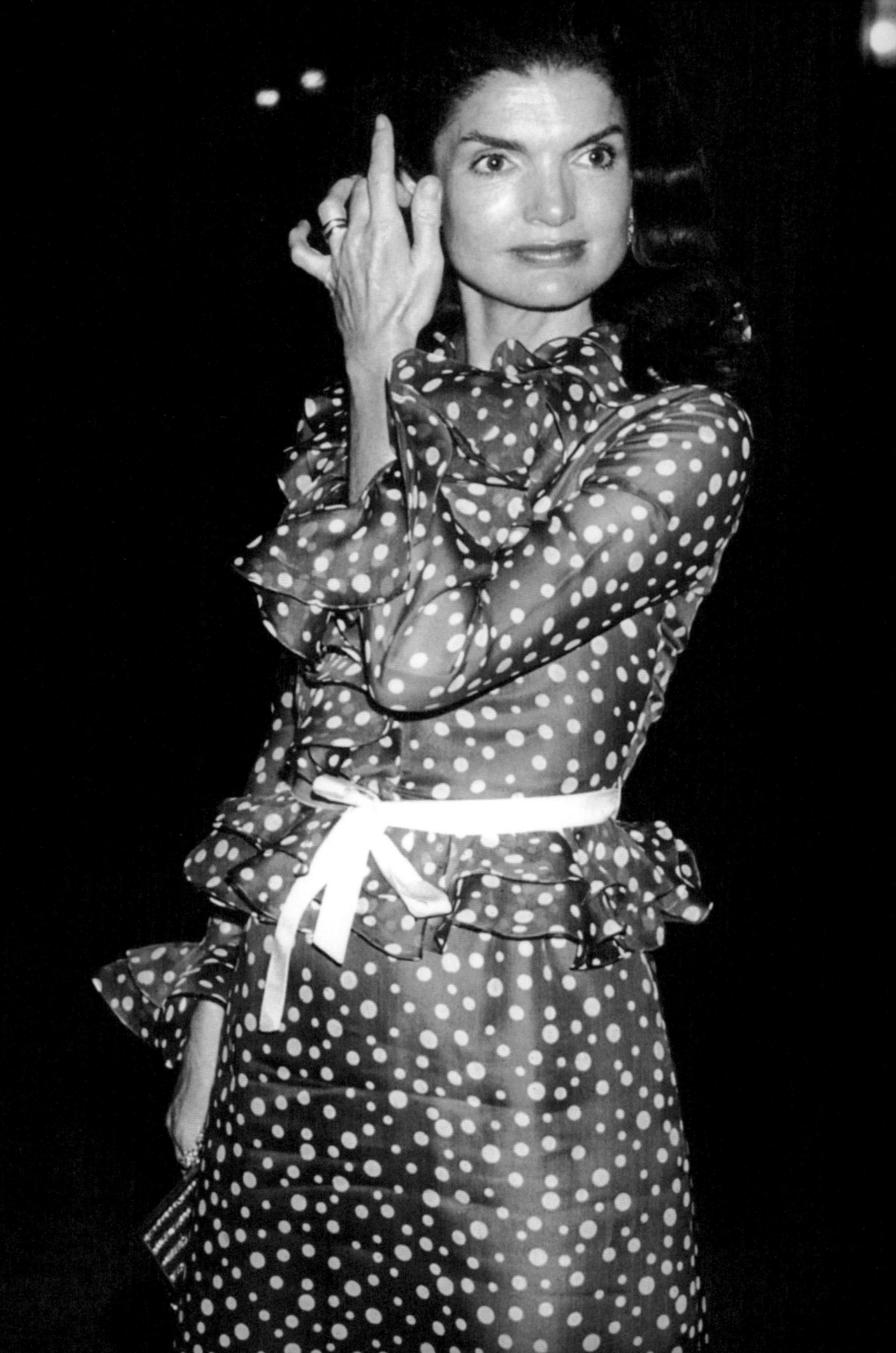

Faye Dunaway
New York City, 1967

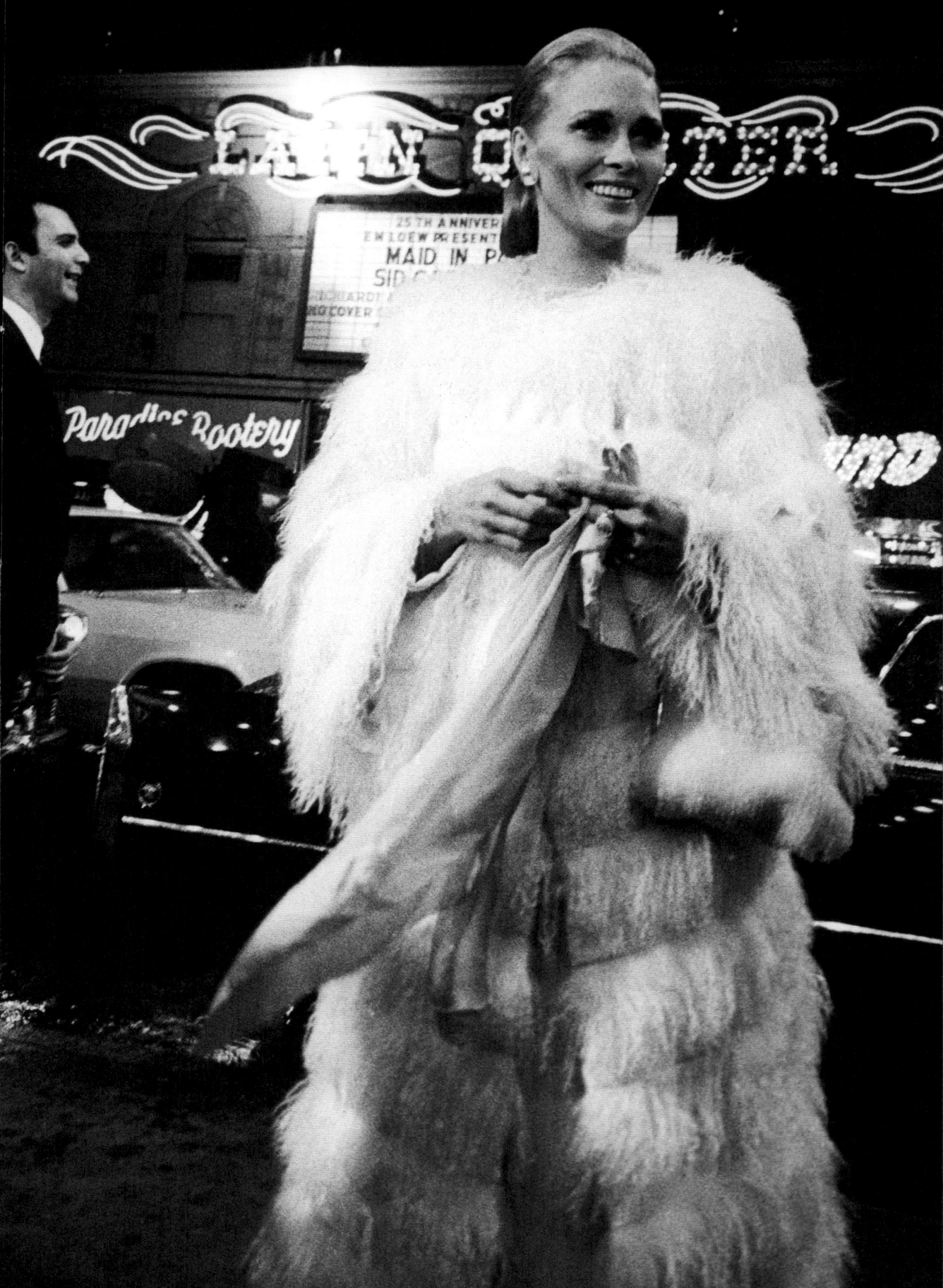

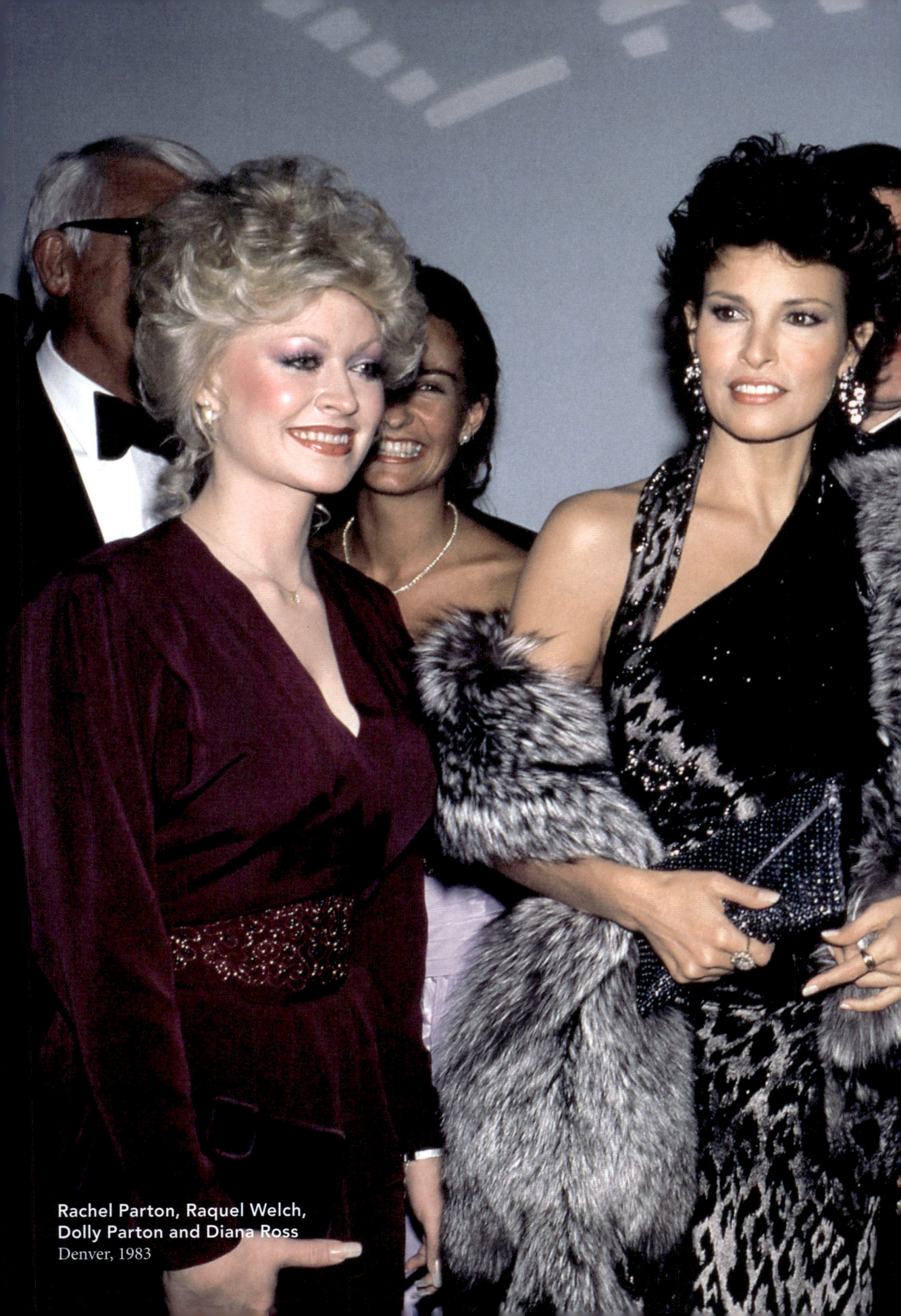

Rachel Parton, Raquel Welch,
Dolly Parton and Diana Ross
Denver, 1983

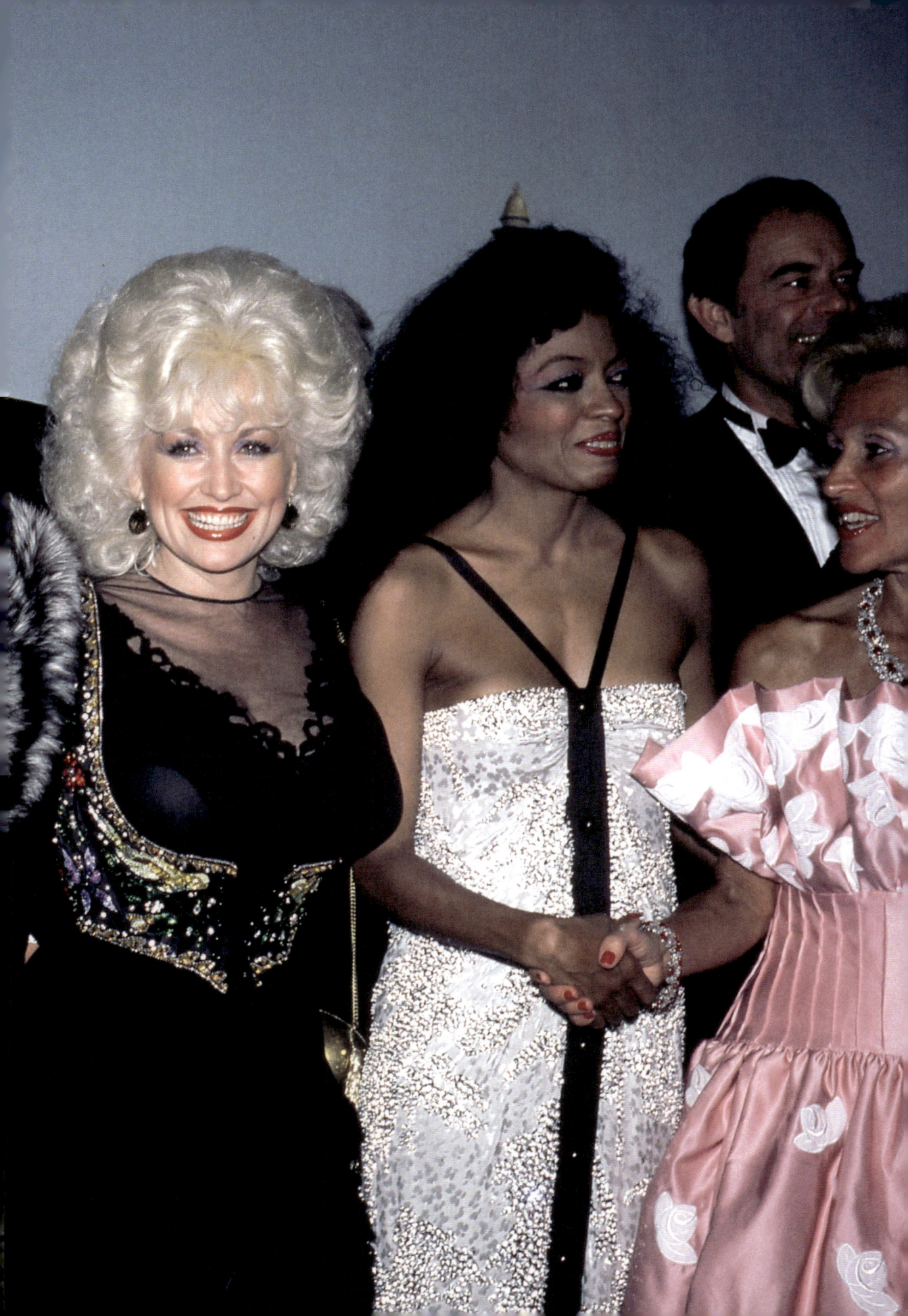

Index

Bailey, Pearl — 176
Baker, Josephine — 135
Ball, Lucille — 127, 154, 219
Barrymore, Drew — 33
Benedetti, Caprice — 106
Bergen, Candice — 144-145
Bergman, Ingrid — 209
Bouquet, Carole — 182
Brinkley, Christie — 23
Campbell, Naomi — 47
Channing, Carol — 61
Charo — 71
Cher — 73, 179
Colbert, Claudette — 77
Crawford, Joan — 165
Dahl, Arlene — 45
Davis, Bette — 63, 168
Deneuve, Catherine — 65
Diana (Princess) — 146
Divine (Harris Glenn Milstead) — 99
Down, Lesley-Anne — 124
Dunaway, Faye — 207, 231
Fältskog, Agnetha — 17, 133
Farrow, Mia — 53, 67
Fawcett, Farrah — 81, 226
Flack, Roberta — 59
Fonda, Jane — 120
Ford, Betty — 151
Franklin, Aretha — 43
Gallagher, Megan — 141
Gayat, Françoise — 157
Gillespie, Cherry — 170
Goldberg, Whoopi — 9
Harper, Jessica — 194
Harry, Debbie — 25, 85, 198
Doody, Alison — 54
Hawn, Goldie — 105
Hayes, Helen — 115
Hepburn, Audrey — 51, 210
Hudson, Tina — 167
Jagger, Bianca — 56, 129, 205
Jones, Grace — 54, 87, 143
Joplin, Janis — 123
Kelly, Grace — 21
Kennedy Onassis, Jackie — 31, 68, 113, 229

Kristel, Sylvia — 40, 95
Lauper, Cyndi — 83
Loren, Sophia — 197
Lyngstad, Anni-Frid — 19, 34
MacLaine, Shirley — 191
Madonna — 137
Midler, Bette — 159
Miller, Ann — 39
Minnelli, Liza — 56, 161
Moreno, Rita — 107
Navratilova, Martina — 139
Newmar, Julie — 221
Olsson, Ann-Margret — 37, 131
Onassis, Christina — 75
Ono Yoko — 117
Parton, Dolly — 15, 232
Parton, Rachel — 232
Pfeiffer, Michelle — 153
Presley, Priscilla — 13, 93
Quinn, Aileen — 27
Rogers, Ginger — 39, 111
Rolle, Esther — 109
Ross, Diana — 89, 90, 120, 193, 232
Silva, Kathy — 201
Soo Soo, Papillon — 54
Streep, Meryl — 149
Streisand, Barbra — 48, 202, 215
Súmac, Yma — 223
Summer, Donna — 101
Tate, Sharon — 189
Taylor, Elizabeth — 78, 103
Tilly, Meg — 29
Trudeau, Margaret — 173, 217
Twiggy, 175
Tyler Moore, Mary — 163
Vanity — 118-119
von Fürstenberg, Diane — 213
Vreeland, Diana — 97
Ward, Rachel — 185
Wedgeworth, Ann — 181
Welch, Raquel — 232
West, May — 225
Westheimer, Ruth — 187
Winfrey, Oprah — 10

About Oscar Abolafia

Oscar Abolafia was a New York-based photographer known for his candid and captivating portraits of celebrities during the 1960s, '70s, and '80s. With a unique ability to move between backstage moments and red-carpet glamour, he photographed some of the most iconic figures of the era — from Elizabeth Taylor and Andy Warhol to Grace Jones and Frank Sinatra. His work appeared in major publications such as *People*, *Harper's Bazaar*, and *Vanity Fair*. What set Abolafia apart was his instinct for intimacy. He didn't just document fame — he revealed the human side of it, often capturing unguarded expressions and moments of rare vulnerability. With charm, trust, and a Leica in hand, Oscar built a visual legacy that continues to resonate with timeless style and authenticity.

Acknowledgements

Oscar Abolafia
Women — Icons by Oscar

© 2025 Terra Publishers, Amsterdam, and
Yoke Abolafia van Berge Henegouwen
Terra is part of Lannoo Publishers
P.O. Box 23202
1100 DS Amsterdam
The Netherlands

terra@lannoo.nl
www.lannoo.com

PHOTOGRAPHY
Oscar Abolafia

DESIGN
Roy Rietstap and Joost Albronda,
Albronda + Rietstap, Amsterdam

With the kind collaboration of Historic
Images, Chris Galbreath, and Connor
Scanlon

First edition: 2025
ISBN: 9789020982503
D/2025/45/212

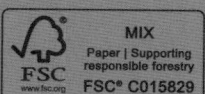

FSC
www.fsc.org
MIX
Paper | Supporting
responsible forestry
FSC® C015829